A Research Agenda for Financial Resources within the Household

Elgar Research Agendas outline the future of research in a given area. Leading scholars are given the space to explore their subject in provocative ways, and map out the potential directions of travel. They are relevant but also visionary.

Forward-looking and innovative, Elgar Research Agendas are an essential resource for PhD students, scholars and anybody who wants to be at the forefront of research.

For a full list of Edward Elgar published titles, including the titles in this series, visit our website at www.e-elgar.com.

A Research Agenda for Financial Resources within the Household

Edited by

FRAN BENNETT

Associate Fellow, Department of Social Policy and Intervention, University of Oxford, UK

SILVIA AVRAM

Senior Research Fellow, Institute for Social and Economic Research (ISER), University of Essex, UK

SIOBHAN AUSTEN

Professor Emerita of Economics, Curtin University, Australia

Elgar Research Agendas

Cheltenham, UK • Northampton, MA, USA

Published by
Edward Elgar Publishing Limited
The Lypiatts
15 Lansdown Road
Cheltenham
Glos GL50 2JA
UK

Edward Elgar Publishing, Inc.
William Pratt House
9 Dewey Court
Northampton
Massachusetts 01060
USA

A catalogue record for this book
is available from the British Library

Library of Congress Control Number: 2023949802

This book is available electronically in the **Elgar**online
Sociology, Social Policy and Education subject collection
http://dx.doi.org/10.4337/9781802204001

ISBN 978 1 80220 399 8 (cased)
ISBN 978 1 80220 400 1 (eBook)
Printed and bound by CPI Group (UK) Ltd, Croydon, CR0 4YY

Contents

Contributors

Siobhan Austen is Professor Emerita of Economics at Curtin University, Australia and Director of the Women in Social and Economic Research group. Her research is currently focused on the gender gap in retirement income, understanding aged care using a capabilities approach and inequality in older-couple households. In her research, Siobhan typically adopts mixed methods, combining the secondary analysis of large-scale, often longitudinal survey data with data drawn from in-depth interviews.

Silvia Avram is Senior Research Fellow at the Institute for Social and Economic Research at the University of Essex. Her research focuses on the causes and consequences of economic inequality and the role played by public policy. Her work draws on both economic and sociological theories and uses quantitative methods, including tax-benefit microsimulation models, and large survey and administrative microdata. Her work has been published in high-ranking journals such as the *Socio-Economic Review* and *Social Science Research.*

Fran Bennett is Associate Fellow of the Department of Social Policy and Intervention, University of Oxford, working on gender and within-household issues, social security and poverty. Her most recent research, with colleagues at the University of Bath, examined universal credit and couples. She has worked and written extensively on social policy issues for non-governmental organisations in particular. She is Fellow of the Academy of Social Sciences and on the policy advisory group of the UK Women's Budget Group.

Tania Burchardt is Associate Director of the Centre for Analysis of Social Exclusion and Associate Professor of Social Policy in the Department of Social Policy at the London School of Economics and Political Science. Her research interests include theories of social justice, including the capability approach, applied welfare analysis and multidimensional disadvantage. She uses both qualitative methods (such as deliberative workshops) and quantitative methods (such as secondary analysis of large-scale survey data).

Sara Cantillon is Professor of Economics and Director of the Centre for Economic Justice at Glasgow Caledonian University. Previously, she was Head of School of Social Justice in University College Dublin and Visiting Professor at the World Bank, Kyoto University, UMass, Amherst and Marie Curie Senior Fellow at Warwick. Her main areas of research are equality, intra-household distribution and care. She is currently the Irish Expert for the European Union Gender Flagship Project and President Elect of the International Association for Feminist Economics.

Monica Costa is an economist and gender and development researcher with a particular focus on the application of gender-responsive budgeting. Her book, *Gender Responsive Budgeting in Fragile States: The Case of Timor-Leste* (2018), is the first international publication addressing the potential of gender-responsive budgeting in fragile states. She has published widely in leading journals and provided advice to a variety of governments in the Asia-Pacific region.

Rita Griffiths is Research Fellow in the Institute for Policy Research at the University of Bath where she specialises in social security policy and family dynamics in the context of means-tested benefits. Prior to moving into academia, as a founding partner of a private-sector research consultancy, she spent more than 20 years delivering qualitative research and evaluation studies on behalf of UK government departments and a range of UK and European public and third-sector bodies.

Anne-Catherine Guio is a senior researcher at the Luxembourg Institute of Socio-Economic Research. Her main research focuses on material deprivation, poverty, social exclusion and wellbeing. She has published extensively in these fields and was co-editor of *Monitoring Social Inclusion in Europe* (2017, with Tony Atkinson and Eric Marlier) and of *Improving the Understanding of Poverty and Social Exclusion in Europe* (2020, with Eric Marlier and Brian Nolan). She is also Deputy Coordinator of the European Social Policy Analysis Network.

Susan Himmelweit is Emeritus Professor of Economics, Open University, a feminist economist whose research has focused on the gender implications of economic and social policy, the economics and policy of care and intra-household inequalities. She was Founding Chair of the UK Women's Budget Group, which analyses the gender impact of government policy, and coordinates its Policy Advisory Group. She is a past president of the International Association for Feminist Economics and was an associate editor of *Feminist Economics*.

Thandie Hlabana is a Senior Lecturer at the National University of Lesotho, in the Department of Sociology and Social Work. She is also a researcher and PhD candidate at the Centre for Water Cultures, University of Hull. She has been president of the Population Association of Southern Africa and secretary general of the Union for African Population Studies. Her research interests include care and social protection for vulnerable groups in Africa and she drafted the 2014 Lesotho National Policy for Older Persons.

Marilyn Howard is an honorary research associate at the University of Bristol. Her work has included researching domestic and financial abuse and social security for Women's Aid. She has also produced policy publications on aspects of social security, gender equality and violence against women and girls for the UK Women's Budget Group, of which she is a member. Her other roles include policy, research and advocacy on social security benefits, including within national and local government.

Eleni Karagiannaki is Assistant Professorial Research Fellow at the Centre for Analysis of Social Exclusion and Faculty Associate at the International Inequalities Institute at the London School of Economics. She has worked on a range of issues relating to poverty and inequality measurement and analysis, with a particular focus on understanding how the tax and benefit systems, the labour market and families interplay to shape socio-economic inequalities.

Gill Main is founder of the Social Research Collective which aims to promote social justice by democratising social research. Prior to this she worked in academia. Her work focuses on child poverty and social exclusion, and centring the expertise of children, young people and parents with experience of poverty in understanding, measuring and addressing it. She was one of the writers of the 2012 *UK Poverty and Social Exclusion Study* and has also worked closely with non-governmental organisations and local government.

Satomi Maruyama is Associate Professor of Sociology in the Graduate School of Letters at Kyoto University, Japan. Her research interests include poverty and gender, and she specialises in qualitative research methods. She is the author of *Living on the Streets in Japan: Homeless Women Break Their Silence* (2018).

Elena Moore is Professor at the Department of Sociology, University of Cape Town. She is the author of *Generation, Gender and Negotiating Custom in South Africa* (2022), *Divorce, Families and Emotion Work* (2017) and *Reform of Customary Marriage, Divorce and Succession in South Africa* (with Chuma Himonga, 2015). She obtained a Wellcome Career Award (2023–2028) to develop a research programme on Family Caregiving of Older Persons in Southern Africa.

Abena D. Oduro is Associate Professor of Economics at the University of Ghana, Legon, Ghana. She is a member of the African Centre for Excellence in Inequality Research. She has co-authored several papers on gender and assets. Her current research interests are in the areas of gender and trade policy and the socio-economic dimensions of climate change adaptation.

Jan Pahl is Professor Emeritus of Social Policy at the University of Kent. Her research on the allocation of money in the household involved several projects over a number of years. The results were published in two books and over 20 articles and chapters in books. She has recently carried out a study of poverty in Canterbury and is working on the contribution that anti-poverty strategies can make in local areas.

Daria Popova is Senior Research Fellow and Deputy Director at the Centre for Microsimulation and Policy Analysis at the Institute for Social and Economic Research, University of Essex. She is a social scientist with a background in quantitative sociology and social policy. Her research interests include gender inequality inside and outside the labour market, impact assessment of social and fiscal policies and the demographic behaviour of households.

Debora Price is Professor of Social Gerontology at the University of Manchester and Fellow of the Academy of Social Sciences. Formerly a barrister, her research focuses on finance over the life course, especially pensions and poverty in late life, financial services for an ageing society, household money and the financial consequences of cohabitation, separation and divorce. She is particularly interested in the political economy of pensions and how pensions and social security systems influence household and family relationships.

Rhonda Sharp is Emeritus Professor at the University of South Australia where she was formerly a Research Chair and Professor of Economics. The focus of her work has been to integrate a gender perspective into economic and social policies and government budgets through research, writing and working with governments, NGOs and international organisations. She was a founding member of the International Association for Feminist Economics and has served as its president. Current research projects include retirement resources in couple households, women and superannuation, and aged care.

Nicola Sharp-Jeffs is an expert in economic abuse as it occurs within the context of coercive control. Nicola set up the charity Surviving Economic Abuse in 2017 and is its Chief Executive Officer. In 2018, Nicola was also appointed Emeritus Fellow of the Child and Woman Abuse Studies Unit, London Metropolitan University, UK.

Supriya Singh is a sociologist of money and migration. She is Adjunct Professor at La Trobe University in Melbourne, Australia. Her recent books include *Domestic Economic Abuse: The Violence of Money* (2021), *Money, Migration and Family: India to Australia* (2016), *Globalization and Money: A Global South Perspective* (2013) and *Marriage Money: The Social Shaping of Money in Marriage and Banking* (1997).

Kate Summers is British Academy Postdoctoral Research Fellow at the London School of Economics. Kate's research is concerned with experiences and perceptions of poverty, economic inequality and related social policies, with a particular focus on social security policy in the UK context. She pre-dominantly uses qualitative methods including in-depth interviews, focus groups and participatory approaches. Her current research centres on developing qualitative methods to study social security policy in a (post-)pandemic context.

Hema Swaminathan is Senior Economist (Gender) at the Asian Development Bank (on leave from the Centre for Public Policy, Indian Institute of Management Bangalore). Swaminathan's recent and ongoing research focuses on inequality in income and wealth distribution between women and men, exploring female labour participation in India and innovating with survey methodology to collect improved data in several domains (individual-level data on asset ownership and wealth, decision-making by women and women's engagement with the labour market).

Frances Woolley is Professor, Department of Economics, Carleton University. Her research centres on families and public policy. Her most cited work is on modelling family decision-making, measuring within-household inequality, feminist economics and tax-benefit policy towards families. She has served as President of the Canadian Economics Association and Co-Editor of the *Review of Economics of the Household* and the *Canadian Tax Journal*. Frances holds a BA from Simon Fraser University, an MA from Queen's University Canada and a PhD from the London School of Economics.

David Young is Research Fellow at the University of Salford. His research focuses on social security policy and the experience of income change and insecurity. His doctoral research at the Institute for Policy Research, University of Bath involved the use of financial diaries to track low-income households' income. He has worked on two qualitative longitudinal projects investigating experiences of claiming social security benefits, including during the COVID-19 pandemic. His wider research interests include temporality, disability assessments and advice services.

Foreword

Jan Pahl

This is an important book about an important topic. The way in which a household controls and allocates its resources makes an impact on the life chances and standard of living of every member of that household. Of course, 'households' do not allocate resources, but as the studies in this book show, patterns of allocation of resources reflect interactions between members of the household as well as structures in the wider society. Fundamentally, this book is about social and economic processes which shape the quality of life of individuals and families all around the world.

A Research Agenda for Financial Resources within the Household is important because it adds to existing knowledge in three different ways. First, it expands the scope of existing work in terms of household type. Most existing research on this topic has assumed a household containing a couple, and perhaps their dependent children, with finances controlled by the couple jointly, by one individual adult or a mix of both. The studies reported here show that children can be active agents in the household economy, while older couples may have to renegotiate patterns of money management. The sharing of money can extend far beyond couple households. What we are dealing with might be described as 'relationship money', as opposed to 'market money', in that patterns of money management represent obligations of love and responsibility and can also be a form of control. Studies on the allocation of money within multi-generational households, or on the sending of remittances between family members living in different countries, reveal the complexities of such situations.

Second, the book is valuable for its global scope. Much of the existing research focuses on the English-speaking world and on money in couple households. This book draws on data from a range of European countries, from India and South Africa and Lesotho and from the global south generally, extending the focus to societies in which many people live with their extended family. The effect is to raise some significant questions. What should be the definition of a 'household' in exploring the access to money of different members of extended family groups? Who within the household/family group should be interviewed and how differently might different individuals respond to questions about household/family finances? What value should be put on the different monies, assets and sources of wealth to which household members may or may not have access? And what are the moralities which shape financial decision-making in this context?

Finally, the book is strengthened by drawing on the many academic disciplines and approaches represented here. The contributors come from disciplines ranging from economics and public policy to sociology and social policy. They bring expertise drawn from business and banking, childhood studies and gerontology and use approaches involving both quantitative and qualitative methods and participatory strategies.

I was particularly interested to see chapters on the relevance of the topic to debates about social security benefits and income maintenance programmes. The results of research should extend knowledge, but in addition they can be used to inform wider debates and ultimately to increase the quality of life of individuals and communities. Here, research about the allocation of money within the household is used to discuss decisions about the unit of assessment for claiming and receiving benefits and about the temporality of social security, for example in terms of benefit waiting periods and the timing of payments. These are significant policy options which can plunge individuals into dire poverty if the implications of particular decisions are not understood.

When I began research on this topic in 1979, the literature review I carried out could identify only one publication specifically concerned with the distribution of income within the family (Young, 1952). That year the United Kingdom government publication *Social Trends*, in its chapter on income and wealth, commented, 'We have no data about the flows of income between people within households' (Central Statistical Office, 1979). As a researcher it was exciting to find a field which seemed so important and in which there was so much to be discovered (Pahl, 1980, 1989). The situation is very different today, with a wealth of research now published on the control and allocation of money within households, as this book makes clear.

However, there is still much to be done. I hope that this book will encourage researchers working on the control of resources within the household to expand their scope into different cultures and into different sorts of households: for example, it would be interesting to explore flows of money within divorce-extended families. In that way *A Research Agenda for Financial*

Resources within the Household will not only make a valuable contribution in its own right but also be a springboard for research in the future on a topic which affects billions of lives across the globe.

Jan Pahl
University of Kent

References

Central Statistical Office (1979) *Social Trends No. 10*, London, HMSO.
Pahl, J. (1980) Patterns of money management within marriage, *Journal of Social Policy*, 9, 3, 313–335.
Pahl, J. (1989) *Money and Marriage*, London, Macmillan.
Young, M. (1952) The distribution of income within the family, *British Journal of Sociology*, 3, 305–321.

Acknowledgements

The editors would like to thank all those who have taken part in the international network on 'money within the household', some of whom we met in Oxford in July 2019. Many of these went on to write chapters for this volume; but those who did not do so also contributed to the thinking behind it, including Ruth Cain, Jackie Goode, Ceri Hughes, Fatma Ibrahim, Nicole Kapelle, Levana Magnus, Charlott Nyman, Sophie Ponthieux and Simone Wong – as well as Jan Pahl, who has kindly written the Foreword to this volume.

We have learned from them all, and from the many others who conduct research into the management and distribution of resources within the household. We should also like to thank our editor at Edward Elgar, Daniel Mather, whose prompt and positive responses to our queries have been much appreciated in the period of preparation for publication.

Introduction to *A Research Agenda for Financial Resources within the Household*

Fran Bennett, Silvia Avram and Siobhan Austen

A brief overview of research on resources in the household

Many scholars have treated the household as unitary, that is, as an undifferentiated unit, in which individuals put their resources without distinction into one pot and then share and use them within the household to the benefit of all (Samuelson, 1956). Such households were often taken to be a couple (traditionally assumed to be female/male) living together, with or without children (the 'family household': Haddad et al., 1997), rather than more complex household forms (Doss, 2021a: 12–14). This assumption of what was often called 'equal sharing' could, it was argued, be explained by a household acting in the same way as an individual and/or by positing an altruistic household head (Becker, 1981). It made modelling simpler in the absence of good quantitative data on what happens inside the household.

More recently, however, both joint and individual interests within households have increasingly been recognised (Sen, 1990). Using the household as the core unit of analysis is more likely to be justified today, therefore, by citing a lack of knowledge about how resources are shared within the household. However, the previous assumption (often conveyed in shorthand as 'equal sharing') often remains unchanged. Thus, for example, measures of poverty and inequality that rely on income are structured in a way that usually fails to provide information on the receipt of income(s) by different individuals within the household (Atkinson, 2019: 73–76).

Policy makers, too, often continue to target households rather than individuals, using a similar rationale about the impossibility of knowing how resources are shared within the household, with this approach often still interpreted as

1

(gender-)neutral non-interference (Howard, 2019). Sometimes, the 'theoretical' assumption that households will have 'worked out' what is best for themselves is given as the rationale for treating the household as a 'black box' that it is not the business of policy makers to inquire into or influence (Bennett, 2013: 582). This reticence may be based on a distinction between public and private, with the belief that governments should not intervene in 'private' matters such as the family. In circumstances of inequality, however, this has implications for those with less power, in particular women and children (Doss, 2021b).

In attempts to expand these limiting perspectives, scholars continue to make advances in theory and methods in researching the management and allocation of resources within households. Some scholars have modelled 'allocation rules' to illustrate the differences in outcomes that would result from different assumptions about intra-household sharing (e.g. Davies and Joshi, 1994). Attempts have also been made from the 1970s onwards to arrive at a more accurate picture of the mix of individual and joint interests within a household, and of the extent of individual income, consumption and/or wealth (e.g. Ponthieux, 2017) – though such attempts may need to make use of some heroic assumptions about allocation, given the lack of primary data. Policy analysts and practitioners have also sought to change the perspectives of policy makers, and policies themselves, to reflect this more nuanced view (e.g. briefings from the UK Women's Budget Group).

Despite the sustained efforts of researchers to explore this area, however, large research gaps persist in our understanding of the management and distribution of resources within households. There continues to be a need for new data, both qualitative and quantitative, on a range of questions. One of these is about how resources enter the household, and in particular their ownership, what they are and how they are seen by household members. Another is how such resources are then managed and distributed within households, raising issues of power – including the obvious ones of decision-making and control, but also the less obvious, such as subversion by the ostensibly less powerful (Agarwal, 2016: 169). A complex area is how management and distribution of resources, whilst apparently separate activities, in practice interact – including in negative ways, such as through the exercise of latent power, causing some topics to be excluded from discussion (Lukes, 1974) and for financial coercion and abuse to occur within some relationships (Postmus et al., 2020).

There is a need for more research into the reasons behind the patterns of resource ownership, management and distribution within households. Further questions arise about how resources are used, in other words by whom and on whom they are spent – including the importance of different roles within relationships, such as acting as a conduit of resources from one household member to another (Daly and Rake, 2003; Doss, 2021b: 309). We also need to explore in more depth how these patterns are linked to the wellbeing of household members, including not only life satisfaction but also capabilities, autonomy and agency (Nussbaum, 2000).

A range of disciplinary routes has been taken in the investigation to date of issues related to resources within the household – including sociology, social policy, economics, international development and development economics, human geography, psychology, anthropology and other fields, with comprehensive recent overviews compiled (in chronological order) by Burton et al. (2007), Bennett (2013), Kulic and Dotti Sani (2017, 2020), Atkinson (2019) and Doss (2021b).

Research has been developed in the global south (e.g. Doss, 2021b) as well as the global north, using different methods to explore the subject. These include theoretical modelling of how households might work in terms of sharing resources and why (Almas et al., 2023) – and/or how outcomes may differ depending on the differential bargaining power of partners; quantitative investigations of intra-household inequality in financial resources and how this links to differential outcomes for household members; and detailed qualitative investigations of the processes involved in managing money within the household. Most research into resources in households has been carried out by academics, and there is also 'grey' literature from non-governmental organisations and think tanks, but financial institutions, banks, journalists and others also inquire into and write about how couples organise and distribute money.

Theoretical frameworks

Theoretical frameworks have been developed (especially in economics, sociology and psychology), and subsequently refined, to explain how resources are handled and shared (or not) within the household, why this may be the case and the resulting outcomes. Such frameworks include theories to explain why one partner in a couple may have more influence in decision-making: resource theory (Blood and Wolfe, 1960), in which the resources brought into the relationship by each partner are seen as critical; and exchange or marital dependency theory (Nyman and Dema, 2007), in which opportunities outside the relationship are viewed as crucial factors. Research in the global south has demonstrated that it is not just bringing in an income but also making a contribution in other ways that is important in giving some leverage over how resources are used. What contribution someone makes to the household, and in what way(s), may of course themselves also be the subject of negotiation.

Besides theories about monies coming into the household, and the relationships between these and differential sharing outcomes, researchers have examined the processes of what is done with money within the household and who benefits (Bennett, 2013). Gender roles and identities ('doing gender') are argued to influence behaviour (West and Zimmerman, 1987). Typologies of different money management practices have been developed (Pahl, 1989), as have ways of looking at the meanings of different forms of money (Zelizer, 1994). The relative influence of country, culture and social norms on what is done with money are debated (e.g. on norms, see Agarwal, 2016: 158–167); and ideology (for example, about male breadwinning), not just the quantity of resources, can be a determining factor in what goes on (Zelizer, 1994).

Measurement and data

Empirical studies by economists have analysed consumption and inferred patterns of intra-household allocation from (individual) consumption data. There are also large-scale quantitative surveys, to investigate empirically different patterns of pooling, partial pooling and separate management of resources within couples, and how decisions are made about using these resources (Lauer and Yodanis, 2011). Small-scale, in-depth, qualitative investigations have explored the day-to-day management of resources and their implications for couples' relationships and individuals' welfare (e.g. Goode, 2010). Research has also recently developed beyond its traditional limitation to female/male (married) couples to engage with other types of relationships and more complex households (e.g. Burgoyne et al., 2011).

However, empirical analysis of intra-household inequalities faces significant challenges due to inherent measurement difficulties and limitations of existing data. First, some theoretical concepts lack a clear or established empirical counterpart (for example, bargaining power). There are also difficulties in capturing subtle differences between ownership, control and use of resources. And there may be differences of view about what might be the most appropriate outcome to measure (consumption, individual utility or wellbeing, or capabilities, for example).

In addition, information about income ownership is often not collected at the individual level. There are lacunae in the allocation of incomes to individuals (for example, wages are allocated, but capital income usually is not). In many regular surveys the ownership of savings, wealth and debt within households is often unclear – although some (though not all) assets may be capable of allocation to individuals, and there are some surveys which do measure individual wealth (cited in Lersch et al., 2022).

Surveys of consumption tend to suffer the same limitation as surveys of income and, if anything, in addition to being less common, data collection on consumption may be even less individualised than collection of income data (Doss, 2021b; Guio and Van den Bosch, 2019). There are some reasons for this, including the difficulties in operationalising individual deprivation, in particular in relation to 'public goods' (available to all within the household) such as housing and, often, spending on children as well (Almas et al., 2023).

Family forms and living arrangements are also changing – including the increasing numbers of 'living apart together' couples and 'blended' families, for example. These changes may mean that the 'family' and the 'household', and exchanges of resources within and between these units, are not very clear, and that using the household as the central unit of analysis is not always appropriate.

Introducing this volume

As co-editors, we were motivated in part by the relative lack of emphasis on intra-household management and distribution of resources in research in recent years, especially perhaps in the global north, compared with two or three decades ago. The most immediate motivation, however, was that we had brought together contributors from different disciplines for participation in an international network and wanted to ensure that the ideas discussed in that network had a longer and more elaborated shelf life.

The book, then, brings together examples of recent scholarship on financial resources within households and garners perspectives on the future research agenda in this key research area. The book deliberately focuses on monetary and material resources (income and assets/wealth), whilst acknowledging that the distribution and management of other resources (such as labour and time in particular) within the household also have significant effects (Davies and Joshi, 1994). As outlined in greater detail below, the book examines the concepts and tools employed in researching this crucial area to date, and the challenges facing researchers in doing so (Part I); investigates studies that exemplify recent developments in extending the scope of this research (Part II); and, because of the significance of the issues involved for policy, analyses the inter-relationships between policy and intra-household distribution and dynamics (Part III). Within each of these parts, the chapters examine the current state of play in particular sub-fields; discuss current or recent research carried out by the author(s) themselves, where relevant; and explore directions for a future research agenda which would build on past and current insights to move in new and innovative directions. The collection is international in scope, focused on both the global south and global north, and cross-disciplinary.

In preparing the book, we asked authors to approach their chapters in a similar way if this was possible given their topic. Thus, all chapters begin by critically discussing the main issues in their sub-field and all end by identifying the most promising directions for future research. However, there is also variation across the chapters, with some focusing on an overview of the most important conceptual and theoretical models and empirical tools, while others address issues that have previously been less explored in the literature (temporality, economic abuse, etc.). There is also variation in relation to the scope of chapters, with some more focused on the authors' own research and others reviewing the subject more widely.

Our intended audience is academics and early-career researchers in particular, but also a wider readership. The book is therefore intended to provide a solid foundation for understanding the topic of resources within the household, drawing on the comprehensive, topical and nuanced knowledge of leading researchers in the field.

Part I: Concepts, tools, measures and challenges

The first five chapters in the book address many of the above issues, covering the main concepts, tools and measures used in, as well as the primary challenges faced by, research into the management and distribution of intra-household resources. Both quantitative and qualitative approaches and themes are reviewed, and the main hurdles faced by researchers, both theoretical and empirical, are discussed. These include conceptualising the household as a 'black box', the inner workings of which remain unknown (and sometimes unknowable); the difficulties of capturing subtle differences between the ownership, control and use of financial resources; and inadequate attention to the ways in which the measurement of key concepts and standard data collection methods affect findings.

In Chapter 1, drawing primarily on the economics literature, Frances Woolley reviews the main theories and empirical strategies used in quantitative research in this area. She discusses two types of models widely used by economists – bargaining models (inspired by game theory) and collective models – scrutinising their strengths and especially their limitations. She then concludes with a detailed discussion of the practical challenges to incorporating the unequal distribution of resources into standard measures of inequality and poverty, such as the practice of surveying only one adult member in the household, lack of information on agency and processes of decision-making within the household, and insufficient longitudinal data to examine changes of decision-making patterns over time.

Fran Bennett (Chapter 2) follows with a review of the literature using qualitative methods, showing how these have been used to capture the meanings that people attribute to money and its management, the ways in which financial resources are intertwined with relationships, roles and identities and how different forms of money are never neutral but instead are imbued with values and beliefs. She contrasts the strengths of qualitative research with those of quantitative studies, highlighting how qualitative methods such as interviews or focus groups are better placed to capture nuances and complexity. She then draws on a qualitative study of financial autonomy in low- and moderate-income families to show how qualitative methods can be used to address questions that quantitative studies cannot address on their own.

Next (Chapter 3), Satomi Maruyama discusses barriers to opening up the household 'black box', using Japan – a patriarchal society with relatively strong gender inequalities in both paid and unpaid work – as a case study. She argues that there are three main barriers that hinder research on intra-household inequality in Japan: unequal gender outcomes being treated as a result of individual free choices rather than reflecting structural constraints; the value of accounting for intra-household inequality in official statistics and for policy making not being recognised; and the technical difficulties in collecting accurate data on individual ownership, control and use of resources. The chapter finishes with a discussion of the most fruitful avenues for future research, including collecting better data and identifying the bias from the continued use of the 'black box' approach in relation to official measures of poverty and inequality.

In Chapter 4, Sara Cantillon and Anne-Catherine Guio focus on the gaps and limitations in the data used for (quantitative) analysis of intra-household distribution. After first reviewing the main outcome measures used in the literature to document intra-household inequality in economic resources, including income, consumption, deprivation and wealth, and the much smaller literature on the pooling, control and management of resources, they argue that existing data suffer from both quality issues and important gaps. Cantillon and Guio show how standard data collection methods may affect the quality of data in known and potentially unknown ways, thereby biasing research results. They also discuss some important gaps, such as the lack of information on financial autonomy and economic independence, lack of information collected from children, the absence of complex families straddling two or more households and the paucity of longitudinal data. They conclude by suggesting potential ways in which the identified data gaps and limitations could be addressed.

Finally, Silvia Avram and Daria Popova (Chapter 5) introduce a new tool, tax-benefit microsimulation models, and show how these models can be used to address some of the data limitations that have affected quantitative research on intra-household inequalities in income. After reviewing the small literature that uses tax-benefit microsimulation models to study gender income inequalities, they give an example based on their own research to showcase the potential of this tool. Lastly, they elaborate on the most promising ways in which the benefits of incorporating tax-benefit microsimulation models into research on intra-household distribution could be maximised.

Part II: Recent research into resources within the household: new directions taken

The second part of this volume contains five chapters illustrating the new directions taken by research into resources within the household in recent years. More specifically, these include investigations into different and more complex households; examinations of assets and wealth in addition to income; turning the spotlight onto financial coercion and abuse within relationships; exploring colliding moralities of money between different generations in complex migrant households; and highlighting the role of children as agents within the household economy. These extensions of research beyond the traditional focus on the female/male couple negotiating income have enriched the field of study. All the authors in this part also suggest ideas for further development of this research in future.

First, Tania Burchardt and Eleni Karagiannaki (Chapter 6) go beyond the single family unit that has usually been the focus of research on resources within the household. They examine the sharing of resources in multigenerational families living together in Europe in complex households, drawing on the European Union Statistics on Income and Living Conditions. Such households have tended to increase in number since the 2008 financial crisis and have always been common in the global south. They reflect on the implications of the differences in how resources are shared in such households for the reliability of traditional measures of poverty and deprivation that usually assume full sharing.

In Chapter 7, Abena D. Oduro and Hema Swaminathan go beyond the usual focus on income in research on within-household resources to review the issues in trying to collect and analyse individual-level data on assets and wealth, in particular in household surveys in the global south. These include conceptualising ownership; determining which assets must be enumerated; who and how many people in the household to interview; how to value assets; and choosing indicators to measure gender inequality. Drawing on recent empirical work in which they were involved, they recommend how researchers can best address these issues and further extend their investigations.

Chapter 8 by Marilyn Howard and Nicola Sharp-Jeffs considers the literature on economic, including financial, abuse and its relation to research on intra-household resource management and distribution. The authors distinguish between control of resources and control over a household member through coercion, which may then continue beyond separation. They argue that economic, including financial, abuse should be incorporated more fully within research into intra-household resources.

Supriya Singh (Chapter 9) argues that literature on intra-household resources has largely considered nuclear households within state boundaries and that literature on migrants has not usually focused on management and control of money within migrant households. She rectifies this by considering the colliding moralities of different ways of dealing with money within complex households in Australia of two generations of migrants from India.

Lastly, Gill Main (Chapter 10) investigates the place of children within resource management and distribution in the household. Research into intra-household sharing predominantly focuses on adults. But she sees this as out of step with childhood studies, which highlight children's agency as co-constructors of family practices. She considers three case studies on how children have been included in studies of intra-household distribution and concludes with recommendations to researchers on filling methodological and empirical research gaps.

Part III: The inter-relationship between resources within the household and policy

The final part of this volume brings together five chapters on the interface between policy and the distribution of resources within the household. The chapters explore the often implicit assumption of policy affecting households – that those within households can/do harmoniously agree on the allocation of resources – before examining how a range of policy settings shape what happens within households, including: who controls financial resources within the household; how issues relating to the use of resources are decided; who is left vulnerable; and who does the work of managing money. The chapters, which span a range of country contexts, highlight the complex and changing ways in which a wide variety of policy settings affect what happens in households, and point to a need for ongoing research into resources within the household to improve outcomes.

In Chapter 11, Elena Moore and Thandie Hlabana discuss issues around social grants, including old age pensions, in South Africa and Lesotho, contexts where poverty rates are relatively high and many households are multigenerational. The authors draw on their studies of the experiences of such households to show how social grants intended for particular recipients (such as an older person or children) are often used to support the basic needs of many others within the household or family, especially when other social grants either are not available or have low value. The pattern of social grants can result in older household members (for the pension) and primary caregivers of children (for the child grant) having significant money management roles and tasks within households; relationship tensions when different household or family members claim a share of benefits; and economic insecurity when the level of benefits is insufficient to meet all needs within the household. The authors highlight the need for improved employment opportunities for young people and advocate the introduction of financial provision for working-age able-bodied individuals without an income.

Chapters 12 and 13 both address intra-household issues associated with policy related to ageing populations. Chapter 12, by Debora Price, addresses key issues affecting older-couple households by exploring declining cognition in old age. Financialisation is part of the policy context of this chapter, as individuals and families are increasingly being tasked with managing their finances in sophisticated ways into old age, without attention having been paid to how money relations within older households are or might be affected by (different degrees of) financial capability, declining cognition and lack of formal capacity for financial decision-making. The chapter demonstrates the need for a range of policy innovations, including those that might, for example, protect a person against legal, but poor (and declining), financial management by their spouse or partner, especially when there are imbalances of power. To support such policy work there is a need for research to fill a number of key gaps, including what happens when a partner controlling money begins to make bad or unwise decisions, or begins to squander assets that could otherwise have been used to provide resources for their remaining joint lives.

Chapter 13, by Siobhan Austen, Susan Himmelweit, Rhonda Sharp and Monica Costa, has a relatively broad focus, attending to questions about the impacts of the process of financialisation of retirement incomes on older-couple households. Its context is Australia, which is ahead of many other countries in its adoption of defined contribution superannuation. Data from in-depth interviews summarised in the chapter show the various risks and difficulties associated with managing and monitoring financial assets in retirement; how the intra-household ownership of and entitlement to such assets is unequally distributed; and how, as a result, many women struggle to have their interests reflected in decisions made over the use of such assets. The results point to a need to push back against financialisation and develop policy alternatives, such as a non-means-tested old age pension. Research is needed that can measure the financial costs and intra-household effects of alternative retirement income policies and draw on cross-national comparisons.

In Chapter 14, by Rita Griffiths, the focus is on the widespread policy practice of determining eligibility and entitlement to government benefits by jointly assessing couples' needs/income/assets. Drawing on research conducted in the United Kingdom, including on the Universal Credit benefits scheme, the chapter identifies a range of negative consequences stemming from this practice, including a reduction in women's personal income, deterrence of family formation, relationship tensions and discouragement of employment by 'secondary' earners within recipient households. The chapter makes a powerful case for new policies that recognise the importance of financial independence. It identifies a need for additional research to support such policy innovation, including studies of employment and family formation in those countries where benefits are more individualised. A call is also made for efforts to standardise concepts and categories across surveys and studies in different countries, so that comparisons of the ways in which different units of assessment operate in different welfare state contexts can be more easily made.

Finally, Kate Summers and David Young explore the temporal aspects of social security money (Chapter 15), highlighting further the ways in which policy design affects what happens in households. The chapter focuses on the effects of both the timing of social security payments (e.g. fortnightly or monthly) and the waiting times associated with, for example, receiving a benefit or resolution of a claim. Drawing on a longitudinal diary study of means-tested benefits in the United Kingdom, it shows how money management within households can be shaped by the 'rhythms' of the flow of benefits; and how a 'monthly-in-arrears' approach to assessing social security benefits can increase instability and insecurity within households and add to relationship tension. The policy implication is that temporal effects need to be considered in policy evaluation and design. To support such efforts, there is also a need (and great scope) for cross-country studies of temporality and its effects.

References

Agarwal, B. (2016) '"Bargaining" and gender relations', in *Gender Challenges: A Three Volume Compendium of Selected Papers*, Vol. 2, Delhi: Oxford University Press: 141–187.

Almas, I., Attanazio, O. and Carneiro, P. (2023) 'Household decisions and intra-household distributions', in S. Lundberg and A. Voena (eds) *Handbook of the Economics of the Family*, Vol. 1, Amsterdam: North Holland/Elsevier: 111–150.

Atkinson, A.B. (2019) 'Inequality within the household', in Atkinson, A.B. (Micklewright, J. and Brandonlini, A. (eds)) *Measuring Poverty around the World*, Princeton: Princeton University Press: 73–76.

Becker, G.S. (1981) *Treatise on the Family*, Cambridge, MA: Harvard University Press.

Bennett, F. (2013) 'Researching within-household distribution: Overview, developments, debates, and methodological challenges', *Journal of Marriage and Family* 75(3): 582–597.

Blood, R. and Wolfe, D. (1960) *Husbands and Wives: The Dynamics of Married Living*, New York: Free Press.

Burgoyne, C.B., Clarke, V. and Burns, M. (2011) 'Money management and views of civil partnerships in same-sex couples: Results from a UK survey of non-heterosexuals', *The Sociological Review* 59(4): 685–706.

Burton, P., Phipps, S. and Woolley, F. (2007) 'Inequality within the household reconsidered', in S.P. Jenkins and J. Micklewright (eds) *Inequality and Poverty Re-examined*, Oxford: Oxford University Press: 103–127.

Daly, M. and Rake, K. (2003) *Gender and the Welfare State: Care, Work and Welfare in Europe and the USA*, Cambridge: Polity Press/Blackwell.

Davies, H. and Joshi, H. (1994) 'Sex, sharing and the distribution of income', *Journal of Social Policy* 23(3): 301–340.

Doss, C.R. (2021a) 'Diffusion and dilution: The power and perils of integrating feminist perspectives into household economics', *Feminist Economics* 27(3): 1–20.

Doss, C.R. (2021b) 'Intra-household decision-making and resource allocation', in G. Berik and E. Kongar (eds) *The Routledge Handbook of Feminist Economics*, Milton Park: Routledge: 303–311.

Goode, J. (2010) 'The role of gender dynamics in decisions on credit and debt in low-income families', *Critical Social Policy* 30(1): 99–119.

Guio, A.-C. and Van den Bosch, K. (2019) 'Deprivation of women and men living in a couple: Sharing or unequal division?', *Review of Income and Wealth* 66(4): 958–984.

Haddad, L., Hoddinott, J. and Alderman, H. (eds) (1997) *Intra-household Resource Allocation in Developing Countries: Models, Methods and Policy*, Baltimore: Johns Hopkins University Press.

Howard, M. (2019) '"Gender-neutral": Universal Credit equality impact assessments', *Blog for Women's Budget Group*, 16 January: https://wbg.org.uk/blog/gender-neutral-universal-credit-equality-impact-assessments (accessed 28 May 2023).

Kulic, N. and Dotti Sani, G. (2017) 'Intra-household sharing of financial resources: A review', EUI Working Paper MWP, 2017/12, Florence: European University Institute: https://cadmus.eui.eu/bitstream/handle/1814/46817/MWP_2017_12.pdf?sequence=1&isAllowed=y (accessed 21 May 2023).

Kulic, N. and Dotti Sani, G. (2020) 'Within-couple distribution of economic resources: A critical review of extant studies and avenues for future research', *Rassegna Italiana di Sociologia* 3: 623–650.

Lauer, S.R. and Yodanis, C. (2011) 'Individualized marriage and the integration of resources', *Journal of Marriage and Family* 73(3): 669–683.

Lersch, P., Struffolino, E. and Vitali, A. (2022) 'Wealth in couples: An introduction to the special issue', *European Journal of Population* 38(4): 623–641.

Lukes, S. (1974) *Power: A Radical View*, London: Macmillan.

Nussbaum, M. (2000) 'Women's capabilities and social justice', *Journal of Human Development* 1(2): 219–247.

Nyman, C. and Dema, S. (2007) 'An overview: Research on couples and money', in J. Stocks, C. Diaz and B Hallerod (eds) *Modern Couples Sharing Money, Sharing Life*, Basingstoke: Palgrave Macmillan: 7–29.

Pahl, J. (1989) *Money and Marriage*, Basingstoke: Macmillan Education.

Ponthieux, S. (2017) 'Intra-household pooling and sharing of resources: A tentative "modified" equivalised income', in A.B. Atkinson, A.-C. Guio and E. Marlier (eds) *Monitoring Social Inclusion in Europe*, Luxembourg: Eurostat: 175–189.

Postmus, J., Hoge, G., Breckenridge, J., Sharp-Jeffs, N. and Chung, D. (2020) 'Economic abuse as an invisible form of domestic violence: A multicountry review', *Trauma, Violence and Abuse* 21(2): 261–283.

Samuelson, P. (1956) 'Social indifference curves', *Quarterly Journal of Economics* 70(1): 1–22.

Sen, A. (1990) 'Gender and cooperative conflict', in I. Tinker (ed.) *Persistent Inequalities: Women and World Development*, Oxford: Oxford University Press: 123–149.

West, C. and Zimmerman, D.H. (1987) 'Doing gender', *Gender and Society* 1(2): 125–151.

Zelizer, V.A. (1994) *The Social Meaning of Money: Pin Money, Pay Checks, Poor Relief, and Other Currencies*, New York: Basic Books.

PART I

Concepts, tools, measures and challenges

1. How much, and why? A critical introduction to the theory and quantitative analysis of intra-household resource distribution

Frances Woolley

Introduction

Intra-household distribution matters. A pioneering paper by Phipps and Burton (1995: 184) found that the estimated after-tax poverty rate for part-nered women increased from 5.9 to 22.5 per cent when equal sharing assumptions were replaced with minimal sharing assumptions (1995: 192), while partnered men's poverty rates fell to just 3.2 per cent. Corsi et al. (2016) reach similar conclusions. The standard practice of assuming equal sharing of resources within households might drastically understate the extent of poverty and deprivation, as well as gender inequality. Understanding resource sharing within households can also lead to better tax, benefit, social and eco-nomic development policy. But how can we know how much each household member commands or consumes?

This chapter considers two paradigmatically different approaches to studying intra-household resource allocation, drawing primarily from the economics literature. The first conceptualizes a household as a group of rational agents acting strategically – here called a 'strategic interaction' approach. This liter-ature encompasses classic bargaining models of the household, such as those of Manser and Brown (1980), Katz (1997) and Chen and Woolley (2001); for overviews of the more recent literature see Doss (2013), Eswaran (2014) or Laszlo et al. (2020).

The second, the collective model, is outcome focused. It does not attempt to model intra-household bargaining and negotiation. Rather, it uses sophisti-cated econometric techniques and assumptions about people's preferences to arrive at precise estimates of how resources are distributed within households. Key findings will be summarized from this literature about intra-household resource allocation and key assumptions underpinning it will be reviewed.

The concluding section outlines serious challenges in adapting standard quantitative measures of inequality and poverty to incorporate the unequal distribution of resources within households. A broader conception of intra-household resource allocation measurement is proposed – one that does not necessarily give a precise answer to the question 'how much?', but may be better able to answer the question 'what matters – and why?'

Households as sites of strategic interactions

Strategic interactions occur when multiple actors make choices that affect one another, within the context of institutions and other structures that constrain their choices. Strategic interaction models focus on the household decision-making process. For example, one model might see work decisions as the outcome of bargaining, whereby household members choose and commit to a division of labour. Another might focus on the challenge of ensuring commitment: for example, someone might be reluctant to work extra hours for pay or in the home, knowing that their partner might respond by reducing their own work effort. A third might identify factors enhancing women's agency, that is their ability to take decisions and act on them, and the consequences of that agency.

One strength of the strategic interaction approach is that it forces analysts to be explicit about their assumptions about how decision-making is structured, and logically work through the implications of the constraints people have, as well as their incentives and preferences. This makes it possible to analyse and predict the impact of rules and institutions – such as divorce laws, property laws, tax and benefit payments, support from extended family or services for domestic violence survivors – on intra-household resource allocation. Thus, a strategic interaction model can explain, for example, how and why women and girls might be made better off by policies paying child benefits to mothers (Lundberg et al., 1997), or worse off by policies limiting their opportunities to own property (Zhang, 2020). This approach can explain how a change in divorce laws can affect resource allocation among still-married couples, by changing the credibility of a divorce threat – and why, if it is not credible, a change in divorce laws might not matter.

Many strategic interaction models take an 'as if' approach. Household members are assumed to act *as if* they were strategic agents – even if they justify their actions (to themselves and/or others) with reference to, say, their astrological sign. Moreover, rational or strategic does not necessarily imply selfish. A person may be highly strategic in promoting their child's wellbeing, for example. The key assumption is consistency in the things people want, facilitating the use of analytical tools to understand their actions.

Strategic interaction models working within a formal analytical framework are limited by what can be analysed using, say, the tools of game theory. Thus, many such models have two decision-makers, usually conceived of as an adult man and woman, husband and wife. The household may have other members – e.g. elders or children – but often these matter only to the extent that the two decision-makers care about them and/or they constrain these decision-makers' choices. So, for example, researchers have studied how women's decision-making power or autonomy affects child outcomes (for a survey, see Richards et al., 2013); but children are seen as passive care recipients, not decision-making agents, in these models (see Main, this volume). Household decision-making does not have to be conceived of so narrowly, however. The famous 'rotten kid theorem' (Becker, 1974) purports to discuss the conflict between parent and child, while Oreffice (2011) considers intra-household decision-making in same-sex households and Gupta et al. (2021) consider the multiple bilateral relationships in extended families.

Formal models of strategic interaction typically simplify resource allocation choices by reducing them to just two or three dimensions, such as leisure, private consumption of goods benefiting one household member only (cigarettes in a one-smoker household, say) or 'public goods' benefiting all household members (such as a warm, safe home). These models are best seen as metaphors: even if a two-dimensional model is not the literal truth, it can still give insights into household decision-making.

A key concept underlying many strategic interaction models is 'cooperative conflict' (Sen, 1987). Household members are better off if they cooperate – sharing groceries and buying in bulk, for example. A 'Pareto-efficient outcome' is one where every household member enjoys the highest level of consumption possible, contingent upon other household members' consumption and any other constraints they face. There are many possible Pareto-efficient outcomes. Each one represents a different way of dividing resources between members of the household. Once one of these Pareto-efficient points is reached, the only way to make one person better off is to make another worse off.

Reaching a Pareto-efficient outcome involves cooperation; but choosing between Pareto-efficient outcomes is inherently conflictual. For example, the household could reach a Pareto-efficient outcome by pooling resources to buy a new, more fuel-efficient cooking stove – disproportionately benefiting the person who gathers fuel and cooks. Alternatively, they could buy a new, more efficient, irrigation system – disproportionately benefiting the person who waters the fields. But a choice must be made; and that involves trade-offs.

Early contributions in the strategic interaction tradition resolved intra-household conflicts using cooperative game theory. This theory posits that no one would accept a cooperative bargain offering them less than they would receive in their fallback position – what they could get if negotiations broke down. It then makes assumptions about how people reach agreements and, on this basis, argues that people will split gains from cooperation evenly.

In cooperative bargaining, the fallback position is crucial to the determination of outcomes. But how should we think of this? It has been interpreted as the payoff to exiting the household (Katz, 1997). This in turn is influenced by divorce laws (Brassiolo, 2016), a person's earning power and income and welfare state provisions such as child benefits, for example, or subsidized childcare. Anything improving the situation of women who leave relationships would be expected to shift outcomes within those relationships in women's favor.

The fallback position can also be interpreted as remaining within the household but acting non-cooperatively, that is doing what maximizes one's own wellbeing contingent on the other party's actions (see, e.g. Chen and Woolley, 2001) or retreating to a 'separate sphere' within the household (Lundberg and Pollak, 1993). In this view, divorce and outside opportunities are less important, but access to resources within marriage – via, for example, employment opportunities or social benefits – is crucial. However the fallback position is conceived, all bargaining models stand in contrast to the traditional economic view of the family that all goods are shared and every household member enjoys the same living standard.

There is evidence in support of the key proposition of bargaining theory that people with better fallback positions enjoy better outcomes. For example, there is research linking benefits paid to mothers to increased spending on goods benefiting women and children (Lundberg et al., 1997; see Doss, 2013 for an overview of this literature). Other outcomes, too, respond to bargaining. For example, Wang (2014) studied a reform expanding private property ownership in China, finding that, when ownership rights were granted to men rather than women, men decreased their share of household chores. And transfers targeted to women have been found to reduce physical violence against women (see e.g. Roy et al., 2019), although there is less consensus on this (see Howard and Sharp-Jeffs, this volume).

This evidence should, however, be interpreted with caution. Resources are multi-dimensional. Consider, for example, the extensive evidence associating transfers to women with increased spending on children (Gitter and Barham, 2008). One might assume that because women choose to spend resources they control on children this makes them better off. However, critical analysis of Mexico's Oportunidades programme, which directs resources to children through mothers, argues: 'there are reasons to doubt how far the programme has succeeded in "empowering women" when its success is so dependent on fortifying and normalizing the responsibilities of motherhood' (Molyneux, 2006: 440). Moreover, as Anderson (2022) argues, empowerment within the household may be unrelated – or even inversely related – to empowerment outside it. Capturing the multi-dimensional nature of intra-household resource distribution is both challenging and a research opportunity.

Another type of evidence in favor of bargaining theory is the link between the influence women report over household decisions and the outcomes of these decisions. For example, Cassidy et al. (2021) find female bargaining power predicting condom use in a country with high HIV rates, while Mohapatra and Simon (2017) find that in rural India the degree to which women influence decision-making influences the decision to invest in improved cooking stoves. Yet these studies beg the question: what determines how much influence each household member has on decision-making?

There is a rich sociological literature suggesting that, while material factors such as women's employment outside the household influence decision-making power, they are not determinative. Kabeer (1997) observes women choosing to surrender control over their earnings to avoid threatening male breadwinner ideology. Each household member's fallback position, and their ability to translate that into beneficial outcomes, is influenced by social norms as well as material resources. As Bradshaw (2013: 84) argues, 'both income and ideology are important for changing women's position within the household'.

Yet this raises a challenge for bargaining theory. If the impact of changes in someone's fallback position is mediated through social norms and ideologies, how do we know when material factors or social norms and ideologies will be more influential? What is the value added of a theory that can rationalize almost any empirical finding by saying that, if something improves women's outcomes, it must have increased their bargaining power? The final section of this chapter discusses how Kabeer (1999) and others have theorized empowerment, that is the expansion of the ability to make strategic life choices, and how this concept can be used to understand household decision-making and resource allocation.

First, however, a class of models is discussed that has largely subsumed and superseded the bargaining model, particularly within the economics and policy literature on intra-household resource allocation: the collective model.

Measuring the intra-household distribution of resources

The collective model of household decision-making responds to two limitations of strategic interaction models. First, the decision-making process within households is often unobserved, so it is difficult to directly test these models' assumptions about strategic interaction. Indeed, some might be uncomfortable with seeing household members as rational agents interacting strategically. There is a long tradition in economics of viewing the household as a place of consensus, either because blood is thicker than water (Samuelson, 1956) or because it is united by a benevolent dictator (Becker, 1974). Another potential drawback of the strategic interaction approach is that it rarely gives a precise answer to the question: 'how much?' – i.e. how much each household member consumes.

The collective approach to intra-household resource distribution starts with mainstream microeconomic methods. First, assumptions are made about the general structure of people's preferences. For example, it is assumed that people's preferences are, in some sense, similar, making it possible to infer one person's demand by observing another's spending. It is also assumed that preferences can be represented using equations of a certain form – equivalent to assuming that decisions are made in certain ways. For example, it is commonly assumed that preferences are 'separable'. This suggests that people make spending decisions by first allocating their spending into broad categories such as 'clothing' or 'transport' and then deciding their spending within each category.

Assumptions are also made about the technology of household production and consumption. An example of a 'consumption technology' is the extent to which goods are shared between household members. For instance, is a television something that is exclusively used by one household member, or can several household members consume it at the same time? These assumptions about preferences and technology make it possible to estimate consumers' demand functions[1] from standard household expenditure data and then – crucially – work backwards from these to people's preferences and make inferences about wellbeing.

A household's demand for electricity or food can be inferred by observing aggregate *household* spending on each. A collective model attempts to estimate *individual*-level demand. For this an 'assignable good' is needed – that (a) is consumed by household members individually; (b) only benefits the person consuming the good; and (c) can be observed (i.e. data are available on how much each household member consumes). Table 1.1 lists some recent papers using the collective approach and lists the 'assignable good' in each. Most use data on clothing purchases, food intake or the amount of time available for 'leisure' (time not spent in paid work or household production).

But how can spending on clothing or food be generalized to resource allocation as a whole? Typically, additional assumptions and more information are needed. One frequent assumption is that the division of resources within the household is determined by a 'sharing rule'. The implication is that private (individual) expenditures not observed in the data are divided in the same way as observable, assignable goods. This is key because it rules out the possibility that consumption of, say, alcohol might be much more unequally divided than clothing.

The sharing rule reflects a consensus reached through 'an unspecified decision process' (Bargain et al., 2014: 264; for an overview see Himmelweit et al., 2013; Ponthieux and Meurs, 2015). This rule is, however, influenced by 'distributional parameters', such as the age difference between spouses or their relative education levels. Once the sharing rule is decided, the household uses a two-stage budget process. First, resources are allocated to each household member's private expenditure and to shared goods, such as housing, according to the sharing rule. Second, each household member chooses how to allocate their private funds between, say, clothing and coffee, contingent upon the sharing rule (Cherchye et al., 2012: 3383–3384).

'Assignable goods' only make up some of household spending. A substantial part goes instead towards 'public goods' or 'collective consumption goods' benefiting all household members – shelter, for example. Typically, collective models assume that these public goods benefit all household members equally. Thus, to identify precisely how income is divided within a household, information is necessary on both the consumption of goods assignable to one

Table 1.1 Collective estimates of resource sharing

Authors	Setting	Assignable good	Sample results
Lise and Seitz (2011)	UK, 1968 to 2001	Expenditures net of housing, durables	Women receive on average 39.6% of full household income, net of public goods expenditure.
Dunbar, Lewbel and Pendakur (2013)	Father/mother/children households in Malawi	Clothing	In a three-child household, men's share = 43–47%; women's share = 17–18%; per child share = 12–13%.
Bargain, Donni and Kwenda (2014)	Cote d'Ivoire	Clothing	'Men's and women's shares of household total expenditure are of the same order of magnitude and positively related to spouses' education. Even if the distribution is slightly more favorable to men, it is not significantly so.' (p.263)
Lechene, Pendakur and Wolf (2019)	Albania, Bangladesh, Bulgaria, Iraq and Malawi	Clothing (all countries) and food (Bangladesh)	Statistically significant differences in resource shares in two out of five countries (several countries not reported). Bangladesh: An average woman is allocated 83% (clothing) or 69% (food) of a man's resources. Iraq: Women's resources 86% of men's.
Lise and Yamada (2019)	Japan	Time use data, reported expenses 'for all of your family' 'you' 'your husband' and 'your child(ren)' (p.2201)	'Evaluated at the mean of the data, the estimate of the weight placed on the wife's utility in the household is 0.44.' (p.2191)

Authors	Setting	Assignable good	Sample results
Cherchye, De Rock, Surana and Vermeulen (2020)	US, PSID data	Leisure; public and private goods	Men's consumption within household 12–17% higher than women's.
Calvi, Penglase, Tommasi and Wolf (2023)	Bangladesh, Mexico	Food (Bangladesh) and clothing (Mexico)	Bangladesh: A woman on average is allocated 77% of men's resources; each child receives 44%. Mexico: a woman's average resource share is 16% higher than a man's.

family member (such as clothing) and the household's total expenditures on goods that are shared. It is also necessary to assume that these goods are shared equally – with no inequality in access to or control over household space, for example.

Table 1.1 shows that several 'collective model' studies of intra-household resource allocation find no evidence that women are disadvantaged in intra-household resource allocation. Lechene et al. (2019) only find statistically significant differences in resource allocation in two out of five countries studied; Bargain et al. (2014) find no statistically significant differences; and Calvi et al. (2023) find differences in only one country. Others do find evidence of gender inequality disadvantaging women. One particularly interesting result is by Dunbar et al. (2013), who estimate that additional spending on children comes mostly at the expense of mothers' consumption – meaning that females' income share in large families is very low. Generally speaking, however, the amount of intra-household inequality reported in the studies in Table 1.1 is less than the amount of gender wage or wealth inequality in the countries/time periods studied.

One striking aspect of these studies is that they draw broad conclusions about intra-household allocation from observations about just a few spending categories, including one or, at most, two 'assignable goods'. As noted earlier, this typically requires some additional assumptions. For example, Lise and Seitz (2011) assume that spouses with equal earnings potential always share consumption equally – assuming away gender norms assigning very different roles and responsibilities to men and women. Cherchye et al. (2020) assume that everyone who is married is better off than if they were single. This allows the use of information on single people's expenditure patterns to draw conclusions about married people's demand functions – but might not be entirely plausible.

Another common assumption is that household decision-making produces Pareto-efficient outcomes, that is, they represent resource allocations where no one person can be made better off without making someone else worse off. However, experimental studies have rejected the assumption that household members always behave efficiently (Kebede et al., 2014; Cochard et al., 2016). Munro (2018: 143) concludes: 'the results of the literature are qualitatively and quantitatively strongly against … efficiency, though there does seem to be some suggestion that the results in high-income countries might be more favourable to efficiency compared to those in low-income societies'.

Some of the assumptions made in collective models are very technical. For example, Cherchye et al. (2020: 3383) write: 'generic identification holds under a specific (weak) non-singularity condition, which pertains to the partial derivatives of the subutility functions'. When assumptions are presented in terms of mathematical equations rather than substantive implications, it can be hard to intuit the meaning of these technical assumptions. This is unsatisfactory because, without some intuitive sense of how results have been reached, it is hard to know how much to trust the quantitative estimates.

The collective approach is, in the language of Kuhn (1962), 'normal science'. The approach does not challenge the basic paradigm of economics. Instead, it treats intra-household resource allocation as a puzzle that can be solved with an imaginative repurposing of standard tools. The basic assumptions of economics – that households reach a consensus on resource allocation, for example, and usually behave efficiently – are maintained. Most importantly, the sharing rule is, in some sense, outside the model: yes, distributional parameters that influence the sharing rule are identified empirically, but there is no understanding of how the sharing rule is arrived at, or how it can be changed – that is, how empowerment can happen.

Directions for future research

If the collective approach does not provide a satisfactory answer to the question of how resources are allocated within households, what is the alternative? To begin with, better answers require better data.

Research on intra-household resource allocation is hampered by the widespread practice of only surveying one person per household (see also Oduro and Swaminathan, this volume). There are some exceptions, such as the Australian HILDA data set used by Austen et al. (2022) to compare the impact of retirement on men's and women's wellbeing, but one-respondent-per-household is the general rule. This creates two problems. First, without data on at least two household members, it is challenging to measure the impact of policies on the relative wellbeing of women, men and children within the same household. Second, men and women living within the same household may report different realities. For example, Doss et al. (2018) show that men and women in the same household answer questions about the value of household property differently. There is also a substantial body of evidence that husbands and wives provide different answers to questions about household decision-making (Anderson et al., 2017). If there are gender differences in various forms of response bias, in access to information about the household's financial situation or even in perceptions of reality, information should be obtained from multiple household members to understand better what is happening inside a household. Thus, a key research priority is to gather information from multiple household members, to provide richer data on intra-household resource distribution and more accurate data on wealth and other financial variables (see Cantillon and Guio, this volume).

A second and related need is for more information on what Kabeer (1999: 435) calls 'agency', which includes 'processes of decision-making, as well as less measurable manifestations of agency such as negotiation, deception and manipulation'. Many early studies of household decision-making were small-scale, qualitative and/or on specific populations. However, since 2003, the United States Demographic and Health Survey (DHS, 2008) has been carrying out large-scale surveys in countries around the world which scale up the concept of agency with questions about intra-household decision-making, such as 'who usually makes decisions about major household purchases – respondent, husband/partner, respondent and husband/partner jointly, someone else' (DHS, 2008: w-51).

There are drawbacks to this type of question. Often a question only captures one type of decision, but decision-making is multi-dimensional. Women have more agency in some spheres of decision-making but less in others. It does not capture gradations of influence, the intermediate space between completely joint and completely solo decision-making. Also, as with any survey, there is a risk of response bias, particularly social desirability bias – the tendency to provide an answer that is socially acceptable, rather than accurate. Yet, the great strength of the question is that it can create an internationally comparable measure of women's agency within the household (World Bank, 2012).

There is considerable scope for expanding on these initiatives by collecting internationally comparable measures of agency in an expanded set of countries. Although many surveys, such as the United States Health and Retirement Study (Tennyson et al., 2022), collect information about decision-making, the precise wording of the question differs from survey to survey, making international comparisons challenging. Here, coordination between statistical agencies and survey sponsors could be of value. Also needed is information about decision-making for a broader group of respondents, not just the women of childbearing age surveyed by the DHS.

One reason that improved data are so important is that this would facilitate the development of indicators of intra-household gender equality. Gender empowerment indicators, such as the United Nations Human Development Report's Gender Development Index and Gender Empowerment Measure (Melikidze et al., 1995), the World Economic Forum's Global Gender Gap Index (World Economic Forum, 2022) and the Organisation for Economic Co-operation and Development's (OECD) Social Institutions and Gender index (OECD, 2023), have been powerful tools in mobilizing action on gender equality and monitoring progress. Typically, these indices include measures of health, such as life expectancy; economic empowerment, such as labour force participation, employment or earnings; education, such as school enrolments, graduation rates or literacy; and political empowerment, such as female representation in legislatures or other decision-making bodies. The OECD Social Institutions and Gender index even attempts to measure the extent of discrimination in the family by comparing international responses to attitudinal questions, including 'When a mother works for pay, the children suffer' (OECD, 2023). Developing gender empowerment indicators that include more and richer information on inequality within the household would be an effective way of drawing attention to intra-household inequality.

A final priority is longitudinal research – studies that track the evolution of decision-making over time. Implicit or explicit in much research on intra-household resource distribution is the notion of empowerment: that it is desirable to increase women's agency so that they have more say, more self-determination. Yet only by tracking decision-making over time is it possible to identify and study changes in agency. Although longitudinal research is expensive, more could be done with existing surveys. For example, the large, longitudinal United States National Health and Retirement Study asks both male and female respondents who has the final say in major household decisions – but does not repeat the question across survey waves, making it impossible to track the evolution of agency of this kind over time.

While there is much to be done, much has also been accomplished: the creation of a large and growing body of literature across multiple disciplines and geographical areas that provides a deep and rich knowledge of intra-household resource allocation.

Note

1. A demand function gives the functional relationship between the quantity of a good demanded, on the one hand, and prices and incomes, on the other hand.

References

Anderson, C.L., Reynolds, T.W. and Gugerty, M.K. (2017). 'Husband and wife perspectives on farm household decision-making authority and evidence on intra-household accord in rural Tanzania'. *World Development* 90: 169–183.

Anderson, S. (2022). 'Unbundling female empowerment'. *Canadian Journal of Economics/Revue canadienne d'économique* 55(4): 1671–1701.

Austen, S., Kalsi, J.K. and Mavisakalyan, A. (2022). 'Retirement and the distribution of intra-household wellbeing'. *Journal of the Economics of Ageing* 23: 100404.

Bargain, O., Donni, O. and Kwenda, P. (2014). 'Intrahousehold distribution and poverty: Evidence from Cote d'Ivoire'. *Journal of Development Economics* 107: 262–276.

Becker, G.S. (1974). 'A theory of social interactions'. *Journal of Political Economy* 82(6): 1063–1093.

Bradshaw, S. (2013). 'Women's decision-making in rural and urban households in Nicaragua: the influence of income and ideology.' *Environment and Urbanization* 25, no. 1: 81–94.

Brassiolo, P. (2016). 'Domestic violence and divorce law: When divorce threats become credible'. *Journal of Labor Economics* 34(2): 443–477.

Calvi, R., Penglase, J., Tommasi, D. and Wolf, A. (2023). 'The more the poorer? Resource sharing and scale economies in large families'. *Journal of Development Economics* 160: 102986.

Cassidy, R., Bruinderink, M.G., Janssens, W. and Morsink, K. (2021). 'The power to protect: Household bargaining and female condom use'. *Journal of Development Economics* 153: 102745.

Chen, Z. and Woolley, F. (2001). 'A Cournot–Nash model of family decision making'. *The Economic Journal* 111(474): 722–748.

Cherchye, L, De Rock, B. and Vermeulen, F. (2012). "Married with children: A collective labor supply model with detailed time use and intrahousehold expenditure information." *American Economic Review* 102(7): 3377–3405.

Cherchye, L., De Rock, B., Surana, K. and Vermeulen, F. (2020). 'Marital matching, economies of scale, and intrahousehold allocations'. *Review of Economics and Statistics* 102(4): 823–837.

Cochard, F., Couprie, H. and Hopfensitz, A. (2016). 'Do spouses cooperate? An experimental investigation'. *Review of Economics of the Household* 14(1): 1–26.

Corsi, M., Botti, F. and D'Ippoliti, C. (2016). 'The gendered nature of poverty in the EU: Individualized versus collective poverty measures'. *Feminist Economics* 22(4): 82–100.

DHS (Demographic and Health Surveys) Program. (2008). DHS model questionnaire – Phase 5 (2003–2008): www.dhsprogram.com/publications/publication-DHSQ5-DHS-Questionnaires-and-Manuals.cfm (accessed 16 May 2023).

Doss, C.R. (2013). 'Intrahousehold bargaining and resource allocation in developing countries'. *World Bank Research Observer* 28(1): 52–78.

Doss, C.R., Catanzarite, Z., Baah-Boateng, W., Swaminathan, H., Deere, C.D., Boakye-Yiadom, L. and Suchitra, J.Y. (2018). 'Do men and women estimate property values differently?' *World Development* 107: 75–86.

Dunbar, G.R., Lewbel, A. and Pendakur, D. (2013). 'Children's resources in collective households: Identification, estimation, and an application to child poverty in Malawi'. *American Economic Review* 103(1): 438–471.

Eswaran, M. (2014). *Why Gender Matters in Economics*. Princeton: Princeton University Press.

Gitter, S.R. and Barham, B.L. (2008). 'Women's power, conditional cash transfers, and schooling in Nicaragua'. *World Bank Economic Review* 22(2): 271–290.

Gupta, S., Ksoll, C. and Maertens, A. (2021). 'Intra-household efficiency in extended family households: Evidence from rural India'. *Journal of Development Studies* 57(7): 1172–1197.

Himmelweit, S., Santos, C., Sevilla, A. and Sofer, C. (2013). 'Sharing of resources within the family and the economics of household decision making'. *Journal of Marriage and Family* 75(3): 625–639.

Kabeer, N. (1997). 'Women, wages and intra-household power relations in urban Bangladesh'. *Development and Change* 28(2): 261–302.

Kabeer, N. (1999). 'Resources, agency, achievements: Reflections on the measurement of women's empowerment'. *Development and Change* 30(3): 435–464.

Katz, E. (1997). 'The intra-household economics of voice and exit'. *Feminist Economics* 3(3): 25–46.

Kebede, B., Tarazona, M., Munro, A. and Verschoor, A. (2014). 'Intra-household efficiency: An experimental study from Ethiopia'. *Journal of African Economies* 23(1): 105–150.

Kuhn, T.S. (1962). *The Structure of Scientific Revolutions*. Chicago: University of Chicago Press.

Laszlo, S., Grantham, K., Oskay, E. and Zhang, T. (2020). 'Grappling with the challenges of measuring women's economic empowerment in intrahousehold settings'. *World Development* 132: 104959.

Lechene, V., Pendakur, K. and Wolf, A. (2019). 'OLS estimation of the intra-household distribution of consumption'. IFS Working Papers W19/19. London: Institute for Fiscal Studies.

Lise, J. and Seitz, S. (2011). 'Consumption inequality and intra-household allocations'. *Review of Economic Studies* 78(1): 328–355.

Lise, J. and Yamada, K. (2019). 'Household sharing and commitment: Evidence from panel data on individual expenditures and time use'. *Review of Economic Studies* 86(5): 2184–2219.

Lundberg, S.J. and Pollak, R.A. (1993). 'Separate spheres bargaining and the marriage market'. *Journal of Political Economy* 101(6): 988–1010.

Lundberg, S.J., Pollak, R.A. and Wales, T.J. (1997). 'Do husbands and wives pool their resources? Evidence from the United Kingdom Child Benefit'. *Journal of Human Resources* 32(3): 463–480.

Manser, M. and Brown, M. (1980). 'Marriage and household decision-making: A bargaining analysis'. *International Economic Review* 21(1): 31–44.

Melikidze, V., Stancliffe, R. and Tarkhan-Mouravi, G. (1995). *Human Development Report 1995: Gender and Human Development*. New York: United Nations Development Programme.

Mohapatra, S. and Simon, L. (2017). 'Intra-household bargaining over household technology adoption'. *Review of Economics of the Household* 15(4): 1263–1290.

Molyneux, M. (2006). 'Mothers at the service of the new poverty agenda: Progresa/Oportunidades, Mexico's conditional transfer programme'. *Social Policy and Administration* 40(4): 425–449.

Munro, A. (2018). 'Intra-household experiments: A survey'. *Journal of Economic Surveys* 32(1): 134–175.

OECD (Organisation for Economic Co-operation and Development) (2023). Social Institutions and Gender (indicator). www .oecd .org/ stories/ gender/ social -norms -and-gender-discrimination/ (accessed 4 May 2023).

Oreffice, S. (2011). 'Sexual orientation and household decision making: Same-sex couples' balance of power and labor supply choices'. *Labour Economics* 18(2): 145–158.

Phipps, S.A. and Burton, P.S. (1995). 'Sharing within families: Implications for the measurement of poverty among individuals in Canada'. *Canadian Journal of Economics* 28(1): 177–204.

Ponthieux, S. and Meurs, D. (2015). 'Gender inequality'. In A.B. Atkinson and F. Bourguignon (eds), *Handbook of Income Distribution,* vol. 2: 981–1146. Amsterdam: Elsevier.

Richards, E., Theobald, S., George, A., Kim, J.C., Rudert, C., Jehan, K. and Tolhurst, R. (2013). 'Going beyond the surface: Gendered intra-household bargaining as a social determinant of child health and nutrition in low and middle income countries'. *Social Science and Medicine* 95: 24–33.

Roy, S., Hidrobo, M., Hoddinott, J. and Akhter Ahmed, A. (2019). 'Transfers, behavior change communication, and intimate partner violence: Postprogram evidence from rural Bangladesh'. *Review of Economics and Statistics* 101(5): 865–877.

Samuelson, P.A. (1956). 'Social indifference curves'. *Quarterly Journal of Economics* 70(1): 1–22.

Sen, A. (1987). 'Gender and cooperative conflicts'. WIDER Working Papers (1986–2000) 1987/018. Helsinki: UNU-WIDER.

Tennyson, S., Hae, K.-Y. and Woolley, F. (2022). 'My wife is my insurance policy: Household bargaining and couples' purchase of long-term care insurance'. *Research on Aging* 44(9–10): 692–708.

Wang, S.-Y. (2014). 'Property rights and intra-household bargaining'. *Journal of Development Economics* 107: 192–201.

World Bank (2012). *World Development Report 2012: Gender Equality and Development.* Washington, DC: World Bank. https:// openknowledge .worldbank .org/ handle/ 10986/4391 (accessed 4 May 2023).

World Economic Forum (2022). *Global Gender Gap Report.* Geneva: World Economic Forum. www.weforum.org/reports/global-gender-gap-report-2022 (accessed 4 May 2023).

Zhang, E. (2020). 'When family property becomes individual property: Intrahousehold property ownership and women's well-being in China'. *Journal of Marriage and Family* 82(4): 1213–1233.

2. Resources, roles and relationships: What qualitative research can reveal about resources within the household

Fran Bennett

Introduction: The contributions of qualitative research in investigating intra-household resources

Qualitative research has been a key tool in the development of literature on the intra-household *management* of resources (i.e. processes, or how it works) and their *distribution* (i.e. outcomes, or how it works out). These issues are at the intersection of several trends, including women's growing financial independence, increasing individualisation of financial risk and – according to Pahl (1999, cited in Goode, 2009) – changes in financial services and technology reducing the need to deal with resources together as a household. In addition, in the global south and increasingly also the north, more complex households exist, which deal with resources in different ways (Burchardt and Karagiannaki, this volume).

One strength of qualitative research is its ability to explore interpretations, feelings and views, thereby facilitating nuanced and complex understandings (Denzin and Lincoln, 1998). This chapter first outlines the main uses of qualitative research in investigating intra-household resources, and then focuses on how it can facilitate the analysis of meanings attached to money; how dealing with money relates to individuals' identities, roles and values; and the functions money performs in relationships, or the 'emotional economy' of family life (Goode, 2010, cited in Bennett, 2013; Singh and Bhandari, 2012).

Common methods employed in qualitative research on intra-household resources include individual interviews (in person, by telephone or online). These may involve members of couples, and can include children (Main, this volume) in lone parent or couple households; they can also involve those living in complex households (Moore and Hlabana, this volume). In the case of couples in particular, joint interviews may be conducted. Interviews can range from structured to unstructured, with semi-structured the most frequent (involving an interview guide but used flexibly). Web-based sources now allow analysis of individuals' communications about intra-household money via online fora (e.g. Moor and Kanji, 2019). Focus groups, and ethnographies and diaries (Ritchie and Lewis, 2003), may also be used. Qualitative longitudinal methods (Neale, 2021) have been employed to explore, for example, gender dynamics in low-income families' experiences of credit and debt (Goode, 2009) and temporality in social security (Summers and Young, this volume). The most common method used, however, is one-off interviews. One concern in relation to couples is that only those at ease in their relationships may agree to participate (e.g. Nyman, 2003). Comparative qualitative research in this area is rare and also challenging (Nyman et al., 2013).

Analysis in qualitative research often focuses on identifying themes (Silverman, 2006), but may be perceived as unable to lead to generalised conclusions holding across diverse contexts. However, its insights can be linked to theory, and thus be more generally applicable. As demonstrated in the project drawn on below (Bennett and Sung, 2013), which used the same database of United Kingdom (UK) couples for quantitative and qualitative analysis,[1] qualitative research can be combined with other methods. Qualitative and quantitative research are also complementary, with qualitative findings suggesting new issues to quantify, and quantitative study revealing new areas to explore in depth.

The following three sections discuss how qualitative research can explore meanings attached to money; the interaction of intra-household management and distribution of resources with relationships, roles and identities; and relevant values and norms.

What qualitative research can reveal

Meanings of money and how it is handled

We focus here on key findings from qualitative research about the potential for diverse meanings of, first, different kinds of money (Daly, 2017) received by different people in the household, and then the pooling or sharing of that money within the household. Different resources may have varying importance in different contexts – for example, the significance of women's property assets in intra-household relationships in the global south may have been underestimated because of assumptions transferred from the global north (Agarwal et al., 2009). But in addition, whilst money in the marketplace has traditionally been seen as a neutral, and endlessly fungible, means of exchange (Bennett, 2013: 582), qualitative researchers argue that its varied social meanings influence how money from different sources is valued and used (Pahl, 1989; Zelizer, 1994). Such meanings can also change over time (Nyman, 2003).

Building on this understanding of different social meanings of money, Nyman (2003) investigated these meanings for ten married Swedish female–male working- or middle-class couples with children; she also explored the implications for the access of individuals in these couples to money and consumption. Partners were interviewed separately. All the couples emphasised the needs of the family and (re)defined at least some forms of money as belonging to the family. But several participants also valued personal ownership of money. Using this individual money for family needs could express love and trust between partners; but it could also be used to maintain the power hierarchy between household members. A study by Hallerod et al. (2007: 144–147) also showed how 'personalised' monies (e.g. gifts or transfers from a partner) could carry expectations about future behaviour by the recipient; Howard and Sharp-Jeffs (this volume) demonstrate how this can become economic and financial abuse.

Money can also be seen differently depending on its recipient. Zelizer (1994) demonstrated how 'pin money' (not earned by the main breadwinner) was undervalued, and Vogler (1998) noted that valuing money differently depending on which partner earned it related to how couples thought about gendered roles (see Sen, 1990). Indeed, perceived ownership of different incomes, or assets, can have more influence than legal ownership within households (Burgoyne and Sonnenberg, 2009; Rowlingson and Joseph, 2010; Austen et al., this volume).

In addition to exploring meanings of different forms of money, researchers have used qualitative methods to reveal different understandings of the pooling, partial pooling or independent management of resources within the household, and of joint or separate monies. Ashby and Burgoyne (2008), drawing on interview data, showed that 'pooled' money could be seen as separately owned, and vice versa. Indeed, as Bisdee et al. (2013) found in interviews with individuals in 45 older couples, 'pooled' money can in practice allow one partner's personal spending to be privileged. In interviews with couples,

Evertsson and Nyman (2014) also uncovered differing interpretations of what their independent management of money meant to each.

These findings demonstrate how merely asking couples whether they pool resources can be insufficient, therefore, and how nuances can be explored through qualitative research to reveal the meanings for individuals. Bjornberg and Kollind (2005), for example, in their study of Swedish couples, found some women suppressing spending on personal items to have more control over joint household spending (see research by Bennett and Sung, 2013); some interviewees with joint monies saw separate finances as a form of separation, whereas those with separate finances could see jointness as surveillance. Diaz et al. (2007) found in research in Spain that, even with all family income put together, this could be used differently by male and female partners, because money from different sources was viewed differently by each. In qualitative comparative research on dual-earner couples, Nyman et al. (2013) emphasised the importance of the political-cultural context for how money is understood, including countries' gender norms and welfare regimes.

Relationships, roles and identities

Qualitative research has demonstrated how children can be active players in how resources are used, especially in low-income families (Ridge, 2002; Main, this volume), as can other members of complex households (Singh, this volume; Moore and Hlabana, this volume). It can also explore how intra-household management and distribution of resources inter-relate with relationship dynamics, household roles (often gendered) and identities (Kirchler et al., 2008). Goode (2010), for example, drawing on a longitudinal study of 12 cases, explored how money management was embedded in the dynamics of couples' relationships, especially when debt was involved. She described couples' 'relational accounting', potentially including financial and emotional exchanges over time as part of relationship building and negotiating (Goode, 2009: 222).

In relation to roles, surveys may ask who has the 'final say' on major purchasing decisions and this can be revealing of power relations. However, psychological research sees decision-making as a more complex process (Kirchler et al., 2008); and Goode (2010) describes decisions as 'coming about' rather than being made. Routines are crucial, especially for established couples; a study of older couples by Bisdee et al. (2013) found that gendered routines of money management responsibilities remained stable, even sometimes in the face of fundamental life changes (Price, this volume).

In addition, in researching roles in relation to money, strategic control and everyday management can be teased apart by qualitative research (Bennett, 2013). As Bjornberg and Kollind (2005) found in qualitative research in Sweden, the administration of household finances represented work, but not necessarily power. But Goode et al. (1998), in qualitative research with families on benefits, noted that control can be exerted at different stages: when income comes in; when decisions are made on allocation; and when spending priorities are shaped within allocation systems. And power and authority may be undermined by practices of secrecy (Price, 2011; Bisdee et al., 2013). Iversen (2003, cited in Bennett, 2013) also suggested that women may exercise some power because of their management skills. However, in the context of low/moderate income, managing the household budget can be about trying to attain peace of mind more than power; women's greater responsibility for day-to-day spending can result in them bearing the brunt of pressures to make ends meet (Bennett et al., 2010).

Moreover, resources which depend on the recipient undertaking a specific role can have complex impacts on intra-household relationships, as Blake (2018) suggests from qualitative fieldwork in a South African township about receipt of the child support grant. As this involves identifying beneficiaries as primary carers, it can result in the renegotiation of diffuse care arrangements and also conveys strong moral imperatives about spending (see also Mokoene and Khunou, 2019). Kelly (2019), researching the disability grant in South Africa's western province, found its centrality to family resources often made the disabled person the 'breadwinner'. This gave opportunities to exercise agency and be valued, but also caused significant stress about dividing the money. Similar tensions emerged in a study of intergenerational care relationships in a township near Cape Town by Button and Ncapai (2019), who interviewed female old age grant recipients and co-resident adult children. Research in Malawi and Lesotho with people receiving social cash transfers (Ansell et al., 2019) concluded that an understanding of how cash transfers intervene in, and are negotiated through, social relations in the 'vulnerable' households targeted is essential to fully grasp their impacts (Moore and Hlabana, this volume). Also, an evaluation of Zambia's child grant programme (Bonilla et al., 2017) found that, despite the increase in financial empowerment for women as beneficiaries, changes in household relationships were limited by entrenched gender norms. One important strength of qualitative methods is their ability to capture nuances such as these.

Qualitative research can also highlight change points in roles in handling money in relationships. When children arrive, money management patterns often alter, typically becoming more joint. Individuals moving from one partnership to another may also decide to do things differently (Goode et al., 1998). This can involve keeping finances more separate (Burgoyne and Morison, 1997), especially if financial conflict was a factor in the break-up. One generation may adopt more 'modern' practices than the previous one (Lewis, 2001, for the UK; Johnson, 2017, for Kenya). Thus, in addition to gender ideology, experiences, attitudes and activity influence decisions and behaviour (Goode, 2009).

There has been less qualitative investigation of money management roles in complex households (though see above about studies in Africa). One example, however, was the exploration by Warner et al. (2017) of Australian families' experiences of negotiating financial and domestic contributions when young adults returned to live with parents. They found (studying ten families, with nine participating parents being women) that few young adults contributed financially and by doing chores; their mothers' expectations were influential. However, unlike Lewis et al.'s findings (2016) for England, this research suggested that parents were concerned by this behaviour.

Finally, in relation to roles and practices, money management has also been viewed as carrying out 'performative' processes, which can be explored via qualitative methods. This approach builds on West and Zimmerman's concept of 'doing gender' (1987), later expanded to incorporate 'doing couple' (Nyman et al., 2013). Here, rather than being static entities, gender relations and coupledom are both seen as being produced by people themselves, through actions that seem to them the 'right' thing to do.

Alongside roles and relationships, identities are also increasingly seen as important. Nyman (1999), in her Swedish study of ten married couples, concluded that – rather than income contribution being central in determining entitlement and access to money, as often argued – deeply rooted, culturally defined traditions, norms and values were key. In particular, women subordinating their own needs did not see this as a sacrifice, because doing things for others was crucial to their (gender) identities (Sen, 1990). Qualitative research with older couples by Bisdee et al. (2013) also suggested a continuing central role for money management in interviewees' gendered identities. And Daly (2017), in analysis of interviews with 51 low-income parents (mostly mothers) in Northern Ireland, suggested seeing spending through the lenses of self-identity as well as practices, related not only to relationships but also to values. This is what we explore next.

Values and beliefs

Qualitative research can investigate values and beliefs and tensions between them in forensic detail. For example, some couples value sharing household expenses 50/50 regardless of any inequality in their incomes – perhaps to avoid the dependence often associated with marriage. As Elizabeth (2001) found in her study of 20 cohabitees in New Zealand, they may therefore emphasise equal *contributions* rather than equal *outcomes*. This can be seen as interpreting equality as equity. Other couples see each partner paying a share proportionate to their income as fairer. Some research, however, has found that partners paying less struggle to feel equal in their contribution, and thus also to feel equal partners in the relationship (e.g. Burns et al., 2008, from interviews with individuals in 22 same-sex relationships in England).

Financial services providers often valorise togetherness, undertaking inquiries concluding that more jointness in couples' handling of money and financial decision-making is preferable (e.g. Van Raaij et al., 2019). Individual independence may here be seen as threatening the sharing necessary for beneficial outcomes from intra-household co-operation. There are clearly genuine concerns about the increasing individualisation of couples' finances, especially for women with children, who often bear a disproportionate share of the costs of children, such as childcare (Pahl, 2005). However, research also reveals how women may use a modicum of separation in household finances to negotiate the balance of jointness and separateness in marriage (Singh and Morley, 2011, from a quantitative/qualitative study in Australia). This can be necessary particularly for partners with commitments to previous relationships, including dependants; couples may manage this by having a mix of individual and joint accounts and designating monies for specific purposes (Burgoyne and Morison, 1997). Lister (2003: 107) warns against interpreting autonomy as 'atomistic individualism', seeing it instead as 'a precondition for genuine, non-exploitative, interdependence'.

Debates continue about whether benefiting equally from household resources, or autonomy in accessing and/or deploying these resources, should be – or is – seen as more desirable (Bennett, 2013). Autonomy may be particularly important for women, traditionally likelier to be subsumed within the family/household unit. Some women in the study in Sweden by Nyman and Reinikainen (2007) saw a lower living standard as acceptable, rather than depend financially on their partners. Bjornberg and Kollind (2005), however, in their research on Swedish couples, found the tensions between autonomy, equality and togetherness being managed more consciously by the women.

The next section explores some of these tensions by drawing on research undertaken by the author and others.

Financial autonomy in low-/moderate-income families

'All in one pot'?

This section draws on qualitative UK-based research in the mid-2000s intended, in part, to investigate whether financial autonomy was meaningful for women and men in low-/moderate-income couples and whether their understandings of it differed. A key purpose of the 'GeNet' project of which this study formed part was to explore the validity of assumptions about togetherness in finances for couples often underpinning both policy measures and analysis, particularly relating to 'welfare reform'.

The research involved separate semi-structured interviews with individuals in 30 female–male low-/moderate-income couples, virtually all working age (and all white) (Bennett and Sung, 2013). Separate interviews should allow individuals to articulate their own views (Pahl, 1989), which can be important for sensitive subjects such as handling money. The focus was on income, although participants were not asked about finances in detail. Data were analysed thematically, using NVivo.

Most participants saw a joint account as important, referring to trust and sharing, practicalities or both (Sung and Bennett, 2007). Indeed, the strikingly common assertion by interviewees was that money was put 'all in one pot' in their household. Thus, togetherness was seen as a central value, mentioned repeatedly (Ribbens McCarthy, 2012). For men especially, focusing on the individual seemed to be associated with failing the family.

'All in one pot' did not, however, mean equality in relation to resources. Indeed, this covered a multitude of practices; and financial togetherness did not prevent a (gendered) hierarchy in some cases, with a few men describing themselves as being at the top.

For these couples, living long term on low/moderate incomes, there were strong drivers towards jointness, and significant obstacles to individual autonomy. For many, sharing resources could be seen as a necessary response to pressures, preventing individual spending from jeopardising tight household budgeting. Independent money management has been associated with factors uncommon for these couples (cohabitation; youth; childlessness), as well as with same-sex couples. All but one couple were married/remarried, they had all brought up children together, most had lived together for some time and more were older than younger. All claimed means-tested benefits – at the time or (a few) previously. Financial autonomy could therefore potentially mean very little. But the study demonstrated that it *was* relevant for them.

Individuals were asked initially not about abstract 'financial autonomy' but instead about the concrete 'money in your own right'. Many men seemed to take their own financial autonomy for granted. Women, however, seemed more aware of tensions between financial togetherness and autonomy, perhaps because of their greater responsibility for managing togetherness (for example, through budgeting for the household) and their lower likelihood of financial independence. 'Money in your own right' had different meanings for participants. Men were more resistant to the idea, perceiving it as opposed to ideals of family togetherness. Some men saw it as just the money in their pocket (sometimes pocket money from their partner) or, alternatively, an amount allowing for more than just the basics. Women, however, were more likely to interpret it as their own money, separate from their partner's or joint household resources.

A framework for exploring financial autonomy

In analysing the data, a framework for investigating financial autonomy was developed, with several dimensions: achieving *economic independence* (Lister, 2003); enjoying *privacy* in one's financial affairs (Pahl, 2005); and having *agency* in relation to financial resources (Bennett and Sung, 2013: 705).

Economic independence can be understood as not having to depend on a partner's resources (Robeyns, 2003: 65). The study investigated individual income, but also feelings of ownership and entitlement more generally in relation to household resources. Most women had paid work, though often part time. But most felt economic independence was relevant for them. For some this was practical, in case something happened to their partner – or if they wanted to leave. Others talked about 'paying their way'. Social security benefits were often seen as money for the family rather than the individual, though those claiming a carer's benefit felt it was theirs. Some couples balanced different income sources between them to try to create more equality. For others, this could give some (limited) autonomy, albeit not economic independence, to individuals in what appeared to be unequal relationships.

Privacy was interpreted as an absence of the control or surveillance of someone's finances often related to economic abuse (Howard and Sharp-Jeffs, this volume). Pahl (1999) saw couples with independent finances as valuing privacy and autonomy, whereas couples pooling incomes value equality rather than privacy – although in practice pooling resources does not necessarily lead to equality in either processes or outcomes (Yodanis and Lauer, 2007). However, leaving this aside, assessing the degree of jointness from the mere existence of joint or individual accounts is challenging. The degree of financial togetherness among couples in our study with no joint account varied widely. In one couple, each partner paid their wages into the other's account, matching their (gendered) roles in managing money; in another, one partner managed the other's individual account entirely. But more women than men had their own account; and more seemed concerned about privacy. However, for women, being able to spend one's money as one wishes can be ambiguous, in that it potentially reinforces the idea of the man as the family provider, with the woman's income being superfluous to family needs ('pin money') (Zelizer, 1994). And privacy may have a negative nature, when combined with unequal power and/or separate decision-making; a few women said they had no knowledge of their partner's financial dealings (Austen et al., this volume).

Agency was perhaps the most complex aspect of financial autonomy examined. Agency can include, for example, negotiation, manipulation and resistance, as well as decision-making (Iversen, 2003, citing Kabeer, 1999: 438). Here, agency was defined to include managing household resources as one potential aspect of financial autonomy. This could be viewed as controversial in that it can still involve financial dependence, but was seen as being true to some participants' descriptions. However, the burden of administration and anxiety often borne by women in low-income households managing the budget and trying to make ends meet (WBG, 2006) was also recognised. Some women had run the household in a partner's absence, which could lead to changes in everyday practices once they were in a couple again in a way which gave them more agency. In general, the boundaries between control and management of resources were found to be fuzzier than often assumed, with management often including some aspects of control (Bennett et al., 2010).

'Agency' also included having access to household resources for 'personal' spending – although for women 'personal' may in practice include spending on the house and/or children (Kamleitner et al., 2018: 268–269); for several women in this study, buying gifts or saving for others was seen as personal spending (Bennett et al., 2010). On the other hand, men's spending on themselves may be defined by them as being for the family (Goode et al., 1998). Men can also see their earnings as family income and thus not fully realise the economic dependence of their partner.

Financial autonomy may therefore have different, often gendered, meanings; and perceptions themselves may affect access to resources (Bennett, 2013). The relationship between the three dimensions of financial autonomy described above can also be complex. For example, women may try to compensate for their loss of economic independence due to childrearing through gaining some control over the household money (Bjornberg and Kollind, 2005). This day-to-day responsibility may result in the exercise of more agency in practice than the decisions on big purchases made in couples, commonly asked about in surveys of household money practices. However, in low-/moderate-income families (Bennett and Sung, 2013), women's money manager role often included limiting their individual financial autonomy (such as not spending on personal items) in order to prioritise the family budget. More women said they saw only their own money as theirs to spend. Thus, as described above, the relationship between economic independence and agency differed between the sexes.

This study was carried out in the mid-2000s. The researchers concluded that policymakers should not discount the aspirations of women in particular for financial autonomy, even in low-/moderate-income couples. But the then UK government's plans for welfare reform failed to take account of this, or of other issues of intra-household dynamics related to family finances. The way in which couples continue to be treated in the UK's means-tested benefits system suggests that the findings of this research still need to be taken fully on board (Bennett, 2021).

Future directions for qualitative research

In terms of *topics*, there has been less qualitative research into assets and debts within households, compared to income and spending – although this is more common in the global south, where land and property are particularly important in (often complex) households (Oduro and Swaminathan, this volume).

In relation to *research participants*, whilst there has been progress in involving children (Main, this volume), men's views often continue to be under-represented (Kulic and Dotti Sani, 2020). This may be because they often seem more reluctant to be interviewed (Bennett, 2013). It may also be because feminist researchers tended to focus on women. Goode and Waring (2011) found 'male pride' concealing a complex relationship between money and masculinity. These gaps in listening to men's voices seem to occur in both the global north and south (e.g. see Moore and Seekings, 2019 about problems in including men's experiences in social protection and intergenerational care in South Africa).

Bennett (2013) identified one methodological challenge as going *beyond studies focusing on a single country* (or method – see Hantrais, 2009). For example, in comparative qualitative research on dual-earner couples, researchers suggested that the meanings of 'joint' or 'separate' money might relate to institutionalised cultural frameworks embodied in different countries' welfare policies (Ludwig-Mayerhofer et al., 2011). But they also revealed the challenges in undertaking such research, including linguistic and cultural difficulties in reaching common understandings of terms (Nyman et al., 2013). They saw a shared understanding of concepts and methodological issues as essential, and comparisons of findings for each country once interpreted as more fruitful than comparing raw data. It is nonetheless hard to find examples that have built on this.

Qualitative research into intra-household resources seems to have enjoyed a heyday in the 1990s/2000s, in particular in English-language journals. Since then, there seems to have been something of a hiatus. But there is still much that remains to explore through such methods, in order to broaden and deepen our knowledge and understanding.

Note

1.   Project 5, Gender Equality Network, funded by the Economic and Social Research Council (RES-225-25-2001).

References

Agarwal, B., Kanbur, R. and Basu, K. (2009) 'Engaging with Sen on gender relations: Co-operative conflicts, false perceptions and relative capabilities', in K. Basu and R. Kanbur (eds), *Arguments for a Better World: Essays in Honour of Amartya Sen, Vol. II: Society, Institutions and Development,* Oxford: Oxford University Press, 157–177.

Ansell, N., van Blerk L., Robson, E., Hajdu, F., Mwathunga, E., Hlabana, T. and Hemsteede, R. (2019) *Social Cash Transfers, Generational Relations and Youth Poverty Trajectories in Rural Lesotho and Malawi,* London: Brunel University.

Ashby, K.J. and Burgoyne, C. (2008) 'Separate financial entitles? Beyond categories of money management', *Journal of Socio-Economics* 37(2), 458–480.

Bennett, F. (2013) 'Researching within-household distribution: Overview, developments, debates, and methodological challenges', *Journal of Marriage and Family* 75(3), 582–597.

Bennett, F. (2021) 'How government sees couples on Universal Credit: A critical gender perspective', *Journal of Poverty and Social Justice* 29(1), 3–20.

Bennett, F. and Sung, S. (2013) 'Dimensions of financial autonomy in low-/ moderate-income couples from a gender perspective and implications for welfare reform', *Journal of Social Policy* 42(4), 701–719.

Bennett, F., De Henau, J. and Sung, S. (2010) 'Within-household inequalities across classes? Management and control of money', in J. Scott, R. Crompton and C. Lyonette (eds), *Gender Inequalities in the 21st Century: New Barriers and Continuing Constraints*, Cheltenham, UK and Northampton, MA, USA: Edward Elgar Publishing, 215–241.

Bisdee, D., Daly, T. and Price, D. (2013) 'Behind closed doors: Older couples and the gendered management of household money', *Social Policy and Society* 12(1), 163–174.

Bjornberg, U. and Kollind, A.-K. (2005) *Individualism and Families: Equality, Autonomy and Togetherness*, London: Routledge.

Blake, R. (2018) 'The price of the grant: The social cost of child support grants for female caregivers and their extended networks', CSSR Working Paper no. 412, Cape Town: Centre for Social Science Research, University of Cape Town.

Bonilla, J., Zarzur, R.C., Handa, S., Nowlin, C., Peterman, A., Ring, H. and Seidenfeld, D. (2017) 'Cash for women's empowerment? A mixed-methods evaluation of the Government of Zambia's child grant program', *World Development* 95, 55–72.

Burgoyne, C.B. and Morison, V. (1997) 'Money in remarriage: Keeping things simple – and separate', *The Sociological Review* 45(3), 363–395.

Burgoyne, C.B. and Sonnenberg, S. (2009) 'Financial practices in cohabiting heterosexual couples: A perspective from economic psychology', in J. Miles and R. Probert (eds), *Sharing Lives, Dividing Assets*, Portland, OR: Hart, 89–108.

Burns, M., Burgoyne, C. and Clarke, V. (2008) 'Financial affairs? Money management in same-sex relationships', *Journal of Socio-Economics* 37(2), 481–501.

Button, K. and Ncapai, T. (2019) 'Conflict and negotiation in intergenerational care: Older women's experiences of caring with the Old Age Grant in South Africa', *Critical Social Policy* 39(4), 560–581.

Daly, M. (2017) 'Money-related meanings and practices in low-income and poor families', *Sociology* 51(2), 450–465.

Denzin, N.K. and Lincoln, Y.S. (1998) *Collecting and Interpreting Qualitative Materials*, London: Sage.

Diaz, C., Dema, S. and Ibanez, M. (2007) 'The intertwining of money and love in couple relationships', in J. Stocks, C. Diaz and B. Hallerod (eds), *Modern Couples Sharing Money Sharing Life*, Basingstoke: Palgrave Macmillan, 100–142.

Elizabeth, V. (2001) 'Managing money, managing coupledom: A critical examination of cohabitants' money management practices', *The Sociological Review* 49(3), 389–411.

Evertsson, L. and Nyman, C. (2014) 'Perceptions and practices in independent management: Blurring the boundaries between "mine", "yours" and "ours"', *Journal of Family and Economic Issues* 35(1), 65–80.

Goode, J. (2009) 'For love or money? Couples' negotiations of credit and debt in low-income families in the UK', *Benefits* 17(3), 213–224.

Goode, J. (2010) 'The role of gender dynamics in decisions on credit and debt in low income families', *Critical Social Policy* 30(1), 99–119.

Goode, J. and Waring, A. (2011) *Seeking Direction: Men, Money Advice and the Road to Financial Health*, London: Money Advice Trust.

Goode, J., Callender, C. and Lister, R. (1998) *Purse or Wallet? Gender Inequalities and Income Distribution within Families on Benefits*, London: Policy Studies Institute.

Hallerod, B., Diaz, C. and Stocks, J. (2007) 'Doing gender while doing couple: Concluding remarks', in J. Stocks, C. Diaz and B. Hallerod (eds), *Modern Couples Sharing Money, Sharing Life*, Basingstoke: Palgrave Macmillan, 143–155.

Hantrais, L. (2009) *International Comparative Research: Theory, Methods and Practice*, Basingstoke: Palgrave Macmillan.

Iversen, V. (2003) 'Intra-household inequality: A challenge for the capability approach?', *Feminist Economics* 9(2–3), 93–115.

Johnson, S. (2017) '"We don't have this is mine and this is his": Managing money and the character of conjugality in Kenya', *Journal of Development Studies* 53(5), 755–768.

Kabeer, N. (1999) 'Resources, agency, achievement: Reflections on the measurement of women's empowerment', *Development and Change* 30(3), 435–464.

Kamleitner, B., Mackhgott, E. and Kirchler, E. (2018) 'Money management in households', in A. Lewis (ed.), *The Cambridge Handbook of Psychology and Economic Behaviour*, Cambridge: Cambridge University Press, 260–284.

Kelly, G. (2019) 'Disability, cash transfers and family practices in South Africa', *Critical Social Policy* 39(4), 541–559.

Kirchler, E., Hoelzl, E. and Kamleitner, B. (2008) 'Spending and credit use in the private household', *Journal of Socio-Economics* 37(2), 519–532.

Kulic, N.M. and Dotti Sani, G. (2020) 'Within-couple distribution of economic resources: A critical review of extant studies and avenues for future research', *Rassegna Italiana di Sociologia*. 3: 623–650.

Lewis, J. (2001) *The End of Marriage? Individualism and Intimate Relations*, Cheltenham, UK and Northampton, MA, USA: Edward Elgar Publishing.

Lewis, J., West, A., Roberts, J. and Noden, P. (2016) 'The experience of coresidence: Young adults returning to the parental home after graduation in England', *Families, Relationships and Societies* 5(2), 247–262.

Lister, R. (2003) *Citizenship: Feminist Perspectives*, Basingstoke: Palgrave Macmillan.

Ludwig-Mayerhofer, W., Allmendinger, J., Hirseland, A. and Schneider, W. (2011) 'The power of money in dual-earner couples: A comparative study', *Acta Sociologica* 54(4), 367–383.

Mokoene, A.K. and Khunou, G. (2019) 'Parental absence: Intergenerational tensions and contestations of social grants in South Africa', *Critical Social Policy* 39(4), 525–540.

Moor, L. and Kanji, S. (2019) 'Money and relationships online: Communication and norm formation in women's discussions of couple resource allocation', *British Journal of Sociology* 70(3), 948–968.

Moore, E. and Seekings, J. (2019) 'Consequences of social protection on intergenerational relationships in South Africa: Introduction', *Critical Social Policy* 39(4), 513–524.

Neale, B. (2021) 'Fluid enquiry, complex causality, policy processes: Making a difference with qualitative longitudinal research', *Social Policy and Society* 20(4), 653–669.

Nyman, C. (1999) 'Gender equality in "the most equal country in the world"? Money and marriage in Sweden', *The Sociological Review* 47(4), 766–793.

Nyman, C. (2003) 'The social nature of money: Meanings of money in Swedish families', *Women's Studies International Forum* 26(1), 79–94.

Nyman, C. and Reinikainen, L. (2007) 'Elusive independence in a context of gender equality in Sweden', in J. Stocks, C. Diaz and B. Hallerod (eds), *Modern Couples Sharing Money, Sharing Life*, Basingstoke: Palgrave Macmillan, 7–29.

Nyman, C., Reinikainen, L. and Stocks, J. (2013) 'Reflections on a cross-national qualitative study of within-household finances', *Journal of Marriage and Family* 75(3), 640–650.

Pahl, J. (1989) *Money and Marriage*, London: Macmillan.

Pahl, J. (1999) *Invisible Money: Family Finances in the Electronic Economy*, Bristol: Policy Press.

Pahl, J. (2005) 'Individualization in couple finances: Who pays for the children?', *Social Policy and Society* 4(4), 381–392.

Price, D. (2011) *Key Findings from the Project 'Behind Closed Doors: Older Couples and the Management of Household Money'*, London: Institute of Gerontology, Kings College London.

Ribbens McCarthy, J. (2012) 'The powerful relational language of "family": Togetherness, belonging and parenthood', *The Sociological Review* 60(1), 68–90.

Ridge, T. (2002) *Childhood Poverty and Social Exclusion: From a Child's Perspective*, Bristol: Policy Press.

Ritchie, J. and Lewis, J. (2003) *Qualitative Research Practice: A Guide for Social Science Students and Researchers*, London: Sage.

Robeyns, I. (2003) 'Sen's capability approach and gender inequality: Selecting relevant capabilities', *Feminist Economics* 9(2–3), 61–92.

Rowlingson, K. and Joseph, R. (2010) *Assets and Debts within Couples: Ownership and Decision-Making*, Dorking: Friends Provident Foundation.

Sen, A. (1990) 'Gender and cooperative conflict', in I. Tinker (ed.), *Persistent Inequalities: Women and World Development*, Oxford: Oxford University Press, 123–149.

Silverman, D. (2006) *Interpreting Qualitative Data: Methods for Analysing Talk, Text and Interaction*, London: Sage.

Singh, S. and Bhandari, M. (2012) 'Money management and control in the Indian joint family across generations', *The Sociological Review* 60(1), 46–67.

Singh, S. and Morley, C. (2011) 'Gender and financial accounts in marriage', *Journal of Sociology* 47(1), 3–16.

Sung, S. and Bennett, F. (2007) 'Dealing with money in low- to moderate-income families: Insights from individual interviews', in K. Clarke, T. Maltby and P. Kennett (eds), *Social Policy Review 19: Analysis and Debate in Social Policy*, Bristol: Policy Press, in association with Social Policy Association, 151–173.

Van Raaij, W.F., Antonides, G. and de Groot, I.M. (2019) *The Benefits of Joint and Separate Financial Management of Couples* (Technical Report), Think Forward Initiative, ING Bank, Netherlands: Amsterdam.

Vogler, C. (1998) 'Money in the household: Some underlying issues of power', *Sociological Review* 46(4), 687–713.

Warner, E., Henderson-Wilson, C. and Andrews, F. (2017) '"It's give and take": Australian families' experiences of negotiating financial and domestic contributions when young adults return home', *Journal of Family and Economic Issues* 38(4), 541–555.

WBG (Women's Budget Group) (2006) *Women's and Children's Poverty: Making the Links*, London: Women's Budget Group.

West, C. and Zimmerman, D.H. (1987) 'Doing gender', *Gender and Society* 1(2), 125–151.

Yodanis, C. and Lauer, S. (2007) 'Managing money in marriage: Multilevel and cross-national effects of the breadwinner role', *Journal of Marriage and Family* 69(5), 1307–1325.

Zelizer, V.A. (1994) *The Social Meaning of Money: Pin Money, Paychecks, Poor Relief, and Other Currencies*, New York: Basic Books.

3. Barriers to opening the 'black box' of intra-household sharing of resources

Satomi Maruyama

Introduction

In research and policy, the household has often been treated as a single unit, with little attention paid to what happens inside it, as argued in the Introduction to this volume. In other words, households have been considered a 'black box' and household members have been assumed to share resources and benefit from them equally. For example, the relative poverty rate, often used to assess poverty, may be calculated using the poverty measure of '50 per cent of median equivalized disposable income', with income captured at the household level. Thus, poverty is measured by assuming that all household members share the same standard of living. However, it is conceivable for a household to be above the poverty line in terms of household income, but with certain household members living in poverty. This is more likely to be experienced by women and children, who tend to have lower incomes under the existing gender structure. However, such inequalities have been obscured within the 'black box' of the household.

In the United Kingdom (UK), Pahl (1989) conducted a study that examined the allocation of resources within the household. The importance of this work has been recognized, especially by feminists. Since then, research looking inside the 'black box' of the household has been accumulating, especially in poverty research. Although the 'black box' may have been partially opened up by studies[1] that followed Pahl, much remains unknown about what happens inside the household. Furthermore, even when it becomes clear that resource allocation is not always equal within households, most poverty measurement, such as the relative poverty rate, still treats households as a unit (see for example Di Meglio et al., 2018), and research focusing on within-household allocation of resources has not revolutionized poverty measurement itself.

In this chapter, the barriers to opening up the household will be discussed, using Japan as a case study.

Japan is a patriarchal society, and the economic status of women remains low in relation to that of men. Although the female employment rate is 71.3 per cent, higher than the Organisation for Economic Co-operation and Development (OECD) average of 60.5 per cent (OECD, n.d.), much of this employment is part time and the wage gap between men and women is the third largest among OECD countries. It was not until the mid-1990s that the percentage of dual-income households in Japan exceeded the proportion of households with a full-time housewife (Japan Institute for Labour Policy and Training, 2023). Husbands in Japan spend only one-sixth as much time in unpaid work as their wives (41 minutes per day on average for husbands, compared to 224 minutes for wives), which is by far the biggest difference proportionately in OECD countries (OECD, n.d.). These factors make gender inequality in Japanese households more severe than in many other countries.

In the 1980s, influenced by Pahl and other British studies of the time, some feminist researchers in Japan began to take an interest in money in the household. They became involved in the establishment in 1986 of the Institute for Research on Household Economics, which has been a critical player in this area of research in Japan. For example, it was on the initiative of this institute that the Japanese Panel Survey of Consumers (JPSC) was set up. The JPSC has been conducted annually since 1993, providing the richest data available on intra-household distribution in Japan, and is perhaps unique worldwide. The survey is undertaken exclusively among women, with approximately 1,500 respondents (initially covering those in their 20s and 30s, and now up to those in their 60s). The survey contains many questions that provide information on intra-household resource allocation: household and individual income; expenditure; savings and debt; type of household money management and disclosure of finances to partners; how decisions are made about money; title holder of housing and insurance; time allocation; life satisfaction, etc.

Most of the analyses of the JPSC in its early stages were carried out by this group of feminist researchers involved in establishing the institute, and these studies are valuable in opening the 'black box' and revealing how resources are allocated within the household in Japan. While the institute and members of the group have since conducted several studies that can shed light on intra-household resource allocation, this interest has largely faded in more recent years. This is probably due to the decline of home economics, the discipline that developed this interest in Japan, and the early death of the key feminist researcher who was active in this area in the early years, with only a few successors to carry on this type of work.

Previous research

Jenkins' pathbreaking work (1991) on the barriers to opening the 'black box' of the household in the UK identified five reasons why the intra-household perspective is ignored in poverty measurement; 30 years on, many of these are still relevant to more general issues of resource allocation within households. Here, we discuss four of these reasons.

First, Jenkins highlighted that, while general poverty studies were based on large quantitative surveys, feminist research that focused on what goes on within households was at that time often based on small qualitative studies, which were often ignored because their representativeness and statistical reliability were questioned. It can be argued that this barrier is less significant today, as large-scale surveys that shed light on intra-household resource allocation are now available in Japan and elsewhere. The results from these large-scale surveys are presented in the following sections of this chapter.

Secondly, Jenkins emphasized that gender inequality within the household was not generally seen as a key issue. Thirdly, he noted that the usefulness of introducing a gender perspective in considering not only the causes of poverty but also policy directions had not been recognized. Fourthly, he analysed the methodological difficulties in ascertaining the actual distribution of resources within households. These points are still applicable to research into within-household resource management and distribution today and their relevance to intra-household issues is discussed in each of the following three sections, using Japan as a case study.

Gender inequality within households is not recognized as a problem

One of the reasons why intra-household resource allocation remains a 'black box' is gender inequality within households not being recognized or, if it is recognized, not being seen as a problem. Jenkins points out that gender inequality within the household is a result of norms arguing that women's traditional roles are those of housewives and carers, or that women themselves may choose to be unequal. Both gender inequality and the failure to see it as a problem persist, although there have been improvements over the past 30 years. Even if women seem to 'choose' inequality for themselves, and tend to behave with self-sacrificing attitudes, their choices may be constrained (Land and Rose, 1985). Therefore, just because a woman herself 'chooses' inequality does not mean that her choice is not problematic.

In Japan, the expression 'wife holds the purse strings' is well known, meaning that the wife is considered to have real power over household money management. However, this is not necessarily the case in practice. Okamoto (2015) made an international comparison of household financial management systems using International Social Survey Program (ISSP) data from 1994, 2002 and 2012. Among the five household management categories, there is a higher proportion of 'female management' and a lower proportion of the 'joint pooling system' in the Asian countries of the Philippines, South Korea and Japan compared to other countries, with Japan being the most prominent example of this. However, when 'the wife holds the purse strings', that is, when the wife manages the household finances, intra-household gender inequality in consumption is most significant; wives themselves may choose to undertake this role and may not be aware of this gender inequality, as the studies presented below point out.

The researcher who has conducted the most comprehensive studies of intra-household distribution in Japan, Mifune, using 1993 JPSC wave 1 data (Mifune, 1995), found that in all types of household management wives' personal expenditure was lower than that of their husbands. In particular, the largest difference in personal expenditure between husbands and wives was found in 'the wife management type',[2] in which wives' personal expenditure was on average only 26.6 per cent of husbands' personal expenditure. This 'wife management type' was the most common in Japan, accounting for 41 per cent of cases. In the UK, women were found in one (qualitative) study to be more likely to manage the money when household income was low (Bennett and Sung, 2013). Cross-national research suggests that in general in countries with higher gender inequality one member of the couple manages money alone (Pepin and Cohen, 2021);[3] Japan fits well into this pattern. The largest amount of personal spending on themselves by wives was in the 'independent management type'; but even then, wives' expenditure was only 76.1 per cent of husbands' expenditure (Mifune, 1995). Husbands who manage a large proportion of the household budget spend relatively little on themselves, which is contrary to some European studies showing that husbands' management of money means husbands spending more (e.g. Cantillon et al., 2016). Mifune (1995) stated on the basis of this study that household financial management responsibilities seem to suppress personal expenditure. Shigekawa (2017) tracks changes in household management types using JPSC data from 1993 to 2014. This analysis shows that, although household finances have become increasingly personalized in recent years, the management type in which the wife manages the household finances is still the most common in Japan, even among younger generations.

Kimura (2001) found that the most unequal type of households in which the wife managed the money have the highest marital satisfaction. She also found that the amount of money available for the wife to spend on herself differs little by money management type. Together with Mifune's (1995) findings, she suggests that wives may voluntarily reduce their own consumption despite being able to spend money for themselves. Sakamoto (2009) also used the JPSC data to examine changes in household finances before and after marriage and childbirth and found that, while the personal consumption of husbands and children increased after childbirth, wives' personal consumption decreased – but that more women were satisfied with the content of their consumption. He suggests that the reason for this may be that the child/ren may have increased mothers' satisfaction. All the above research recognizes the existence of gender inequality within the household but suggests that wives themselves are either choosing this inequality themselves or are satisfied with it.

The idea that wives do not question intra-household inequalities applies not only to personal expenditure but also to the ownership of assets. As will be seen below, in Japan analysis shows that the legal title in terms of ownership of the asset(s) does not necessarily correspond to the couple's perception of who owns it, and this has also been noted in the UK (Joseph and Rowlingson, 2011). Mifune (1999) shows the difference between the percentage of assets held in the name of the husband or the wife: 71 per cent of household assets were owned by husbands and 29 per cent by wives. However, 94 per cent of husbands believed that their wives – and 86 per cent of wives believed that they – had the right to use the assets held in their husbands' names. In other words, husbands perceived assets to be shared even if they were held in their personal names. In addition, 63 per cent of husbands and 51 per cent of wives believed that the name was a formality and were not concerned by this. From this evidence, Mifune pointed out that, although wives' rights to assets were substantially recognized, there was little awareness of the disparity between husbands and wives regarding nominal assets, and even wives rarely questioned this situation, possibly due to gender bias (Mifune, 1999: 211).

As discussed in the above studies, Japanese married women tend to earn less, manage more of the household money and spend less on themselves, although they also have higher levels of marital satisfaction. Thus, it would appear that women voluntarily choose inequality. However, such behaviors will be influenced by gender norms and social structures that are economically disadvantageous for them. The low income of wives themselves reflects a gender structure in which wives are often responsible for unpaid work at home and in which the wage system is disadvantageous to them. As discussed above, this is particularly the case in Japan, where women work longer hours than men in unpaid work and earn considerably lower wages. It can therefore be assumed that most of the household income is earned by the husband and that the wife, due to her responsibility for managing the household budget, is constrained in spending money on herself. This can be described as 'adaptive preferences', as Sen argues – that is, familiarity with living in disadvantageous social and economic circumstances may induce people to accept and endure negative situations (Sen, 1999). People can have various aims and goals other than the pursuit of personal happiness; they can behave altruistically, willingly accept inequalities and be content with their deprivations (Sen, 1990). The literature on the 'ethic of care' also points out that women tend to find value in caring for others more than men do (Gilligan, 1982).

Gender inequalities in intra-household distribution are overlooked in Japan not only by ordinary people but also in terms of policy. This is reflected in the failure of Japanese policy to address economic abuse, another aspect of inequality in the distribution of household resources (Howard and Sharp-Jeffs, this volume). According to a national survey (Gender Equality Bureau, 2021) that asked those who had been married if they had experience of family violence, of the four forms of violence – physical assault, psychological abuse, economic pressure and sexual coercion – 8.6 per cent of the women reported that they had experienced 'economic pressure', such as not being given living expenses, having their savings used without permission and being prevented from working outside the home. This means that a significant number of women have experienced economic abuse. In Japan, however, economic abuse is rarely considered an issue of poverty or deprivation resulting from inequalities in the distribution of resources within the household. In addition, while there are policies related to physical violence, such as shelter placement and protection orders, there are no preventative or response measures relating to economic abuse. Thus, the existence of gender inequalities in intra-household resource allocation is rarely recognized in Japanese policy.

The value of focusing on individuals within households is not recognized

The second reason the household has remained a 'black box' is that the value of incorporating a gender perspective, and acknowledging the inequalities within households, for developing improved policies and poverty measurement has not been recognized.

From a policy perspective, it has been pointed out that even if the amount of money coming into a household is the same, the effect on the wellbeing of individuals in the household may differ depending on who is the recipient of resources (Robeyns, 2003); therefore, inequality in the allocation of resources within the household should not be ignored. For example, in the late 1970s in the UK, a study was conducted on a policy change in child benefit, in which a deduction from (usually) the father's taxes was replaced by a cash payment to (usually) the mother, resulting in an increase in expenditure on clothing for women and children, even though household income itself did not change (Lundberg et al., 1997). This research demonstrated the potential for policy decisions about which person in the household should receive benefits to reduce inequality within the household and influenced subsequent policy decisions in the UK.

In Japan, however, there is little debate about the appropriate recipient of social security benefits within a couple, and it is taken for granted that the benefits are paid to the head of the household, usually the individual with the higher income.[4] Japan's child benefit is a typical example, in most cases being paid to fathers. Therefore, even during periods of separation before divorce, or when fleeing family violence, the child benefit often goes to the husband, depriving the mother and the child of an income source before some necessary procedures to redirect the benefit are completed. Another example is the one-off 100,000 yen universal benefit implemented in 2020 to cope with the loss of income during the COVID-19 pandemic. The benefits for all family members were paid together to the head of the household, usually a man, in order to provide the benefit quickly. At this time, discussions around the husband receiving the benefits in cases of separation or domestic violence brought the issue of the appropriate recipient of benefits within a couple to light for the first time in Japan.[5] Thus, even though it is crucial to think about who should be the recipient of benefits within the household, especially for households experiencing disharmony, the usefulness of looking within the household has not been fully recognized to date in this policy area in Japan.

Not only in relation to policy but also in poverty measurement, the main-stream way of treating households as a single entity has only changed very recently, and only slightly in some countries – and this has not yet happened in Japan. As will be discussed in more detail in the next section, the material deprivation indicators that have come to be used as a means of measuring poverty show different results when individual-level indicators are adopted, as opposed to the household-level indicators that have traditionally been employed (Cantillon and Nolan, 2001; Cantillon and Guio, this volume). This result has led to the introduction of individual-level indicators in addition to household-level indicators in the European Union Statistics on Income and Living Conditions (EU-SILC), but this has only been done recently in the EU and is still nowhere to be seen in Japan.

Technical difficulties in capturing the distribution of resources within a household

A third reason why the household remains a 'black box' in relation to the allocation of resources is that revealing this allocation is technically difficult in practice, even if the importance of shedding light on it is recognized in principle.

One of the technical difficulties is the data limitations. A wide range of household surveys has been conducted around the world, but most of them capture household finances as a whole, except for personal income, and there are few individual-level surveys that can reveal the distribution of resources within a household, such as income pooling and transfers between household members.

The same is true in Japan, where the Japanese government prides itself on con-ducting detailed monthly household surveys since the 1940s, but where only a few individual-level household surveys have been conducted. One of these is the JPSC, mentioned earlier. This is the source of the richest data capturing money within the household in Japan, although it is not perfect because it consists of only 1,500 female respondents; in other words, it is not paired data, asking both husbands and wives simultaneously about household finances and comparing the results.

The institute conducting the JPSC has also conducted several ad hoc surveys to compensate for this limitation, one of which is the Contemporary Nuclear Family Survey. This was undertaken in 1999 and 2008 for nuclear families, using paired data in which husbands and wives were asked separately about their household finances. Using this paired data, Tanaka (2010), for example, examined husbands' and wives' perceptions of money, and showed that only about 60 per cent of couples agreed on the amount of money in the household, such as income and assets, and only 40 per cent on the individual cumulative contribution to the household since their marriage, including income, care work and housework. There was thus a significant gap in the perceptions of household finances between husbands and wives.

In addition to data limitations, another technical problem is the difficulty in assigning household consumption to each family member, even if data were available on an individual basis. Clothing and shoes are often used as proxy indicators for personal consumption because it is easy to identify who they are for, but it is questionable whether personal consumption can be captured by the consumption of 'assignable goods' (Woolley, this volume). Indeed, what people in a household consume includes 'public goods' shared by family members, such as housing and heating, and it is not easy to calculate the amount of food consumed by each individual.

Furthermore, studies in Japan have shown contradictory results between capturing each individual's consumption of 'assignable goods' and using other indicators. For example, the JPSC asks for the amount of personal comsumption in September as a question that can reveal the allocation of individual resources, and using this indicator shows that the wife's personal expenditure averages only 36.5 per cent of the husband's personal expenditure (Mifune, 1995). On the other hand, the Intra-Household and Intergenerational Survey, conducted by the same agency as the JPSC as a one-off exercise in 2006 among women of the same age group, asked about consumption of certain 'assignable goods' (clothing, shoes, culture and entertainment expenses), and using this indicator showed that wives' personal consumption was generally higher than that of their husbands (Sakamoto, 2008).[6] These contradictory results may indicate that further research is needed on how to capture inequalities in intra-household resource allocation in consumption.

One way to overcome these problems is to use non-monetary indicators rather than personal consumption. EU-SILC, the key statistics on poverty in the European Union (EU), have used deprivation indicators that measure the lack of 'socially perceived necessities' among the population. These indicators have been used to measure living standards in a non-monetary way since 2009. Also, as mentioned in the previous section, deprivation indicators were originally captured at the household level, but it has been pointed out that deprivation indicators at household and individual levels should be different (Cantillon and Nolan, 2001; Cantillon, 2013; Cantillon and Guio, this volume), and EU-SILC has been incorporating individual-level deprivation indicators since 2015. In Japan, however, deprivation indicators have not yet been introduced in official surveys at the national level, perhaps reflecting a lack of government interest in poverty – although they are now being considered. Japan therefore lags far behind the developments in poverty measurement in other countries and is yet to distinguish household-level from individual-level deprivation indicators.[7]

Although some progress has been made in resolving these technical issues, it is thus clear that more will need to be done to open the 'black box' that is the household, in particular in Japan.

Future research agenda

To make visible more comprehensively and systematically what is happening within the household in relation to the management and distribution of resources, three further research directions are proposed here.

First, more research would need to show that focusing on the resources and standard of living enjoyed by individuals in households leads to different results from those found in traditional studies that consider households as a single entity. For example, Karagiannaki and Burchardt (2020) compare household- and individual-level deprivation indicators in the EU and show that the risk of deprivation decreases by more than 25 per cent when inequalities in deprivation within households are missed (see also Burchardt and Karagiannaki, this volume). As the EU-SILC began to include individual-level deprivation items in its survey in 2015, more data will be available for similar studies in the future. As such findings accumulate, the need to focus on intra-household resource allocation will become more obvious, and conventional research will no longer be able to ignore the existence of inequalities within households. This would probably lead to a change in the way poverty is measured, including in countries such as Japan that do not currently research or analyse deprivation data on an individual basis.

Second, further development is needed in how intra-household management and distribution can be captured. In this field of research, European scholars have made a distinction between outcomes (consumption, deprivation, wellbeing, etc.) and the processes of how resources are treated within households (management and financial control) (Bennett, 2013). As discussed above, outcomes have often been captured by the amount of 'assignable goods' consumed, such as clothing and shoes, where it is clear who is consuming them, or by individual-level deprivation indicators, while processes have often been captured by answers to questions about who makes the decisions on major purchases. However, the validity of the method of capturing outcomes by consumption of 'assignable goods' needs further examination, as other indicators have shown contradictory results, and the complexity of processes of management and control within the household may not be captured by one-off answers to such questions (Bennett, this volume).

Furthermore, Japanese studies have found that marital satisfaction was highest in couples where the wife's personal consumption is the lowest compared to the husband's and where the wife manages the household finances (Kimura, 2001). In these cases satisfaction does not necessarily seem to be driven by higher consumption. It has been argued that capabilities are more important for individual wellbeing than consumption, because capabilities emphasize substantive freedoms, or what people are able to be or do in their lives that they have reason to value (Sen, 1990). Recently, there has been some discussion about the need for indicators to measure capability and financial autonomy to capture inequalities in within-household distribution (e.g. Burchardt and Holder, 2011, for the UK), but these indicators have not yet been fully developed. The development of such indicators would allow us to capture new aspects of how individuals behave and fare within households in relation to the management and distribution of resources and would contribute to further deepening and extending our exploration of the 'black box' that is the household.

Notes

1. Bennett (2013) reviewed research in these areas.
2. In the JPSC, money management types are divided into 18 subcategories, which Mifune (1995) organizes into seven broad categories. This typology is unique and cannot simply be compared to the money management typologies used in Pahl (1989), EU-SILC and the ISSP, as it reflects who earns the money, how much is pooled, who manages the pooled money and how much individuals keep for themselves, etc.
3. Pepin and Cohen (2021) found this pattern by examining the relationship between money management type and women's status in 20 countries using the 2012 ISSP, though Japan is not included in these 20 countries.
4. The head of household may be changed on request, but it is advantageous for tax and social security purposes for the head of household to be the partner with the higher income. In the case of compound families, this is decided on application.

Couples in common law marriages, which are very rare in Japan, are treated exactly like married couples in relation to the social security system, though the partners are not treated as married couples for the tax system and have no inheritance rights in relation to each other.

5. As a result of growing public disquiet, in the above case benefits were available on application to those who were not the head of the household.

6. The survey shows that wives' personal consumption, calculated in terms of clothing, shoes, culture, entertainment and socializing expenses, is higher in 13 out of 16 cases in which the husband and wife have different employment statuses; but in terms of leisure time, wives consume less than their husbands, regardless of their employment status. Wives also spend less on personal consumption when living with the husband's parents than they do when living separately from parents or living with their own parents (Sakamoto, 2008).

7. In Japan, deprivation indicators for children have been introduced in many child poverty surveys by local authorities, through the efforts of some researchers, but this has not been done for adults.

References

Bennett, F. (2013) 'Researching Within-Household Distribution: Overview, Developments, Debates, and Methodological Challenges', *Journal of Marriage and Family*, 75(3): 582–597.

Bennett, F. and Sung, S. (2013) 'Dimensions of Financial Autonomy in Low-/Moderate-Income Couples from a Gender Perspective and Implications for Welfare Reform', *Journal of Social Policy*, 42(4): 701–719.

Burchardt, T. and Holder, H. (2011) 'Developing Survey Measures of Inequality of Autonomy in the UK', *Social Indicators Research*, 106(1): 1–25.

Cantillon, S. (2013) 'Measuring Differences in Living Standards within Households', *Journal of Marriage and Family*, 75(3): 598–620.

Cantillon, S. and Nolan, B. (2001) 'Poverty within Households: Measuring Gender Differences Using Nonmonetary Indicators', *Feminist Economics*, 7(1): 5–23.

Cantillon, S., Maitre, B. and Watson, D. (2016) 'Family Financial Management and Individual Deprivation', *Journal of Family and Economic Issues*, 37(3): 461–473.

Di Meglio, E., Kaczmarek-Firth, A., Litwinska, A. and Rusu, C. (2018) 'Living Conditions in Europe: 2018 Edition', Brussels: Eurostat.

Gender Equality Bureau (2021) Research Report on Gender-Based Violence. www.gender.go.jp/research/kenkyu/konnan/pdf/seikatsukonnan.pdf (accessed 22 May 2023).

Gilligan, C. (1982) *In A Different Voice: Psychological Theory and Women's Development*, Cambridge, MA: Harvard University Press.

Japan Institute for Labour Policy and Training (2023) 'Long-Term Labour Statistics in Graphs'. www.jil.go.jp/kokunai/statistics/timeseries/index.html (accessed 22 May 2023).

Jenkins, S. (1991) 'Poverty Measurement and the within-Household Distribution: Agenda for Action', *Journal of Social Policy*, 20(4): 457–483.

Joseph, R. and Rowlingson, K. (2011) 'Her House, His Pension? The Division of Assets among (Ex-)Couples and the Role of Policy', *Social Policy and Society*, 11(1): 69–80.

Karagiannaki, E. and Burchardt, T. (2020) 'Intra-Household Inequality and Adult Material Deprivation in Europe', *Case Paper 218*, London: Centre for Analysis of Social Exclusion, London School of Economics and Political Science.

Kimura, K. (2001) 'Household Jointness and Husband–Wife Relationships', *Journal of Household Economics*, 49: 14–24.

Land, H. and Rose, H. (1985) 'Compulsory Altruism for Some or an Altruistic Society for All?', in P. Bean, J. Ferris and D. Whynes (eds), *In Defense of Welfare*, London: Tavistock: 74–99.

Lundberg, S., Pollak, R. and Wales, T. (1997) 'Do Husbands and Wives Pool Their Resources? Evidence from the United Kingdom Child Benefit', *Journal of Human Resources*, 32(3): 463–480.

Mifune, M. (1995) 'Economic Relationship within the Household and the Gap between Couples: Money and Working Hours', *Japanese Journal of Research on Household Economics*, 25: 57–67.

Mifune, M. (1999) 'Women, Distance from Property, and Family Community', *Journal of Legal Sociology*, 51: 206–211.

OECD (n.d.) OECD Time Use Database. https://stats.oecd.org/Index.aspx?datasetcode =TIME_USE# (accessed 22 May 2023).

Okamoto, M. (2015) 'Household Management System in Japan and Other Countries: Analysis of Panel Date and Multinomial Logistic Regression Analysis', *Japanese Journal of Research on Household Economics*, 107: 54–63.

Pahl, J. (1989) *Money and Marriage*, Basingstoke: Macmillan.

Pepin, J. and Cohen, P. (2021) 'Nation-Level Gender Inequality and Couples' Income Arrangements', *Journal of Family and Economic Issues*, 42(1): 13–28.

Robeyns, I. (2003) 'Sen's Capability Approach and Gender Inequality: Selecting Relevant Capabilities', *Feminist Economics*, 9(2–3): 61–92.

Sakamoto, K. (2008) 'Structure of Consumption and Leisure Allocation within Households', in C. Horioka and Institute for Household Economics Foundation (eds), *An Economic Analysis of Intrahousehold Distribution and Intergenerational Transfers*, Kyoto: Minerva Publishing: 21–47.

Sakamoto, K. (2009) 'Changes in Household Financial Management and Household Behavior with Family Formation', *Journal of Household Economics*, 84: 17–35.

Sen, A. (1990) 'Gender and Cooperative Conflict', in I. Tinker (ed.), *Persistent Inequalities: Women and World Development*, Oxford: Oxford University Press: 123–148.

Sen, A. (1999) *Development as Freedom*, Oxford: Oxford University Press.

Shigekawa, J. (2017) 'Changes in Household Management Types among Husbands and Wives: Has Individualization of Household Finances Progressed?', *Journal of Household Economics*, 114: 38–47.

Tanaka, K. (2010) 'Husbands and Wives' Mutual Recognition of "Household Economics" and Evaluation of Marital Relationships and Well-Being', *Journal of Household Economics*, 86: 38–44.

4. Data about money within the household: Exploring the challenges and gaps

Sara Cantillon and Anne-Catherine Guio

Introduction

Accumulated empirical evidence has shown that investigating – rather than assuming *a priori* – the processes and attributes of the sharing, management, distribution and expenditure of household resources is critical to understanding the wellbeing and capabilities of individual household members. If different individuals within households do experience different living standards, this also has significant policy implications, not least for understanding poverty and framing anti-poverty policies. Indeed, many studies show that estimates of inequality and poverty based on household income and equal sharing are biased downward (Davies and Joshi, 1994; Crespo, 2017). Relying only on household income and the assumption of equal sharing could lead to understating the nature and extent of gender differences in living standards and to obscuring the experience of poverty for some adults and children. Several studies show that there may be hidden poverty among wives, particularly in non-poor households across many countries in the global north (Fritzell, 1999 for Sweden; Meulders and O'Dorchai, 2011 for Belgium; Phipps and Burton, 1998 for Canada; Corsi et al., 2016 for Europe). A review of evidence from low- and middle-income contexts by Richards et al. (2013) examined intra-household bargaining power and demonstrated the importance of women's decision-making and access to and control over resources.

Getting inside the 'black box' of the household to examine differences in, *inter alia*, living standards and access to and control over resources among household members is, however, conceptually and methodologically challenging. This chapter discusses some key issues in relation to methodological approaches, data collection tools and measurement methods, alongside data quality and gaps. Although international comparative quantitative data are scarce, country-specific surveys within Europe and the ad hoc modules included in the European Union Statistics on Income and Living Conditions (EU-SILC) in recent years have revealed important insights, specifically regarding income pooling, management and deprivation.

Where we are now: Data and measures

There are several ways to measure resources and living standards, including income, consumption and deprivation. All face difficulties when it comes to measurement at the individual level. Below we review some quantitative studies of intra-household distribution. Our primary focus in reviewing the different elements – resource pooling, control and management within the household, as well as unequal living standards and their interactions – is to highlight some challenges in terms of data quality and gaps.

Unequal sharing of resources and living standards

The literature has used data on individual income, consumption, material deprivation and wealth to challenge the unitary household model and to more closely examine the actual intra-household distribution of living standards.

Intra-household inequality in income

Some studies moved away from the assumption of equal sharing by simulating alternative distributions of income within households (Bennett, 2013). These generally compute poverty or inequality indicators using alternative measures of personal income, comparing them with usual estimates based on equal sharing (e.g. Meulders and O'Dorchai, 2011; Corsi et al., 2016). By assuming various scenarios regarding individualisation, such studies aim to quantify the possible order of magnitude of intra-household inequality, generally relying on assumptions concerning how partners divide their own income – often with an individualised part reserved for themselves and a residual part ceded to a common pot (Avram and Popova, this volume) – and gauging whether and how inequalities in 'personal' income are translated into inequality in living standards, usually measured through consumption or deprivation indicators.

Intra-household inequality in consumption

A challenge of moving from income-based approaches to approaches measuring directly intra-household differences in consumption is measuring individual consumption adequately. Attributing household consumption to each household member is extremely difficult (Cantillon and Nolan, 1998; Guio and Van den Bosch, 2019). Various forms of consumption are 'public goods' within the household, in that use by one individual does not reduce their availability to others (housing, heating) and others are partly public and partly private (television, car). Whilst some consumption is, in principle, solely private (e.g. food), it may be difficult to measure individual consumption precisely. Studies have shown differences in consumption between individuals in households across all three categories, including the quality and quantity of food consumed (Hoddinott and Haddad, 1995; Goode et al., 1998; Chant, 2007; Bernard et al., 2020).

Intra-household inequality in deprivation

One way to get round difficulties in accurately measuring individual consumption has been the use of non-monetary indicators. These measure the lack of 'socially perceived necessities' among the population (Townsend, 1979; Mack and Lansley, 1985). Although these deprivation indicators were typically collected only at household level, a growing number of surveys also gather them at individual level, allowing for some exploration of intra-household differences.

Cantillon and Nolan (1998) pioneered this approach using 1989 Irish survey data containing items of deprivation at the household and individual levels. Focusing on married partners who both completed individual questionnaires, Cantillon and Nolan showed greater differences between spouses in the possession or lack of personal items/activities (e.g. clothing, shoes, leisure) than in those whose use is commonly shared within households (e.g. car), although gender differences do exist. Divergent answers were most common for items such as time for socialising, a hobby/leisure activity and access to personal spending money. For most of these, more women than men were disadvantaged. While the gap between the deprivation levels of spouses was not found to be systematically related to household income, class or age, the analysis did show that if the woman had an income of her own the gap was smaller. Other measures of individual deprivation include the Individual Deprivation Measure (IDM), across 15 items, which aims to capture gendered differences in the experience of poverty, as well as differences by other markers of identity or social status, such as age, ethnicity or location. Pilot studies undertaken in Nepal and the Philippines indicated higher IDM scores for women than men, except for leisure (Bessell, 2015).

In 2017, the European Union (EU) adopted an official indicator of material and social deprivation containing 13 items; of these, six items are collected at individual level (for those aged over 15) and the remainder at household level. Guio and Van den Bosch (2019) analysed the individual items for couples. They show that the proportion of couples in the EU in which there is a one-sided enforced lack (i.e. where one partner does not have the item because she/he cannot afford it and the other has it, or does not for other reasons) is limited (from 2 to 7 per cent, depending on the item). When aggregating the six items into an individual deprivation scale, and considering the difference between partners' scores, they found no difference in most couples. Where there was a difference, the intra-couple gender deprivation gap might be to the detriment of either partner but was more frequently to the woman's. Multivariate analysis showed that each partner's work status and their share of individual income in total household income were important determinants of this gap. Cantillon and Maitre (2019) found similar results for The Republic of Ireland using the same source. When focusing on asymmetric experiences only (i.e. one partner is deprived and the other is not), women consistently experience more deprivation. For example, for lack of regular leisure, 9.5 per cent of households contain a deprived woman (and a non-deprived man), compared to only 5.7 per cent of households containing a deprived man (and a non-deprived woman). For personal spending money, the corresponding figures are 7.1 and 5.2 per cent.

Deprivation indicators, usually focused on poverty, are currently the main instrument available to explore within-household inequalities. However, it is challenging to include a large enough range of activities and items in surveys to sufficiently capture differences between partners in non-deprived households, as well as any differences in quality and individuals' freedom of choice in relation to them. The absence of a deprivation gap does not necessarily imply equality in the use of resources within households, nor equivalent access in quantity and quality to items and activities.

Individual deprivation indicators have also been used to measure intergenerational differences within a household (Burchardt and Karagiannaki, this volume). Comparing deprivation levels between different ages, however, requires further validation of the items for the whole adult age range, to ensure comparability of these indicators (Guio et al., 2017). While older people may have different tastes and priorities compared to those of younger adults, a common set of suitable and valid items still seems appropriate. For children, however, the development of specific indicators, different from those for adults, is required, which brings additional data collection challenges. The EU officially adopted a child-specific deprivation measure in 2018, composed of 12 indicators for children's consumption or activities and five for household deprivations from which children may suffer (inadequate heating, no internet, etc.). Using this measure is a step forward as, before 2018, all children were attributed their household's deprivation status. It can show, for example, how parents in poverty tend to sacrifice their own needs to avoid deprivation for their children (Main and Bradshaw, 2016).

Intra-household inequality in wealth

Living standards are also determined by asset ownership and wealth, especially in the long term. As Oduro and Swaminathan (this volume) show, an increasing body of literature documents the gap between women's and men's wealth accumulation. The previous literature mainly compared wealth accumulation *between* households and failed to record disaggregated information about asset ownership (Deere and Doss, 2008). Data on wealth are usually collected for the household, with the wealth attributed equally to each partner or treated as belonging to the household member identified as the 'most financially knowledgeable person' (Ruel and Hausei, 2013). Both assumptions lead to wealth inequality measures biased by gender.

The increasing availability of data on individual adults' wealth has facilitated the emergence of a literature on within-household wealth inequality (Frémeaux and Leturcq, 2020; Nutz and Lersch, 2021; Oduro and Swaminathan, this volume). This indicates that wealth can be possessed jointly or individually by partners within couples and that individuals may restrict partners' access to personal wealth. The within-couple wealth gap appears to be influenced by age at union formation, partnership type, life-course events and institutional factors such as inheritance laws, marital property regimes, pension rights, taxation systems and/or housing market characteristics (Lersch et al., 2022). Oduro and Swaminathan (this volume) analyse individual-level asset and wealth data in the global south using household surveys, highlighting key issues.

Income pooling, control and management of resources

As argued by Bennett (2013: 585), 'between incomes and outcomes, processes of control and management of money intervene'. In addition to income sharing and inequality in living standards, studies have attempted to measure actual income pooling and management practices, using both qualitative and quantitative data. The quantitative data necessary for identifying the distribution and impact of management modes and within-household financial decision-making are not usually included in generalist surveys. Including dedicated modules in some international surveys allowed for significant progress (e.g. EU-SILC 2010; International Social Survey Programme module 2012, 2022). Using the EU-SILC module, Ponthieux (2017) showed that at EU level the proportion of 'full pooling' couples, in which neither partner reported keeping any personal income separate, was about 59 per cent on average, with large country variations. The probability of full pooling was positively and significantly associated with marriage, presence of children, the time a couple had lived together and low household income level, but decreased when both partners were employed (Ponthieux, 2017). Some countries have added their own ad hoc modules exploring intra-household issues to ongoing surveys – e.g. the Intra-Household Distribution of Resources module within the 2019 Scottish Social Attitudes Survey.

Linking management and sharing of resources

As Bennett (2013) emphasised, it would be misleading to use households' allocation systems to infer a 'sharing rule' determining consumption and wellbeing. Results concerning the impact of different forms of money arrangement on individual living standards confirm that the relationship is not straightforward. Vogler and Pahl (1994) showed that the wife controlling finances did not protect her against deprivation; however, male control, especially in the form of a housekeeping allowance given to the wife, did benefit men in comparison with women. Gender equality (measured in deprivation indicators) was highest in households with joint control of pooled money and lowest in either low-income households or higher-income households in which males controlled the finances. Cantillon et al. (2015) found that under full pooling the woman's risk of individual deprivation tended to be higher, controlling for income level and other factors. Under partial pooling, the risk of individual deprivation was lower. This strand of quantitative research is demanding, as data on financial arrangements and income pooling are complex to collect and reconcile, due to inconsistencies between partners' answers (see the next section). Furthermore, Cantillon (2013) showed that management arrangements varied across not only households but also different spending areas.

Gaps in data and challenges in data quality

The previous section demonstrated that, whatever the empirical approach, good-quality data are required. Here we discuss some methodological challenges hindering good data collection, considering ways in which methods and/or modes of collection affect the accuracy of responses. We also identify intra-household distribution issues for which data are currently non-existent or insufficient, including those involving reconstituted families, children in shared custody, longitudinal perspectives, and how income, pooled or otherwise, is spent and who benefits from it.

Data collection challenges

Challenges arise in relation to both individual- and household-level data needed to study intra-household processes and outcomes, not least that the data collection methods themselves are not neutral. For most household-level questionnaires, one person responds for the whole household, and his/her answers are taken to reflect the situation of the household unit. The 'identity' of the household respondent (age, gender, labour market situation, etc.) is not considered and, to our knowledge, no sensitivity analyses are performed regarding the impact of the household respondent's profile on replies given to 'household' questions in large-scale surveys on income and living conditions with only one respondent.[1]

Information collected at the individual level may also not be neutral. One issue is the impact of data collection methods on responses. For example, the presence of a partner or of another household member during the interview may affect responses about individual deprivation, management of resources and autonomy in decision-making (Cantillon and Nolan, 1998, 2001; Cantillon and Newman, 2005; Guio and Van den Bosch, 2019). Ideally, each household member should be surveyed on his/her own. In most large-scale surveys, the presence of other members is not recorded. In the Living in Ireland Survey this is recorded, showing that the presence of another household member significantly influences the wife's responses to questions about deprivation and/or financial management and responsibility, but does not affect the husband's replies (Cantillon, 2013).

In many low-income countries, the measurement of intra-household differences in the most extreme forms of deprivation (e.g. access to food or healthcare) is even more challenging. Women may not be allowed to meet the survey interviewer in person or may not reply freely to their questions in the presence of another household member. If this information is collected through telephone-based surveys, gender gaps in access to and control of technologies may affect the quality and representativeness of the data collected. A pilot survey in Somalia on intra-household differences in food insecurity illustrates this, as most respondents to the telephone-based remote survey were adult males, talking about experiences faced by female household members (World Food Programme, 2021).

Guio and Van den Bosch (2021) show that the mode of interviewing also affects the deprivation gap between partners in couples in Europe, with self-administered and computer-assisted web interviewing questionnaires showing a larger deprivation gap (to women's disadvantage). The privacy of these two interviewing modes may indeed help to improve accuracy, particularly when deprivation differs between partners (Guio and Van den Bosch, 2021: 243). Furthermore, restrictions on conducting face-to-face interviews due to the COVID-19 pandemic have led to temporary changes in modes of data collection, with the increase in non-contact collecting modes potentially affecting the measurement of within-household inequalities.

In Guio and Van den Bosch (2019), multivariate analysis indicates that the use of proxy interviews (when another household member can reply to an absent household member's individual questionnaire) affects the (collected) deprivation status of the absentee in some countries, decreasing the probability of seeing a disadvantage vis-à-vis the absentee's partner. In EU-SILC, the percentage of proxy interviews varies between countries (and, often, over time within countries) and is more likely to affect younger sample members and males (Lynn, 2022). This could imply systematic bias in comparing subgroups with a different propensity to be absent and in studying intra-household variations. Research on intra-household wealth distribution has also shown the impact of using proxy instead of self-reporting (Oduro and Swaminathan, this volume). It is therefore vital to limit the use of proxies for questions about deprivation, control over resources, wellbeing and/or wealth.

Sometimes information cannot be collected directly from the person most affected. For example, EU child deprivation data are collected from the adult responding to the household questionnaire (the household respondent).[2] This may cause problems of inaccuracy of data from parents (due to, for example, shame in admitting the lack of something, and possible omissions and errors) and the different perspectives parents and children may have (Main, 2018; and this volume). Moreover, one parent may know more about their children's situation than the other, so the identity of the household respondent may matter. Data should be collected on each child within a household. Some surveys, such as EU-SILC, only collect information for the children as a whole (if at least one child lacks an item, it is assumed that all children in that household lack it). It is therefore impossible to study differences in deprivation between children living in the same household – for example, between girls and boys, children of different ages, and/or half-siblings from different unions (Guio and Van den Bosch (2021)).

Particular attention must be given to drafting survey questions. Qualitative research can tease out differing perceptions (Bennett, this volume). In addition, focus groups can help to test and refine question wording for use in quantitative surveys. Cantillon (2013) used these to phrase questions about personal deprivation, ensuring that the respondent understood that these related to his/

her own consumption, not the whole household's. Such issues are particularly challenging in cross-country surveys, which require optimum translation of complex concepts, adapted to each linguistic and cultural context (Lynn and Lyberg, 2022).

Another important issue relates to the inconsistencies between answers from the partner responding to the household questionnaire and those from each partner to the individual questionnaires. Ponthieux (2013) shows large differences in household and personal responses to questions on income pooling: the share of responses in which the individual's answer is consistent with that of their household ranges from under half in six countries to over 90 per cent in the Netherlands. In another context (Bangladesh, Uganda and Guatemala), Alkire et al. (2013) showed that among couples interviewed about who makes decisions on joint agricultural activity, male and female responses were identical in only 43 per cent of cases.

Another challenge when measuring within-household inequalities is collecting accurate data on individualised income. It is not always possible to attribute all income sources to individuals. This is easier with some income components (e.g. wages or some income replacement benefits). Even in some of these cases, however, eligibility for and the amount of a social transfer may depend on the household's or cohabitants' resources and/or characteristics; individuals cannot be treated as a unit independent from their household. The individualisation of other income components is complex, especially when they are intended for more than one household member and/or the household as a whole (e.g. some housing allowances or minimum income schemes), the couple (property income or self-employment income in cases of shared property or activity), or children. In many surveys, there is no information about who receives these kinds of transfers. Furthermore, some income components are aggregated at the household level by the data producer, even if they may be received at the individual level in some countries (e.g. minimum income schemes and other social assistance support). Moreover, in many countries, individual incomes are jointly taxed at couple or household level, i.e. income taxes are computed at household level. In such cases, neither survey nor administrative data allow for the computation of the net amounts of individual income components, requiring the use of microsimulation methods (Avram and Popova, this volume).

Data gaps

Despite the tradition in collecting information (albeit imperfectly in large-scale surveys) on income, wealth, etc., information on concepts such as financial autonomy or economic independence is rarely – and often only partially – collected. Collecting data on women's empowerment and autonomy of decision-making is crucial, particularly in countries where most resources are in kind and individual income data may not give a true picture of living standards. Bridging this data gap, Alkire et al. (2013) proposed various domain-specific measures of empowerment (e.g. decision-making about agricultural production, ownership of productive resources, control over the use of income or time allocation), based on questions that can be fielded in individual or household surveys (Bessell, 2015).

As we have attempted to show, even when data are collected, there is often only partial evidence of the complexity of processes taking place relating to resources in the household. How incomes are actually used (whether pooled or kept separate – or, often, a bit of both) remains unobserved in surveys; as discussed earlier, the income kept separate by someone may be used exclusively for him/herself and/or for expenditures benefiting another household member. Although it is extremely difficult to collect this type of information, experimental data collection, such as the use of personal electronic expenditure data, could be considered a useful tool. The United Kingdom (UK) Household Longitudinal Survey ran an experiment using bank account data, asking people for their receipts (Jäckle et al., 2019). Similarly, a study in Iceland analysed the relationship between the intra-household distribution of income, household spending and financial arrangements using bank account data. As all bank accounts in Iceland are individual rather than joint, the researchers could observe individual spending and debt holdings of all household members in ways previously not feasible (Olafsson and Pagel, 2018). This would be impossible in many other countries, where joint accounts are common and access to bank account data raises significant data protection issues.

Most data collection conventions do not acknowledge the (increasing) complexity of household units. Documenting all relationships between household members in complex households (multigenerational households or reconstituted families) is crucial to understand their sharing of resources (Burchardt and Karagiannaki, this volume). Investigation of the 'statuses' of members who may live sometimes in one household and sometimes in another requires methodological development and additional data collection. This is particularly relevant for children of separated parents. Haux and Luthra (2019) discuss the challenges of the evolving phenomenon of shared care – particularly for longitudinal surveys, as much of their value rests on asking the same questions over time. The authors explore UK data from the Understanding Society survey to examine how shared care is negotiated and practised, as well as the appropriateness of, and future changes to, existing questions in the survey about care arrangements. In most surveys, these children are recorded as full members of the household being surveyed, regardless of the amount of time they spend there. In traditional poverty and inequality analysis, income is adjusted for household size to take into account economies of scale, without considering the fact that children in shared custody share their time between two households. To disentangle this, additional data on time spent with each parent, and the existence and degree of sharing of expenditures, and of child benefits/child tax allowances/tax credits and of any transfers between households, should be collected. When these data are available (e.g. in EU-SILC 2021), the information collected is usually too limited. Information on parents' situation before the separation, on decisions about custody arrangements and their evolution over time, and on both parents' involvement would be needed.

Furthermore, Main (2018) argues that it is problematic to use the household as the measurement unit when children are the object of interest. One reason is that children's access to resources may vary across the households they reside in – and different children within the same household may also have variable access to resources, depending on their non-resident parents' contributions. Some studies adopt a strict residential criterion, whilst others include all (resident and non-resident) family members. If the focus is the social, psychological, and material living conditions of the child, it may indeed make sense to identify all sibling relationships (full, half, step) that children of separated parents may have and uncover how these span households (Toulemon, 2013).

Understanding the *dynamics* of within-household inequalities is also crucial to highlight important drivers and draw out policy recommendations. There are, however, only a few longitudinal studies that investigate changes in the patterns of control, management, and use of resources over time, or the impact of trigger events on such arrangements (for example, childbirth, illness, job loss, retirement, repartnering, etc.), due to lack of panel data covering a sufficiently long period. Lott (2017) provided interesting insights into the evolution of money management in Germany, using longitudinal data from the German Socio-Economic Panel. This study explored whether couples abandoned independent money management when particular life events occurred or when partners' relative resources changed. It shows that an increase in women's incomes is associated with independent money management.

There is also a lack of longitudinal data on factors explaining wealth accumulation and on the long-term effects associated with pooling or separating wealth and economic resources. As articulated by Lersch et al. (2022: 636): 'Is separate wealth good or bad for women and men later in life, and how does the answer depend on individuals' socio-demographic characteristics and life courses?'

As explained by Oduro and Swaminathan (this volume), it is also important to collect information on the institutional and legal frameworks that affect women's ability to own property.

Future research

The chapter has identified many methodological challenges, which require further research. Recognising the sensitivity of questions related to deprivation, control over resources, wellbeing, or empowerment and autonomy is a necessary step, but insufficient without adequate investment in improvements to methods. We argue that both the breadth and quality of existing approaches and tools need to be developed to enhance the quality and societal impact of research on these issues as well as its policy relevance.

The chapter extensively illustrated various methodological challenges hindering good data collection. We argued that it is crucial to better investigate the ways in which the methods employed affect the accuracy of responses. This includes, for example, controlling for the impact of modes of collection on the measurement of within-household inequalities. Also, the impact of the presence of other people during the interview or the use of proxies should be scrutinised. We proposed that the reasons for inconsistencies between answers given by people living together responding to the same question(s) should be systematically investigated. We showed that particular attention must be given to drafting survey questions, using qualitative research when needed to test and refine question wording for use in quantitative surveys.

The chapter has also identified significant data gaps which prevent the adequate measurement of the complexity of the processes that take place within households in relation to resources. Filling in these gaps requires the development of new research tools and cross-fertilisation between qualitative and quantitative research.

This includes, for example, using experimental data collection, such as personal electronic expenditure data, to measure how incomes are actually used by individuals living together. It encompasses going beyond the boundaries of the household to better take into account the evolving reality of families, for example by taking into account all the flows of resources and expenditure that span across separated parents or multigenerational families.

We discussed the importance of collecting and analysing new longitudinal data in order to improve our knowledge of the dynamics of within-household inequalities, the complexity of wealth and income sharing, and changes in the patterns of control, management and use of resources over time, as well as the impact of trigger events on such arrangements.

In view of the challenges and gaps thus identified, the key question is how to transform our current analyses and knowledge into real improvements in the collection of data and the construction of indicators. The importance of accurate data collection on within-household resource distribution, outcomes and processes can only be demonstrated if the available data are used and translated into robust indicators published in official statistics. We hope that this will in turn lead to data improvements and investment in the areas currently insufficiently covered and thereby create a virtuous circle.

Notes

1. The World Bank (15 July 2013) notes this lack of research on the impact of choice of respondent in household surveys: https://blogs.worldbank.org/impactevaluations/whats-right-way-pick-respondent-household-survey (accessed 3 March 2023). There is some evidence that responses about the household will vary depending on respondents' characteristics, but this is indirect in relation to household finances.
2. There are exceptions: the UK Household Longitudinal Survey collects its youth data from 10- to 15-year-olds, with questions meant to be answered by them.

References

Alkire, S., Meinzen-Dick, R., Peterman, A., Quisumbing, A.R., Seymour, G. and Vaz, A. (2013). 'The women's empowerment in agriculture index', OPHI Working Paper No. 58. Available at: www.ophi.org.uk/wp-content/uploads/ophi-wp-58.pdf (accessed 9 January 2023).

Bennett, F. (2013). 'Researching within-household distribution: Overview, developments, debates, and methodological challenges', *Journal of Marriage and Family*, 75(3): 582–597.

Bernard, R., Tzamourani, P. and Weber, M. (2020). 'How are households' consumption plans affected by the COVID-19 pandemic?', *Bundesbank Research Brief, No. 35*, Frankfurt: Deutsche Bundesbank. Available at: www.econstor.eu/bitstream/10419/249772/1/2020-35-research-brief-data.pdf (accessed 10 March 2023).

Bessell, S. (2015). 'The individual deprivation measure: Measuring poverty as if gender and inequality matter', *Gender and Development*, 23(2): 223–240.

Cantillon, S. (2013). 'Measuring differences in living standards within households', *Journal of Marriage and Family*, 75(3): 598–610.

Cantillon, S. and Maitre, B. (2019). 'Economic autonomy within households', Political Economy Research Institute Workshop Series, University of Massachusetts, 24 September.

Cantillon, S. and Newman, C. (2005). 'Bias in interview data created by presence of a third party: Methodological issues in a study of intra-household deprivation', *Radical Statistics*, 90: 33–44.

Cantillon, S. and Nolan, B. (1998). 'Are married women more deprived than their husbands?', *Journal of Social Policy*, 27(2): 151–171.

Cantillon, S. and Nolan, B. (2001). 'Poverty within households: Measuring gender differences using nonmonetary indicators', *Feminist Economics*, 7(1): 5–23.

Cantillon, S., Maître, B. and Watson, D. (2015). 'Family financial management and individual deprivation', *Journal of Family and Economic Issues*, 37(3): 461–473.

Chant, S. (2007). *Gender, Generation and Poverty: Exploring the 'Feminisation of Poverty' in Africa, Asia and Latin America*. Cheltenham, UK and Northampton, MA, USA: Edward Elgar Publishing.

Corsi, M., Botti, F. and D'Ippoliti, C. (2016). 'The gendered nature of poverty in the EU: Individualized versus collective poverty measures', *Feminist Economics*, 22(4): 82–100.

Crespo, S. (2017). 'What if couples do not share all their incomes? Consequences for the measurement of inequalities in welfare', *Cahiers québécois de démographie*, 46(1): 73–99.

Davies, H. and Joshi, H. (1994). 'The foregone earnings of Europe's mothers?', in O. Ekert (ed.), *Standards of Living and Families: Observation and Analysis*. Paris: INED John Libbey Eurotext: 101–135.

Deere, C.D. and Doss, C.R. (2008). 'The gender asset gap: What do we know and why does it matter?', *Feminist Economics*, 12(1–2): 1–50.

Frémeaux, N. and Leturcq, M. (2020). 'Inequalities and the individualization of wealth', *Journal of Public Economics*, 184(6): 1–18.

Fritzell, J. (1999). 'Incorporating gender inequality into income distribution research', *International Journal of Social Welfare*, 8(1): 56–66.

Goode, J., Callender, C. and Lister R. (1998). *Purse or Wallet: Gender Inequalities and Income Distribution within Families on Benefits*. London: Policy Studies Institute.

Guio, A.C. and Van den Bosch, K. (2019). 'Deprivation of women and men living in a couple: Sharing or unequal division?', *Review of Income and Wealth*, 66(4): 958–984.

Guio, A.C. and Van den Bosch, K. (2021). 'Deprivation among couples: Sharing or unequal division?', in A.C. Guio, E. Marlier and B. Nolan (eds), *Improving the Understanding of Poverty and Social Exclusion in Europe*. Eurostat Statistical Working Papers. Luxembourg: Publications Office of the European Union: 235–250.

Guio, A.C., Gordon, D., Najera, H. and Pomati, P. (2017). 'Revising the EU material deprivation variables'. Available at: www .poverty .ac .uk/ sites/ default/ files/ attachments/Revising-the-EU-deprivation-variables_Eurostat_2017.pdf (accessed 9 January 2023).

Haux, T. and Luthra, R.R. (2019). 'What is shared care?', Understanding Society Working Paper, 2019-12 Colchester: Institute for Social and Economic Research,. University of Essex.

Hoddinott, J. and Haddad, L. (1995). 'Does female income share influence household expenditure? Evidence from Cote D'Ivoire', *Oxford Bulletin of Economics and Statistics*, 57(1): 77–96.

Jäckle, A., Burton, J., Couper, M. and Lessof, C. (2019). 'Participation in a mobile app survey to collect expenditure data as part of a large-scale probability household panel', *Survey Research Methods*, 13(1): 23–44.

Lersch, P.M., Strufolino, E. and Vitali, A. (2022). 'Wealth in couples: Introduction to the special issue', *European Journal of Population*, 38(4): 623–641.

Lott, Y. (2017). 'When my money becomes our money: Changes in couples' money management', *Social Policy and Society*, 16(2): 199–218.

Lynn, P. (2022). 'The effect of proxy responses on non-response error', in P. Lynn and L. Lyberg (eds), *Improving the Measurement of Poverty and Social Exclusion in Europe: Reducing Non-Sampling Errors*. Luxembourg: Publications Office of the European Union: 107–123.

Lynn, P. and Lyberg, L. (eds) (2022). *Improving the Measurement of Poverty and Social Exclusion in Europe: Reducing Non-Sampling Errors*. Luxembourg: Publications Office of the European Union.

Mack, J. and Lansley, S. (1985). *Poor Britain*. London: George Allen and Unwin.

Main, G. (2018). 'Fair shares and families: A child-focused model of intra-household sharing', *Childhood Vulnerability*, 1(1–3): 31–49.

Main, G. and Bradshaw, J. (2016). 'Child poverty in the UK: Measures, prevalence and intra-household sharing', *Critical Social Policy*, 36(1): 38–61.

Meulders, D. and O'Dorchai, S.P. (2011). 'Revisiting poverty measures towards individualisation', *Journal of Income Distribution*, 20(3–4): 75–102.

Nutz, T. and Lersch, P.M. (2021). 'Gendered employment trajectories and individual wealth at older ages in Eastern and Western Germany', *Advances in Life Course Research*, 47: 1–11.

Olafsson, A. and Pagel, M. (2018). 'Family Finances: Intra-Household Bargaining, Spending, and Financial Structure.', Columbia Business School/Copenhagen Business School Working Paper.

Phipps, S.A. and Burton, P.S. (1998). 'What's mine is yours? The influence of male and female incomes on patterns of household expenditure', *Economica*, 65(260): 599–613.

Ponthieux, S. (2013). 'Income pooling and equal sharing within the household: What can we learn from the 2010 EU-SILC module?', Eurostat Methodologies and Working Papers, Luxembourg: Publications Office of the European Union.

Ponthieux, S. (2017). 'Intra-household pooling and sharing of resources: A tentative "modified" equivalised income', in A.B. Atkinson, A.C. Guio and E. Marlier (eds), *Monitoring Social Inclusion in Europe*, Luxembourg: Publications Office of the European Union: 175–190.

Richards, E., Theobald, S., George, A., Kim, J.C., Rudert, C., Jehan, K. and Tolhurst, R. (2013). 'Going beyond the surface: Gendered intra-household bargaining as a social determinant of child health and nutrition in low and middle income countries', *Social Science and Medicine*, 95, pp 24–33.

Ruel, E. and Hausei, R.M. (2013). 'Explaining the gender wealth gap', *Demography*, 50(4): 1155–1176.

Toulemon, L. (2013). 'Les pères dans les statistiques', *Informations sociales*, 176(2): 8–13.

Townsend, P. (1979). *Poverty in the United Kingdom*. Harmondsworth: Penguin.

Vogler, C. and Pahl, J. (1994). 'Money, power and inequality within marriage', *Sociological Review*, 42(2): 263–288.

World Food Programme (2021). *Somalia Annual Country Report 2020, Country Strategic Plan 2019–2021*. Available at: https://docs.wfp.org/api/documents/WFP-0000137210/download/ (accessed 9 January 2023).

5. Peering into the black box: Using microsimulation methods to evaluate the gendered impact of taxes and transfers

Silvia Avram and Daria Popova

Introduction

Research on income distribution and living standards measured by income usually focuses on household rather than individual income. Similarly, official indicators used for policy purposes (e.g. the at-risk-of-poverty indicators in the European Union (EU) or Households Below Average Income statistics in the United Kingdom (UK)) are constructed based on household incomes, adjusted for household size. As noted in the introduction in this volume, this choice has been justified theoretically by assuming that households constitute a single decision-making unit, as in the unitary model (Becker, 1974). While this assumption has the advantage of simplicity, it entirely obscures any intra-household dynamics, treating the household instead as a 'black box' (Maruyama, this volume).

The inadequacy of the unitary household model has been recognised for some time. Empirical studies have found the assumptions of complete pooling and equal sharing to be generally unsupported and theoretical alternatives such as bargaining and collective models have been proposed (for an overview, see Ponthieux and Meurs, 2015 and Woolley, this volume). Some studies have used an assumption of minimal income pooling to derive alternative (individual-level) measures of disposable income and poverty (Jenkins, 1991; Sutherland, 1997; Fritzell, 1999; Davies and Joshi, 2009; Meulders and O'Dorchai, 2010), yet this approach has not become mainstream in income distribution analysis.

Practical limitations in household surveys or register data[1] have constrained the use of individual disposable income measures. Unlike earnings, data on many non-labour forms of income are not collected at individual level. This is particularly so for transfers targeted at families/households rather than individuals, such as family or housing benefits, but also for individual non-labour incomes collected, for convenience, at the household level (e.g. property income or private transfers). Information on who receives non-individual incomes is usually lacking and these incomes generally can only be allocated at the individual level based on assumptions. Even if relatively accurate measures of individual income can be constructed, measuring the intra-household allocation of resources requires information about income pooling and sharing. Such information cannot be retrieved from income registers and is typically also lacking in surveys of income and living conditions.

Although not without limitations, tax/benefit microsimulation models can make an important contribution to research on intra-household distribution by addressing some of the existing data challenges. Microsimulation describes a technique whereby a set of rules is consistently applied to a collection of individual units to simulate changes in their state or behaviour (Figari et al., 2015). Tax/benefit models are a class of microsimulation models using individual and household microdata together with detailed information on fiscal legislation to simulate tax liabilities and benefit entitlements at the individual/family/assessment unit[2] level. This chapter explains how tax/benefit microsimulation models can be applied to analyse intra-household income inequality.

What is microsimulation and how can it be used to research the intra-household distribution of resources?

Tax/benefit microsimulation has a long history in income distribution analysis. Its development was motivated primarily by the need to evaluate policy reforms before implementation, both for their distributional consequences – to achieve a better understanding about winners and losers – and to obtain more accurate forecasts of their budgetary impact. Today, the uses of tax/benefit microsimulation extend well beyond *ex ante* policy evaluation (for a review of the many ways in which microsimulation has been used in both academic research and policy analysis, see Figari et al., 2015). Yet to date their potential in tackling the existing limitations in intra-household distribution research has not been fully exploited.

Tax/benefit microsimulation models are a tool to apply tax liability and benefit entitlement rules to a household sample to understand how taxes and benefits affect household disposable income (i.e. income after payment of direct taxes and receipt of all benefits). To accurately simulate fiscal liabilities and benefit entitlements, these models require comprehensive information about individual and household characteristics driving these entitlements and liabilities, including but not limited to household size and composition, market incomes, history of paying social insurance contributions, labour market status, disability status, etc. Based on this information and on legislative rules, such tax/benefit models can then simulate the amount of fiscal liabilities and benefit entitlements at the assessment unit level (see below about benefit take-up).

Why use tax/benefit microsimulation models?

In the context of intra-household distribution, tax/benefit microsimulation models have several advantages. First, they can improve the accuracy of income information in surveys. Several studies have shown that means-tested benefits tend to be under-reported in surveys, at least in developed countries (Meyer and Sullivan, 2003; Brewer et al., 2017). By simulating means-tested benefit entitlements, such microsimulation models can improve the accuracy of income measures at the bottom of the distribution. They can also be used to impute benefit entitlements and tax liabilities at the individual/assessment unit level whenever information is only collected at the household level in surveys. For example, the EU Survey of Income and Living Conditions (EU-SILC), the primary data source for income distribution analysis in many European countries, only collects information about taxes paid at the household level, even when tax liabilities are individual. Tax/benefit microsimulation models can be used to reconstruct tax liabilities at the individual level, subject to the relevant characteristics being captured in the microdata. Finally, microsimulation models can be used to construct measures of fiscal/tax advantages not directly observable in survey data, such as tax allowances or tax credits.

A second advantage of tax/benefit microsimulation models, of relevance to this volume in particular, is that they can facilitate the construction of individualised measures of income based on transparent assumptions. Whilst they cannot provide information about who is receiving and/or controlling an income source within the household beyond what is collected directly in surveys, they can use assumptions about how non-individual-level incomes are shared and distributed among household members to draw conclusions about individual income levels and living standards. They can also vary these assumptions and test how sensitive the results are in relation to income pooling and sharing. Finally, if information on actual income pooling and sharing patterns is available in a survey, tax/benefit models can be combined with this information to arrive at individual income measures that more accurately reflect the living standards of individuals within the household. We present an example later in the chapter.

Tax/benefit microsimulation models can be particularly useful in the evaluation of gender mainstreaming, i.e. in the assessment of the impact of a policy measure from a gender perspective (EIGE, 2016). Most policy evaluation studies struggle to fully capture gender differences in the effects of policies. Such assessment is only straightforward for single women and men. When measures of living standards, poverty or inequality are based on household incomes, women and men living in the same household are, by definition, assumed to have the same (equivalent) living standard. If household members do not fully share their incomes in practice, the living standards of women, who typically have lower labour incomes and assets, may be overestimated and those of men underestimated. Tax/benefit microsimulation models can help to capture the gender dimension of proposed policy reforms by enabling the construction of accurate individual income measures.

The importance of individual income

Disposable income (income after direct taxes and transfers) is probably the most widely used measure of economic resources in both scholarly work and policy analysis. In rich, and most middle-income, countries inequality and poverty measures are primarily computed on this basis. Disposable income measured at individual level is particularly salient in the context of intra-household research.

First, individual income represents a measure of economic independence or autonomy, seen as important in its own right (Pahl, 2005; Dema-Moreno and Díaz-Martínez, 2010; Bennett and Sutherland, 2011), especially with rising family instability. Adults who contribute few or no economic resources are vulnerable as withdrawal of financial support from their partner can leave them economically deprived, as attested by the significant negative economic consequences of union dissolution for some women (Brewer and Nandi, 2014; Popova and Navicke, 2019).[3] Second, individual income is often correlated with other measures of economic resources. Several studies have shown that women's consumption and living standards are related to their share of earnings or income within the household (Cantillon, 2013; Himmelweit et al., 2013; Bonke, 2015; Guio and Van den Bosch, 2020). It should be noted, though, that individual disposable income measures do not capture non-monetary aspects of intra-household inequality – for instance, gender inequalities in time use and unpaid work. Second, individual disposable income measures on their own do not capture differences between receiving, controlling and benefiting from income. For instance, a certain level of intra-household inequality in individual incomes received does not necessarily imply the same level of consumption inequality, as transfers between partners can occur without explicit income pooling; on the other hand, the person receiving an income does not necessarily control how it is spent or benefit from it directly.

Limitations of using tax/benefit microsimulation models

Tax/benefit microsimulation models therefore have tremendous potential in income distribution analysis; but they also have some limitations. First, the accuracy and reliability of simulations depend on the information in the underlying microdata. When pieces of information are not available (e.g. long social insurance contribution histories, details on disability status, detailed expenditure, etc.), assumptions must be made to enable the simulations to be run (Figari et al., 2015). Aggregate results also depend on the underlying microdata being representative – for example, the inability of surveys to adequately capture high-income earners leads to underestimation of tax revenues (Sutherland, 2018). For intra-household research, results may be biased if lack of accurate information affects some household members more than others – for example, assumptions about social insurance contribution histories may be more realistic for men, who are more likely to be in stable employment, than for women, who are more likely to have interrupted labour market careers.

A model's restricted scope can also be a limitation. The existing tax/benefit models have been used primarily to produce accurate measures of cash benefit entitlements and direct tax liabilities to assess the impact of these on disposable incomes. Some attempts have been made to extend these models to cover wealth and wealth taxes (Kuypers et al., 2019), indirect taxes (De Agostini et al., 2017) and non-cash benefits (Figari and Paulus, 2015; Hufkens et al., 2020). Traditionally, however, these have not been part of tax/benefit models, although it is possible to incorporate them.

Existing tax/benefit microsimulation models differ in how they account for behavioural responses to policy rule changes (Bourguignon and Sparado, 2006). Static or arithmetic models are perfectly adequate to evaluate the first-round effects of policy changes and, under certain conditions, might be a good approximation of a final policy effect. Studying the medium- or long-term effects, however, requires static microsimulation models to be linked with behavioural models, for instance to model labour supply changes following policy reforms.

Another relevant issue is the sensitivity of microsimulation analysis to assumptions about benefit non-take-up and tax non-compliance. These are behavioural aspects that cannot be internally captured by tax/benefit micro-simulation models. Instead, simulations can be calibrated to correspond to a non-take-up benchmark based on external information; and/or researchers may run sensitivity analyses to account for possible non-take-up scenarios. In addition to the direct underestimation or overestimation of incomes of entitled/liable households, non-take-up and non-compliance are important because they are likely to relate to intra-household dynamics. Non-take-up may be more or less likely depending on which household member is entitled to the benefit. Similarly, tax compliance/non-compliance may depend on intra-household dynamics and how household members manage and control money.

Overview of existing research on intra-household resources using tax/benefit microsimulation models

To overcome the conceptual and methodological problems posed by meas-uring income at household level, several studies have used tax/benefit micro-simulation models to explore how the distributional outcomes for women and men would change depending on assumptions about the pooling and sharing of common resources (Sutherland, 1997; Bennett and Sutherland, 2011; Figari et al., 2011; Avram et al., 2016; Doorley and Keane, 2020; Fuenmayor et al., 2020; Avram and Popova, 2022a, 2022b). All the studies relied on some modifications of the *minimal income pooling* assumption to derive individual measures of disposable income and poverty. In each case, it was assumed that individual incomes (e.g. earnings, individual benefits) are retained by their recipients, while household incomes (e.g. family benefits, housing allowances) are distributed among household members following some sharing rules, and the costs of children are split between their parents or assigned to one parent (e.g. the mother).

Sutherland (1997) pioneered this approach in a UK study in which she showed that this kind of simulation resulted in women being disproportionately represented in the bottom quantiles of the individual income distribution. Bennett and Sutherland (2011) simulated a hypothetical reform abolishing all non-means-tested earnings replacement benefits for working-age people in the UK and let the means-tested system fill some of the gap. Assuming equal sharing of means-tested incomes within the couple, the reform resulted in women in couples 'losing' less in absolute terms than men; but as a proportion of individual incomes women in couples lost more than men. These findings highlight the importance of non-means-tested benefits for the financial independence of women living in couples.

Several microsimulation studies carried out comparative analyses for a range of European countries using EUROMOD, the tax/benefit model for the EU (Figari et al., 2011; Avram et al., 2016; Doorley and Keane, 2020; Fuenmayor et al., 2020; Avram and Popova, 2022a). EUROMOD is a tax/benefit model simulating benefit entitlements and tax liabilities for all EU member states, from the mid-2000s to the present day, using some common assumptions (Sutherland and Figari, 2013). All the EUROMOD-based studies showed that women's individual disposable incomes are consistently lower than men's. However, the gender gap in earnings appears to be higher, suggesting an equalising effect of taxes and transfers on disposable incomes. All studies find significant cross-country variation in the redistributive effect of policies and the resulting ratio of female to male disposable incomes (the latter ranging from Germany's 60 per cent to Finland's 84 per cent). Old-age pensions and survivor benefits have the largest equalising effect among older people, whilst personal income taxes are most important for the working-age population.

Avram et al. (2016) and Avram and Popova (2022a) have tested the sensitivity of gender income ratios to various assumptions about splitting non-individual income components. In particular, they assigned them to the primary earner, or the secondary earner, or split them equally among the adults in the assessment unit. Overall, the choice of scenario made little difference to the calculation of gender income ratios because of the small share of collective income components (such as family benefits, social assistance and housing benefits) in disposable income; yet it was important for one-earner couples and couples with children, who are more likely to be eligible for these types of benefits.

Avram and Popova (2022b) used EUROMOD to reconstruct measures of individual income prior to separation and to create a counterfactual scenario by splitting all heterosexual couples in the data and simulating all benefits and taxes each individual would be entitled to if living in separate households. They find that, assuming complete income pooling during the partnership, replacement rates after separation (i.e. the ratio of post-separation to pre-separation disposable income) appear to be lower for working-age women than for working-age men. If minimum income pooling is assumed, women have higher replacement rates after separation compared to men.

Apart from point-in-time analyses, tax/benefit microsimulation models have also been used to assess the distributional impact of policy changes over time.

Doorley et al. (2021) assessed the gendered impacts of COVID-19 on earnings and disposable incomes using the Irish component of EUROMOD, finding that the redistributive effect of the Irish tax/benefit system on the gender gap in income doubled during the pandemic. A study by EIGE (2023) used EUROMOD to assess the pandemic's impact on gender income inequality in all EU member states. It finds that the labour market shock in 2020 affected women's individual incomes less compared to men's incomes. The effects of EU governments' discretionary policies to counteract the adverse impacts of the pandemic on disposable incomes (i.e. furlough schemes and benefit top-ups and/or tax reductions) were positive for both women and men of working age in almost all EU countries, and more favourable for women. This has resulted in a reduction in gender income inequality for the working-age population in 14 EU member states, compared to the pre-COVID-19 scenario.

It should be noted that existing tax/benefit microsimulation research on intra-household inequality is generally limited to rich countries such as EU member states and the UK, due to the absence of quality microsimulation models in the global south until recently. With the development of tax/benefit microsimulation models by CEQ,[4] SOUTHMOD[5] and LATINMOD,[6] the lack of tax/benefit models for many low- and middle-income countries is no longer a constraint.

Using microsimulation to examine the effect of income pooling on the gender income gap

In this section, we use our own research to show how microsimulation can be combined with survey information about household income pooling to measure individual income.

In 2010, EU-SILC implemented an *ad hoc* module on intra-household sharing of resources (for a review and analysis of the data see Ponthieux, 2013). Information collected included the system of managing finances used by the household, based on the classification originally developed by Pahl (Pahl, 1983; Vogler and Pahl, 1994), and the share of personal income kept separate by the respondent. Ponthieux (2017) used the latter piece of information to derive partial income pooling measures for a selection of European countries. We follow her approach here, but in addition we combine the survey information with the tax/benefit microsimulation model EUROMOD to derive gender income ratios under complete income pooling, minimal pooling and partial pooling. Microsimulation allows us to compute accurate measures of personal income, as well as to better identify and allocate collective income sources. EUROMOD uses the cross-sectional version of EU-SILC as its underlying data, allowing us to merge information from the 2010 *ad hoc* module on intra-household sharing into the data.

Using EUROMOD and EU-SILC, we derive three income measures. The first assumes complete income pooling and equal sharing and corresponds to income measures traditionally used in distributional analyses, as well as for policy-reporting purposes, as explained in the introduction. It is derived by pooling all the income of all household members and then dividing the total household income by the household equivalent size, calculated based on the 'OECD-modified' scale (the scale, developed by the Orgaisation for Economic Co-operation and Development (OECD) assigns a weight of 1 to the first adult, a weight of 0.5 to subsequent adults and a weight of 0.3 to children, defined as individuals aged under 14). Because it assumes that all household income is pooled and shared among all household members, this measure cannot capture any intra-household income inequalities.

The second measure we derive assumes minimal income pooling, in line with the studies based on EUROMOD reviewed above. All adults are assumed to keep all income received in a personal capacity (earnings and individual benefits, including income replacement benefits and other benefits based on an individual's own status) and pay individual taxes, and only incomes received in common (typically means-tested benefits and benefits targeted at children) are split equally between the adult members of the unit receiving those incomes. We use EUROMOD to calculate personal income components not captured individually in EU-SILC, notably parental leave benefits, taxes and social insurance contributions, as well as to assign common benefits (social assistance, housing benefits, family benefits, etc.) to individuals entitled to receive them (i.e. only those household members who are part of the assessment unit for that benefit). We then use a special equivalisation strategy to maintain comparability with the first income measure; for a detailed description of the methodology, see Avram and Popova (2022a). While not necessarily capturing exactly the total income available to spend for each household member, this individualised income measure can be used to examine inequality in economic resources among members of the same household. It also arguably reflects aspects of well-being such as economic independence and autonomy that are not captured by focusing on consumption.

Finally, our third measure combines the two previous approaches. Neither complete nor minimal pooling is a realistic assumption for most households. Previous research has shown that household members do often pool their incomes, especially when relationships are long term and/or there are children (Bonke, 2015; Präg et al., 2019). We use information on the share of personal income kept separate to calculate a measure of individual incomes under partial pooling. We calculate personal income as the sum of all incomes received in a personal capacity, as in the minimal income pooling scenario above. We then split this personal income into a part kept separate and a part shared (equally) with the other household members. We do not have information on the exact share of income that is kept separate (and not pooled) by the respondent. Instead, EU-SILC allows respondents to select one from the following five options: all income, more than half, about half, less than half and none. We translated these answers into the following percentages: 100, 75, 50, 25 and 0. We continue to split all common benefits equally among members of the recipient unit.

Finally, we compute gender income ratios, defined as average female disposable income divided by average male disposable income for working-age individuals (defined as aged 18–64 years), older people (aged 65+ years) and four household types. Figure 5.1 presents these income ratios for Germany, but the same analysis could be performed in any country with valid data on personal income sharing.

Results show that, as expected, gender income ratios are much lower (and hence gender income inequality higher) when we assume minimal pooling (shown as triangles in Figure 5.1). In the case of working-age individuals, the income ratio falls from 93 per cent assuming complete pooling (shown as circles in Figure 5.1) to 56 per cent assuming minimal pooling. The difference reflects women's significantly lower earnings. Similarly, gender differences in pensions are reflected in even lower gender income ratios among older people assuming minimal pooling. Similar results are obtained for one- and two-earner couples, with or without children. The difference between gender income ratios based on complete and minimal pooling is higher for couples with children, especially for one-earner couples.

Assuming partial pooling (squares in Figure 5.1) generates income ratios that are between the other two scenarios but much closer to complete pooling than minimal pooling, suggesting that most respondents declare that they pool most of their personal income. One-earner couples have the lowest income ratios when assuming partial pooling: 81 and 84 per cent, respectively, for those with and without children. Of course, pooled income may not benefit all members of the household equally. Unfortunately, we do not have sufficient information on how income is spent to be able to examine this more closely. Nonetheless, our analysis demonstrates how pooling assumptions affect meas-

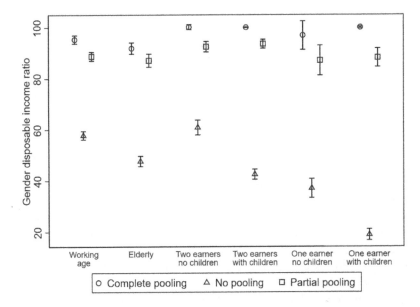

Note: Authors' calculations based on EUROMOD I4.0+ and EU-SILC 2010 *ad hoc* module. The vertical bars show 95 per cent confidence intervals.

Figure 5.1   Gender income ratios in Germany under various pooling assumptions, 2015

ured gender income inequality. It also shows how microsimulation models can be combined with information about income pooling and sharing to generate more accurate measures of individual income.

Conclusions and some suggestions for future research

Treating households as single units does not provide an accurate picture of the economic well-being of women and men and can be particularly misleading when we try to understand the gendered impacts of public policies on individuals and/or their behaviour. In this chapter we have argued that tax/benefit microsimulation models offer a powerful tool for peering inside the 'black box' of the household, by allowing us to construct more accurate measures of individual/personal incomes and by enabling the estimation of gender-specific policy effects.

Further improvement of the measurement of individual incomes requires better data collection, primarily on who receives (and thus may be more likely to control) each income source, on the actual income pooling and sharing practices in a household, and on income sources that cannot be simulated but can be very important for some groups (such as income from capital). Future research could explore how new survey instruments can be embedded in existing studies in order to address these challenges and/or how accurate income information can be added from administrative registers to supplement information collected via surveys.

Whilst gender mainstreaming is now widely endorsed by international organisations such as the EU and the United Nations (United Nations, 2002; EIGE, 2016), in practice a gender dimension is yet to be routinely included in policy evaluation exercises. Scholars could exploit the full potential of tax/benefit microsimulation models to capture the gender impacts of fiscal policies, including their effect on individual disposable incomes and work incentives. In addition to gender, researchers could also explore how tax/benefit microsimulation models can shed light on other dimensions of inequality within the household, such as redistribution across generations, and where necessary incorporate intersectionality (EIGE, 2023).

An accurate understanding of how welfare state policies affect women and men requires the scope of simulations to be enlarged to cover the impact of wealth taxes, indirect taxes and public services. Public services may be especially important to women who in their absence may be faced with restricted labour market choices and/or increased demands on their time. Future scholarship should examine how the provision of public services contributes to or mitigates existing gender economic inequalities.

Finally, a fruitful direction for future research will be to exploit the new microsimulation models for the global south in the study of gender inequality within the household in order to research intra-household management and distribution of resources in a wider range of countries.

Notes

1. Register data refers to data that are collected and maintained by official government agencies or other organisations in order to track various aspects of social life. Register data are typically considered to be more accurate and reliable than

self-reported data in surveys, as they are collected directly from official records rather than relying on individuals to report their own information.

2. An assessment unit is a group of individuals that together are jointly entitled to a cash transfer (benefit unit) or liable for a tax payment (tax unit).

3. Though note that such studies tend to assume complete income sharing in the partnership pre-dissolution.

4. Commitment to Equity (CEQ) – a database of studies of the impact of taxation and social spending on inequality and poverty for low- and middle-income countries developed by the CEQ Institute. See www.commitmentoequity.org.

5. SOUTHMOD – a multi-country tax/benefit microsimulation model for the global south developed by UNU-WIDER, the EUROMOD team at the University of Essex and Southern African Social Policy Research Institute. See www.wider.unu .edu/project/southmod-simulating-tax-and-benefit-policiesdevelopment.

6. LATINMOD – a multi-country tax/benefit microsimulation model for six Latin American countries sponsored by Centro Estratégico Latinoamericano de Geopolítica, Quito, Ecuador, with the collaboration of EUROMOD. See www .celag.org/latinmod-un-simulador-integrado-de-politicas-fiscales-en-america -latina/.

References

Avram, S. and Popova, D. (2022a) 'Do taxes and transfers reduce gender income inequality? Evidence from eight European welfare states'. *Social Science Research* 102: 102644.

Avram, S. and Popova, D. (2022b) 'Intrahousehold income inequality and the gender income gap after union dissolution: A comparative study of European countries'. RC28 Spring Conference 2022, London School of Economics.

Avram, S., Popova, D. and Rastrigina, O. (2016) 'Accounting for gender differences in the distributional effects of tax and benefit policy changes'. Research note 3/2015. Luxembourg: Directorate-General for Employment, Social Affairs and Inclusion, European Commission.

Becker, G.S. (1974) 'A theory of social interactions'. *Journal of Political Economy* 82(6): 1063–1093.

Bennett, F. and Sutherland, H. (2011) 'The importance of independent income: Understanding the role of non-means-tested earnings replacement benefits'. ISER Working Paper No. 2011-09. Colchester: Institute for Social and Economic Research, University of Essex.

Bonke, J. (2015) 'Pooling of income and sharing of consumption within households'. *Review of Economics of the Household* 13(1): 73–93.

Bourguignon, F. and Sparado, A. (2006) 'Microsimulation as a tool for evaluating redistribution policies'. *Journal of Economic Inequality* 4(1): 77–106.

Brewer, M. and Nandi, A. (2014) 'Partnership dissolution: How does it affect income, employment and well-being?' ISER Working Paper No. 2014-30. Colchester: Institute for Social and Economic Research, University of Essex.

Brewer, M., Etheridge, B. and O'Dea, C. (2017) 'Why are households that report the lowest incomes so well-off?' *The Economic Journal* 127(605): 24–49.

Cantillon, S. (2013) 'Measuring differences in living standards within households'. *Journal of Marriage and Family* 75(3): 598–610.

Davies, H. and Joshi, H. (2009) 'Sex, sharing and the distribution of income'. *Journal of Social Policy* 23(3): 301–340.

De Agostini, P., Capéau, B., Decoster, A., Figari, F., Kneeshaw, J., Leventi, C., Manios, K., Paulus, A., Sutherland, H. and Vanheukelom, T. (2017) 'EUROMOD extension to indirect taxation: Final report'. EUROMOD Technical Note No. EMTN/3.0. Colchester: Institute for Social and Economic Research, University of Essex.

Dema-Moreno, S. and Díaz-Martínez, C. (2010) 'Gender inequalities and the role of money in Spanish dual-income couples'. *European Societies* 12(1): 65–84.

Doorley, K. and Keane, C. (2020) 'Tax-benefit systems and the gender gap in income'. IZA Discussion Papers, No. 13786. Bonn: Institute of Labor Economics.

Doorley, K., O'Donoghue, C. and Sologon, D. (2021) 'The gender gap in income and the COVID-19 pandemic'. IZA Discussion Paper No. 14360. Bonn: IZA Institute of Labor Economics.

EIGE (European Institute for Gender Equality). (2016). *Gender Impact Assessment: Gender Mainstreaming Toolkit*. Vilnius: European Institute for Gender Equality.

EIGE (2023). *Evidence to action: gender equality and gender mainstreaming in the COVID-19 recovery*. Vilnius, European Institute for Gender Equality. https:// eige .europa.eu/ publications-resources/publications/evidence-action-gender-equality-and -gender-mainstreaming-covid-19-recovery?language_content_entity=en (accessed 3 July 2023)

Figari, F. and Paulus, A. (2015) 'The distributional effects of taxes and transfers under alternative income concepts: The importance of three "I"s'. *Public Finance Review* 43(3): 347–372.

Figari, F., Immervoll, H., Levy, H. and Sutherland, H. (2011) 'Inequalities within couples: Market income and the role of taxes and benefits in Europe'. *Eastern Economic Journal* 37(3): 344–366.

Figari, F., Paulus, A. and Sutherland, H. (2015) 'Microsimulation and policy analysis'. In A.B. Atkinson and F. Bourguignon (eds), *Handbook of Income Distribution*. Amsterdam: Elsevier: 2141–2221.

Fritzell, J. (1999) 'Incorporating gender inequality into income distribution research'. *International Journal of Social Welfare* 8(1): 56–66.

Fuenmayor, A., Granell, R. and Savall Morera, T. (2020) 'Tax-benefit systems and gender gap: An across-Europe study'. *Hacienda Pública Española/Review of Public Economics* 235(4): 87–118.

Guio, A.-C. and Van den Bosch, K. (2020) 'Deprivation of women and men living in a couple: Sharing or unequal division?' *Review of Income and Wealth* 66(4): 958–984.

Himmelweit, S., Santos, C., Sevilla, A. and Sofer, C. (2013) 'Sharing of resources within the family and the economics of household decision making'. *Journal of Marriage and Family* 75(3): 625–639.

Hufkens, T., Figari, F., Vandelannoote, D. and Verbist, G. (2020) 'Investing in subsidized childcare to reduce poverty'. *Journal of European Social Policy* 30(3): 306–319.

Jenkins, S.P. (1991) 'Poverty measurement and the within-household distribution: Agenda for action'. *Journal of Social Policy* 20(4): 457–483.

Kuypers, S., Figari, F. and Verbist, G. (2019) 'Redistribution in a joint income–wealth perspective: A cross-country comparison'. *Socio-Economic Review* 19(3): 929–952.

Meulders, D. and O'Dorchai, S.P. (2010) 'Revisiting poverty measures towards individualisation'. DULBEA Working Papers 10-03. Brussells: Universite Libre de Bruxelles.

Meyer, B.D. and Sullivan, J.X. (2003) 'Measuring the well-being of the poor using income and consumption'. *Journal of Human Resources* 38(4): 1180–1220.

Pahl, J. (1983) 'The allocation of money and the structuring of inequality within marriage'. *The Sociological Review* 31(2): 237–262.

Pahl, J. (2005) 'Individualisation of couple finances: Who pays for the children?' *Social Policy and Society* 4(4): 381–391.

Ponthieux, S. (2013) 'Income pooling and equal sharing within the household: What can we learn from the 2010 EU-SILC module?' Eurostat Methodologies and Working Papers. Luxembourg: Publications Office of the European Union.

Ponthieux, S. (2017) 'Intra-household pooling and sharing of resources: A tentative "modified" equivalised income'. In A.B. Atkinson, A.-C. Guio and E. Marlier (eds), *Monitoring Social Inclusion in Europe*. Luxembourg: Eurostat: 175–189.

Ponthieux, S. and Meurs, D. (2015) 'Gender inequality'. In A.B. Atkinson and F. Bourguignon (eds), *Handbook of Income Distribution*. Amsterdam: Elsevier: 981–1146.

Popova, D. and Navicke, J. (2019) 'The probability of poverty for mothers after childbirth and divorce in Europe: The role of social stratification and tax-benefit policies'. *Social Science Research* 78: 57–70.

Präg, P., Begall, K. and Treas, J. (2019) 'Understanding the marriage–cohabitation gap in income pooling: Evidence from 29 European countries'. *SocArXiv*, https://doi.org/10.31235/osf.io/rqzj3.

Sutherland, H. (1997) 'Women, men and the redistribution of income'. *Fiscal Studies* 18(1): 1–22.

Sutherland, H. (2018) 'Quality assessment of microsimulation models: The case of EUROMOD'. *International Journal of Microsimulation* 11(1): 198–223.

Sutherland, H. and Figari, F. (2013) 'EUROMOD: The European Union tax-benefit microsimulation model'. *International Journal of Microsimulation* 6(1): 4–26.

United Nations. (2002). *Gender Mainstreaming: An Overview*. New York: United Nations.

Vogler, C. and Pahl, J. (1994) 'Money, power and inequality within marriage'. *The Sociological Review* 42(2): 263–288.

PART II

Recent research into resources within the household: New directions taken

6. Many mouths under one roof: Multigenerational families in Europe sharing resources within households

Tania Burchardt and Eleni Karagiannaki

Introduction

The assumption that family and household are the same is oversimplistic, in at least two respects: firstly, because many families extend beyond the household, encompassing a 'kin' network of interdependence (Singh, this volume); and, secondly, because many households contain a single person or couple and any dependent child/ren but also additional members. This chapter concerns the second of these features of 'the household'.[1] In the European context, these 'additional' people are most commonly adult children who have not yet left the parental home (or who left and returned), or the parent(s) of a householder, and these households can be termed multigenerational. But in other contexts coresidence with other relatives is also common, for example in South Africa and Lesotho (Moore and Hlabana, this volume). Decades of research have established that resources are not always shared to the equal benefit of all members of a household (see Bennett, 2013, for a review). But less is known about resource sharing within multigenerational households – the focus of this chapter.

The way in which sharing resources within a household can produce variable poverty risks for its members is captured by our conceptual framework. First, there are inputs to the household's resources. Some are individual – crucially, earnings and pensions; some are for a family unit – such as most social assistance benefits and some taxes/tax credits; and some are household level – such as many housing assets and housing-related benefits.

Next, there is the household. An example is a household composed of three 'family' units: (1) a pensioner couple, who are the parents of (2) a middle-aged daughter, who is a lone parent with two sons, one a teenager and the other

97

(3) a 25 year old, working but still living at home. Everyone in the household stands to benefit from the economies of scale of living together. For example, only one rent must be paid, which is considerably less than the total rent for three separate households. And there may also be further sharing of incomes and/or expenditures, benefitting those with fewer resources of their own. The financial arrangements, degree of control over different resources and the process of negotiating decisions within the household, sometimes called money management and control, are important in determining who benefits from coresidence. But here we concentrate on the outcome – the living standard of different household members – rather than the process. So we examine the associations between three factors: inputs (what, who and how much); household composition; and the living standard arising from different patterns of resource sharing.

The living standard is not directly observable. Although overall inequalities in living standards are of interest, outcomes at the bottom of the distribution are a particularly pressing public policy concern. The focus here is on material deprivation (lacking goods and services widely considered necessary for a decent living standard) and risks of poverty (resources lower than a specified threshold, such as 60 per cent of median population income).

These inputs, sharing and outcomes all exist within a wider context, including the housing and labour markets, tax and benefit systems, availability of care services (for children and older or disabled people) and social norms (for example, about gender roles, independence and marriage and filial duties). Young adults' decisions about whether to continue residing with their parent(s), or to return after being away – and parents' decisions about this – may be influenced by all of these (see Iacovou, 2010; Lewis and West, 2016), and by the relationship itself. Similarly, older people's decisions about whether to remain living independently or to coreside with their son/daughter are shaped by a range of considerations (Burgess and Muir, 2020).

The wider context also influences how resources are shared once the household is formed. As research on couples has found (Cantillon et al., 2016), who brings money into the household influences who controls it. In a multigenerational household, we must think about sharing not only within a couple but also across family units. Financial benefits of coresidence can flow up or down the generations (or both).

In research on poverty, the conventional assumption is that the total income of all household members is shared to the equal benefit of all. This is reflected in the use of 'equivalised' household income as the standard metric. One corollary is that all members of a given household are attributed the same poverty status. However, we know that (male) earners may in practice not fully share their earnings with (female) non-earning partners (Pahl, 1989; Cantillon, 2013); and that, in low-income families, parents may sacrifice their own standard of living to protect their children from hardship (Middleton et al., 1997; Main and Bradshaw, 2016). So in reality there can be variations in experienced poverty, or achieved living standards, within a household.

Avram and Popova (this volume) explore the implications of relaxing the 'equal sharing' assumption, with a focus on gender equality, in different countries. This chapter explores how different assumptions about sharing within multigenerational households affect poverty estimates for children, working-age adults and pensioners. The next section reviews the state of knowledge. The chapter then homes in on European countries to describe how the risk of poverty and deprivation as conventionally calculated differs between multigenerational households and others, drawing on original analysis of the European Union Statistics on Income and Living Conditions (EU-SILC). The next section explores the implications for poverty estimates of varying the standard 'equal sharing' assumptions for different types of multigenerational households. The final section summarises key findings and identifies important avenues for future research.

Sharing of resources in multigenerational households

Multigenerational living is, or has been, the norm in some lower- and middle-income countries but is coming under increasing pressure from population ageing, rural–urban migration and changing expectations of younger generations (see, e.g., Samanta et al., 2015, on India and Zeng and Xie, 2014, on China). The social expectation that families will look after older kin is in some cases reinforced by legal requirements and/or fiscal incentives (e.g. Czech Republic, France, Singapore), or partially offset by arrangements to encourage older people's independent living (e.g. Japan) (ILC Global Alliance, 2012), with resulting differences in levels and types of multigenerational living. The social security system and women's participation in the formal labour market are also important (Albuquerque, 2011, on Portugal).

Interest in multigenerational households in high-income countries was rekindled by many young people being prevented from leaving home through unemployment and high housing costs following the 2008 financial crisis, and others being encouraged to return (e.g. Whelan, 2016, on Australia), including some who already had children, leading to an increase in grandparent–parent–grandchild households. Pilkauskas et al. (2020) reported that in 2018 one in 10 children in the United States lived with parents and grandparents.

Higher rates of multigenerational living among migrants and some ethnic minorities is common, including in Germany (Flake, 2012) and Australia (Easthope et al., 2017); the experiences of Indian migrants in Australia in multigenerational households are explored by Singh (this volume). Cultural norms and preferences play a part, but so too do higher risks of poverty, with coresidence often a means to lower and shared costs.

A few studies have investigated this sharing in multigenerational households. When older people's incomes are a higher proportion of total income in multigenerational households, spending on foods that older people value has been found to be higher in Japan (Hayashi, 1995), and older people's poverty to be lower in Greece (Gosling and Karagiannaki, 2004) – although Easthope et al.'s (2015) interviewees (in Australian cities) make clear that feelings of control matter, not just financial flows. Amorim (2019) finds higher expenditure on children's education and other activities, and lower expenditure on child care, in multigenerational households including grandchildren compared to families with only one adult generation, controlling for other household characteristics. She concludes that these living arrangements are 'an adaptive strategy' for low-income and single parents; but her findings also suggest significant pooling of time and material resources within these households, to children's benefit. Verbist et al.'s analysis (2020) for European countries is similar, showing that countries with relatively well-developed pensions and less generous child benefits tend to have more multigenerational households including grandparents and grandchildren, suggesting a potential flow of resources from older to younger generations. However, Iacovou and Davia (2019) find that older coresident offspring, particularly in low-income households, may also be contributing to the household's finances, demonstrating that the net flow of resources is not always from older to younger.

The extent to which coresidence benefits children, young adults or older people within the household, even considering just material benefits such as protection from poverty or deprivation, is an open question that can only be resolved empirically. It is to this question we now turn, with reference to Europe in particular.

Composition and resources of households

In this and the following section we draw on analysis of EU-SILC data for around 30 European countries. EU-SILC is an annual collection of micro-data, comprising household survey data and, for some countries, register data. It covers many topics, including household composition, sources and levels of income and living standards. We use 2014 data because that survey incorporated an ad hoc module to obtain more information about adults' and children's material deprivation. The definitions used are shown in Box 6.1.

Box 6.1   Definitions of key terms

adult deprivation   adults who lack and cannot afford at least two out of seven items: replace worn-out with (some) new clothes; have two pairs of properly fitting shoes; get together with friends/family for drink/meal at least monthly; regularly participate in leisure activities; spend a small amount each week on oneself; have internet connection for personal use at home; and have regular use of public transport.

child deprivation   children in a household that lack and cannot afford at least three of 11 child items: some new (not second-hand) clothes; two pairs of properly fitting (including one pair of all-weather) shoes; fruits and vegetables once a day; one meal with meat, chicken or fish (or vegetarian equivalent) per day; books at home suitable for their age; outdoor leisure equipment; indoor games; regular leisure activity; celebrations on special occasions; invite friends round to play; and go on holiday away from home for at least one week per year.

dependent child   how 'dependence' is constituted varies across countries and within countries across systems (e.g. education, taxes and benefits, marriage law), but we apply a common definition across all countries in our child deprivation analysis: any child aged 19 years or under, or aged 20–25 and in full-time education, and living with a parent. For analyses of adult deprivation, a slightly more restrictive definition of a dependent child is applied: any unmarried person under age 18 unless s/he reports employment/self-employment income.

family unit   an adult, plus his/her partner (if any) and any dependent child(ren). A 'family unit' can be a single individual.

household   people living in the same private dwelling and sharing some expenditures (e.g. jointly responsible for, or contributing to, rent or heating costs). This definition is specified by EU-SILC and is commonly applied in household surveys, with minor variations.

household deprivation   individuals living in a household that lacks and cannot afford at least three out of nine items: pay the rent, mortgage or utility bills; keep the home adequately warm; face unexpected expenses; eat meat or proteins regularly; go on holiday; have a television; have a washing machine; have a car; and have a telephone.

income   unless otherwise specified, income is equivalised disposable household income, i.e. all sources of income minus direct taxes and social insurance contributions, adjusted for differences in household size and composition by the Modified OECD Equivalence scale. This scale, used by Eurostat, gives the first adult in the household a weight of 1.0, each second adult or child aged 14+ 0.5 and each child aged 0–13 0.3 (see ONS, 2015).

multifamily household   a household consisting of more than one family unit.

multigenerational household   a multifamily household in which at least two adults are related as parent and child. The most common examples here are parents (with or without dependent children) living with young adult offspring; and elderly parents living with their son/daughter (plus any partner and any dependent children).

parents, siblings and grandparents   'parents' include step-parents and parents' partners. 'Siblings' include coresident step-/half-siblings. Grandparents are also inclusively defined.

poverty   having an income lower than a threshold measured as 60 per cent of the median equivalised disposable household income in the country.

Over one third of adults in our sample lived in multigenerational households, ranging from one in six in Sweden to nearly four in six in Serbia. Just over one in 10 children did so, varying from 0.25 in 10 in Germany to four in 10 in Serbia. In general, Eastern European and Baltic countries have high, Southern European countries medium, Western European countries low and Nordic countries very low levels.

Children in one-parent families are much more likely to live in multigenerational households than their two-parent family counterparts. However, the proportion of children in one-parent families varies widely, from 6 per cent in Greece to 22 per cent in the United Kingdom (UK) and 24 per cent in Latvia.

Nearly twice as many children live with their parents and grandparents as with parents and older (adult) siblings; only a very small proportion live with both. Differences across countries in children's rates of multigenerational living are driven much more by differences in coresidence with grandparents than in coresidence with older siblings.

For each family type, individuals in one-family households have on average much higher incomes than those in multigenerational households (Box 6.1 gives the definitions of income, household-, adult- and child-level deprivation we use).[2] The less well off are much more likely to coreside than the better off. For example, couples with children living by themselves have an average income 44 per cent higher than couples with children living with others, even taking account of differences in household size. Higher incomes are in turn associated with lower risks of material deprivation; those living in one-family households are therefore generally at much lower risk than those in multigenerational households.

These results do not imply that coresidence has a deleterious effect on children's, or adults', living standards – in fact, it is often the reverse. Rather, they strongly suggest that worse-off families select into multigenerational living to benefit from economies of scale in living costs – and, perhaps, the sharing of incomes or expenditures with members of the wider household. Other motivations are also likely to play a part, including cultural norms, shared care and both parties' preferences. But in general, individuals and families who can afford to, tend to live in independent households.

Implications for poverty and deprivation

In contrast to conventional household-level approaches, using deprivation measures that can vary between individuals within a household (such as whether they have a small amount of money each week to spend on themselves) facilitates an investigation of whether full sharing of resources takes place in multigenerational households – at least those towards the bottom of the income distribution.

Comparing adults living in households with otherwise similar characteristics, including the same income level, the risk of being individually deprived is generally higher for women than men; this rises with age to about 60 and then falls slightly, and is higher for tenants and non-householders than owner-occupiers.[3] Controlling for all these characteristics, plus family type, having an individual income constituting a lower percentage of total household income puts that person at greater risk of individual deprivation.[4] Having no individual income increases the risk of individual deprivation by five percentage points, other things being equal, compared to being the sole contributor to household income. Given the rate of individual deprivation of 19 per cent for this sample, five percentage points is a substantial shift. The implication is that having one's own income gives greater control over resource allocation within the household and that this is protective.

However, the relationship between individual income share and the likelihood of individual deprivation, controlling for household income, varies across family and household type. There is no significant association between elderly singles' or couples' income shares and their risk of individual deprivation in multifamily (including multigenerational) households – a result consistent with the sharing of resources between elderly family units and the rest of the household, at least in lower-income households.[5] When an elderly person's income is low, sharing is therefore highly protective against deprivation. On the other hand, financial support may flow in the opposite direction, down the generations, especially in those countries where pensions are more generous than unemployment and/or family benefits (Moore and Hlabana, this volume).

However, for lone parents and single adults in multifamily (including multigenerational) households, and for couples in multifamily households, the association between individual income and individual deprivation risk, at a given level of household income (controlling for other characteristics), is strong. For example, a lone parent in a multifamily household with no individual income has an individual deprivation risk 15.5 percentage points higher than a similar lone parent who is the sole contributor to household income. This is very large, suggesting a far from complete sharing of resources within these types of multifamily households.

Children typically do not have income in their own right. But we can estimate the extent to which they may be protected through multigenerational living arrangements by comparing their deprivation risk predicted on the basis of, first, the whole household income and, second, their own family unit's income – in both cases taking account of the number of people for whom the income must provide.[6] We distinguish between children in households including adult siblings and those including grandparents.

In every case, a higher deprivation risk is predicted if the children were to have to rely on their own family unit's income alone. The difference for children in one-parent families living with grandparents is particularly large; so coresidence with grandparents is potentially a significant protective factor for them.

This protective effect is apparent across Southern and Eastern European countries and the Baltic states, with some variations (see Karagiannaki and Burchardt, 2022, Table 7). The potential impact for children of living with adult siblings is more mixed across countries. In Denmark, Germany and Greece, for example, such children in two-parent families have higher predicted probabilities of deprivation based on their household income than if they relied on their parents' income alone. That is, the 'extra mouth to feed' costs more than the average additional income these adult siblings are bringing in – and food is not the only additional cost.

Assumptions about sharing have profound implications for poverty estimates for people in multigenerational households. Figure 6.1 offers the results of a series of simulations of different sharing assumptions for poverty estimates for Europe as a whole and for different subgroups. The scenarios are: (A) no sharing (implausible, but useful as a baseline); (B) economies of scale only (i.e. all benefit from lower costs, but no sharing beyond that); (C) partial sharing across families (likely to be the most realistic); and (D) full sharing (the default in conventional poverty analysis). Specifically under (C), we model complete sharing within a family unit, but sharing between family units limited to the economies of scale enjoyed by the household, divided proportionately to the number of people in each family unit.

Looking first at the whole population, if there were no economies of scale from shared living arrangements and no sharing of resources within households (A), the poverty rate would be 47 per cent, compared to the conventional estimate assuming full sharing (D) of 17 per cent. Almost half the difference between these two extremes is due to the effect of economies of scale, as allowing for these – but still assuming no sharing of resources beyond reduced costs for the household (B) – produces a poverty estimate of 33 per cent. If we go one step further and allow for sharing within each family unit in the household, but not between family units (C), the estimated poverty rate falls to 21 per cent. The difference between (C) and (D) can be understood as the potential that multigenerational households (and other multifamily households) have to reduce poverty among their members through fully sharing resources; as noted above, however, in practice that is unlikely.

Women face slightly higher poverty rates than men even under the assumption of full sharing, because women living alone (especially lone parents) are more likely to be poor than men living alone. However, these gender differences in

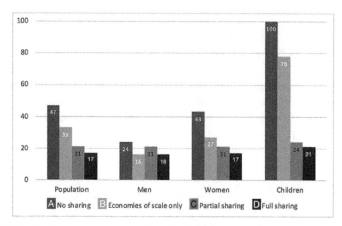

Note: Estimates based on a poverty threshold fixed across all simulations at 60 per cent of median equivalised disposable household income.
Source: Authors' calculations using EU-SILC 2014 cross-sectional data UDB ver. 2014-2 1-8-16.

Figure 6.1   Simulated poverty rates in Europe, by population subgroup and sharing assumptions, 2014

poverty estimates become much wider when we remove the assumption of resource sharing within family units (simulations (B) and (A)). If household members retain their own incomes, and benefit from shared living arrangements only insofar as these reduce everyone's costs (B), the estimated poverty rate for women is 11 percentage points higher than for men.

Children have (typically) no individual income so, in the absence of any sharing, all children would live in poverty (A). Assuming full sharing, conventional estimates (D) put child poverty in Europe at about 21 per cent. However, that calculation assumes full sharing *across* family units within households; if that did not occur (C), child poverty rates would be three percentage points higher. This difference – equivalent to a 14 per cent increase in child poverty – can be seen as the potential contribution multigenerational households can make to reducing child poverty, over and above the benefits of reduced costs.

Overall, these simulations suggest that economies of scale from shared living arrangements make a larger contribution to poverty reduction than the potential contribution from the sharing of resources across families within households.

Discussion and directions for future research

To understand the exposure of children and adults to poverty and deprivation, we need to understand the resources available to them in practice. To that end, this chapter has examined the difference between the resources of the household as a whole and of each family unit within it. This difference is important for at least three reasons: firstly, because households containing more than one family unit, in particular multigenerational households, are more common than often supposed; secondly, because the formation of multigenerational households is systematically related to one or more parties having limited resources; and thirdly, because complete sharing of resources within these households cannot be presumed. Although the empirical data above relate to European countries, the principle of paying attention to the potential role of the need to share resources in shaping household composition, and the importance of tracing – where possible – flows of resources between narrowly defined family units and the wider household they live in, are relevant to many other geographical contexts.

We have noted the prevalence of multigenerational households in European countries, especially but not exclusively in Eastern Europe, the Baltic states and Southern Europe. Coresidence of children with parents and grandparents is common, as is coresidence with grown-up siblings who have returned to, or never left, the parental home. We have also shown that multigenerational households in Europe are disproportionately found among those with lower equivalised disposable household incomes and higher risks of deprivation. Although multiple factors may contribute to a decision to coreside, those who can afford to live independently generally do so, whether they are elderly, young adults or families with dependent children.

We do not observe directly how resources are shared within households. However, using individual- and child-level rather than exclusively household-level deprivation indicators suggests that the person (or family) bringing income into a multigenerational household generally retains some advantage in spending allocations, but that dependent children are prioritised by everyone, including grandparents.

These findings indicate how much more could be investigated about resource sharing in multigenerational households, and the consequences for different people's living standards. One important avenue for further research is qualitative: exploring in depth how decisions about coresidence between generations (or independent living) were made and, once coresidence is established, how money is considered, controlled and managed within the household. Given the differences reported here between multigenerational arrangements with grandparents versus those with adult siblings, such research might be most fruitful if focused on particular type(s) of multigenerational household. In addition, given the significant influence of the institutional context – including housing and labour markets and the tax/benefit system – on household formation and resource sharing, comparing the accounts of families in different countries about their decision-making could be valuable. Ghodsee and Bernadi (2012) for Bulgaria, and Easthope et al. (2015) for Australia, as well as chapters in this volume, provide interesting insights along these lines to build on.

Another avenue for further research is the development of family-based equivalence scales taking into account the wider household context. The UK's Social Metrics Commission (2018) proposed the replacement of household-based poverty measures with measures based on the incomes of all family-related people in a household. But in our opinion this does not adequately distinguish between economies of scale in the costs of living from which everyone in a household is likely to benefit, even if each family unit retains complete control over its own income, and spending on behalf of others, which we argue is discretionary and variable. Instead, we suggest that it would be worthwhile to work on an equivalence scale that differentiates between one-family and multifamily households, and that reflects empirically informed assumptions about partial sharing at both household and family levels. This would facilitate assessments of poverty risk reflecting the experiences of families in different types of household more closely.

Finally, this chapter has focused mainly on the bottom of the distribution, where multigenerational households are concentrated, and on income poverty and material deprivation as outcomes. But there are multigenerational households throughout the distribution. It would be interesting to explore the consequences of applying partial or minimal sharing rules to the incomes of multigenerational households for estimates of population income inequality as a whole. Particularly in countries with a large share of multigenerational households, such as Eastern and Southern European and Baltic countries, current estimates of population income inequality based on an assumption of full sharing may underestimate inequality in the resources from which people actually benefit.

Families and households are invariably more heterogeneous and complex than models allow. But moving beyond simply counting the mouths under one roof to recognising at least some ways in which the financial arrangements people make within a household tend to be structured should help us to approach a better approximation of the real world.

Notes

1. Some of the research underlying this chapter was funded by the Economic and Social Research Council (ESRC) (grant number ES/P000525/1). It uses data from Eurostat, EU-SILC 2014. The responsibility for conclusions lies entirely with the authors, not Eurostat, the European Commission or any national statistical authorities. We are grateful to ESRC, Eurostat and our project Advisory and User Group Carlotta Balestra, Fran Bennett, Hans Dubois, Maria Iacovou, Peter Matejic and Holly Sutherland. We also benefitted from discussion at the 'Money within the Household' international workshop at the University of Oxford in 2019.
2. For research on EU-SILC material deprivation measures see e.g. Guio, 2009; Deutsch et al., 2015; Guio and Marlier, 2017.
3. Probit regression on the likelihood of having enforced lack of two or more of the individual adult deprivation items, controlling for log of equivalised household income, country, age, age squared, sex, family and household type, housing tenure, householder status, individual's income as percentage of total household income and whether the interview was provided by a proxy respondent. For details see Karagiannaki and Burchardt, 2020, Table 4.
4. Individual income is construed as earnings, pensions and any benefits paid to an individual, net of taxes; if taxes are recorded at household level, we allocate these in proportion to each individual's share of total taxable income.
5. Sharing behaviour may differ at different points in the income distribution; see Ponthieux, 2013.
6. Predicted deprivation probabilities based on *household* income are calculated using regression coefficients from pooled probit models predicting these for children in different family types as a function of the number of children of different ages in the household, total equivalised disposable household income, family type and country dummies. Standard errors are clustered at household level to account for multiple children per household. Predicted deprivation probabilities based on *family* income are calculated using the *same* regression coefficients but inputting the values for total equivalised family income rather than household income.

References

Albuquerque, P. (2011) 'Grandparents in multigenerational households: The case of Portugal', *European Journal of Ageing*, 8(3): 189–198.

Amorim, M. (2019) 'Are grandparents a blessing or a burden? Multigenerational coresidence and child-related spending', *Social Science Research*, 80: 132–144.

Bennett, F. (2013) 'Researching within-household distribution: Overview, developments, debates, and methodological challenges', *Journal of Marriage and Family*, 75: 582–597.

Burgess, G. and Muir, K. (2020) 'The increase in multigenerational households in the UK: The motivations for and experiences of multigenerational living', *Housing, Theory and Society*, 37(3): 322–338.

Cantillon, S. (2013) 'Measuring differences in living standards within households', *Journal of Marriage and Family*, 75: 598–610.

Cantillon, S., Maître, B. and Watson, D. (2016) 'Family financial management and individual deprivation', *Journal of Family and Economic Issues*, 37: 461–473.

Deutsch, J., Guio, A.-C., Pomati, M. and Silber, J. (2015) 'Material deprivation in Europe: Which expenditures are curtailed first?', *Social Indicators Research*, 120(3): 723–740.

Easthope, H., Liu, E., Burnley. I. and Judd, B. (2017) 'Changing perceptions of family: A study of multigenerational households in Australia', *Journal of Sociology*, 53(1): 182–200.

Easthope, H., Liu, E., Judd, B. and Burnley, I. (2015) 'Feeling at home in a multigenerational household: The importance of control', *Housing, Theory and Society*, 32(2): 151–170.

Flake, R. (2012) *Multigenerational Living Arrangements among Migrants*, Ruhr Economic Paper no. 366. https:// papers .ssrn .com/ sol3/ papers .cfm ?abstract_id = 2159706 (accessed 22 July 2022).

Ghodsee, K. and Bernardi, L. (2012) 'Starting a family at your parents' house: Multigenerational households and below replacement fertility in urban Bulgaria', *Journal of Comparative Family Studies,* 43(3): 439–459.

Gosling, A. and Karagiannaki, E. (2004) *Intra-Household Allocation and the Living Standards of the Elderly in Greece*, CEPR Discussion Paper No. 4776, London: Centre for Economic Policy Research.

Guio, A.-C. (2009) *What Can Be Learned from Deprivation Indicators in Europe?*, Eurostat Methodologies and Working Papers, Luxembourg: Publications Office of the European Union, https:// ec .europa .eu/ eurostat/ web/ products -statistical -working-papers/-/ks-ra-09-007 (accessed 22 July 2022).

Guio A.-C. and Marlier, E. (2017) 'Amending the EU material deprivation indicator: Impact on size and composition of deprived population', in A.B. Atkinson, A.-C. Guio and E. Marlier (eds), *Monitoring Inclusion in Europe*, Luxembourg: Eurostat: 193–208.

Hayashi, F. (1995) '*Is the Japanese Extended Family Altruistically Linked? A Test Based on Engel Curves*', Journal of Political Economy, 103(3): 661–674.

Iacovou, M. (2010) 'Leaving home: Independence, togetherness and income', *Advances in Life Course Research*, 15(4): 147–160.

Iacovou, M. and Davia, M.A. (2019) 'Who supports whom? Do adult children living at home share their incomes with their parents?', *Advances in Life Course Research*, 40: 14–29.

ILC Global Alliance (International Longevity Centre Global Alliance) (2012) *Global Perspectives on Multigenerational Households and Intergenerational Relations*, ILC Global Alliance Report. www.academia.edu/ download/ 32872049/ Global_Alliance _Intergenerational_Relations_March_2012.pdf (accessed 22 July 2022).

Karagiannaki, E. and Burchardt, T. (2020) *Intra-household Inequality and Adult Material Deprivation in Europe*. CASEpaper 218. London: London School of Economics.

Karagiannaki, E. and Burchardt, T. (2022) *Living Arrangements, Intra-household Inequality and Children's Deprivation: Evidence from EU-SILC*. CASEpaper 227. London: London School of Economics.

Lewis, J. and West, A. (2016) 'Intergenerational relations between English students, graduates living at home, and their parents', *Social Policy and Administration*, 51(7): 1248–1266.

Main, G. and Bradshaw, J. (2016) 'Child poverty in the UK: Measures, prevalence and intra-household sharing', *Critical Social Policy*, 36(1): 1–24.

Middleton, S., Ashworth, K. and Braithwaite, I. (1997) *Small Fortunes: Spending on Children, Childhood Poverty and Parental Sacrifice*, York: Joseph Rowntree Foundation.

ONS (Office for National Statistics) (2015) 'Equivalised income', in *Family Spending in the UK*. www .ons .gov .uk/ peoplepop ulationand community/ personalandhou seholdfinances/ incomeandwealth/ compendium/ familyspending/ 2015 (accessed 25 November 2022).

Pahl, J. (1989) *Money and Marriage*. Basingstoke UK: Macmillan Education.

Pilkauskas, N.V., Amorim, M. and Dunifon, R.E. (2020) 'Historical trends in children living in multigenerational households in the United States: 1870–2018', *Demography*, 57(6): 2269–2296.

Ponthieux, S. (2013) *Income Pooling and Equal Sharing within the Household: What Can We Learn from the 2010 EU-SILC Module?* Eurostat Methodologies and Working Papers Eurostat Publications Office. https://data.europa.eu/doi/10.2785/21993 (accessed 12 January 2023).

Samanta, T., Chen, F. and Vanneman, R. (2015) 'Living arrangements and health of older adults in India', *Journals of Gerontology: Series B*, 70(6): 937–947.

Social Metrics Commission (2018) *A New Measure of Poverty for the UK: Final Report of the Social Metrics Commission*. https:// soc ialmetrics commission .org .uk/ social -metrics-commission-2018-report/ (accessed 22 July 2022).

Verbist, G., Diris, R. and Vandenbroucke, F. (2020) 'Solidarity between generations in extended families: Old-age income as a way out of child poverty?', *European Sociological Review*, 36(2): 317–332.

Whelan, S. (2016) 'Multigenerational households: Economic considerations', in H. Easthope and E. Liu (eds), *Multigenerational Family Living: Evidence and Policy Implications from Australia*, Abingdon: Routledge.

Zeng, Z. and Xie, Y. (2014) 'The effects of grandparents on children's schooling: Evidence from rural China', *Demography*, 51(2): 599–617.

7. Individualising wealth and asset measures in the Global South: Challenges and new directions for research

Abena D. Oduro and Hema Swaminathan

Introduction

The investigation of gaps between men and women in wages, earnings and income has dominated research on gendered economic inequality (Ponthieux and Meurs, 2015). Literature on gender gaps in assets and wealth is of relatively recent origin (Deere and Doss, 2006). Individuals' asset portfolios define their opportunities and reflect structural inequalities and discrimination that they may have encountered. Thus, unlike a snapshot of income, data on assets provide information about an individual's long-run standard of living. Assets are significant in other ways, too. Assets such as land confer social status and recognition. They can be used as collateral to access credit and drawn upon to maintain consumption if the individual suffers an economic shock. Assets, or the lack thereof, are critical for determining whether a household or individual is chronically poor or can transition out of – or into – poverty (Carter and Barrett, 2006).

This chapter aims to discuss the individualisation of asset and wealth measures and reviews the latest developments in collecting such data from household surveys. We touch briefly on how this can extend understanding of gender inequality and intra-household resource allocation and reflect on potential ways to extend this critical body of research. The standard definition of assets (physical and financial) is based on the 2008 System of National Accounts.[1] An asset is a physical or financial item, such as a house, livestock or money in a financial account, that generates benefits such as income for its owner(s). Wealth typically refers to the value of such assets net of debt and liabilities. Gross wealth includes only the value of assets without taking account of such deductions.

The issues involved in individualising measures of assets and wealth to estimate gender gaps are relevant globally (Deere and Doss, 2006; Lersch et al., 2022), but here we focus on the global south, for several reasons. In the global north, with greater economic development and urbanisation, the asset portfolio of households tends to differ, comprising largely private pension or retirement funds and property (Hays and Sullivan, 2022; Office for National Statistics, 2022), and ownership and the associated security of tenure and rights over assets are more likely to be well defined. Finally, we emphasise the relevance of household surveys in obtaining data on assets and wealth in countries where administrative data may not be easily accessible or maintained over time.

Evidence on intra-household asset and wealth distribution

There is greater inequality in the distribution of wealth compared to consumption expenditure or income (Atta-Ankomah et al., 2020; Kenya National Bureau of Statistics, 2020; Chancel et al., 2021). In addition, there is mounting empirical evidence of a gender gap in asset ownership and wealth biased against women (e.g. Doss et al., 2011, for Ecuador, Ghana and Karnataka (India); Deere et al., 2012, for Latin America; Joshi et al., 2022, for Asia; and Schneebaum et al., 2018 and Lersch et al., 2022, for Europe). Assets may be purchased, inherited, received as gifts, acquired by being married to an asset owner or acquired through state allocation and titling programmes (formalising previously informal property rights). Gender gaps in asset ownership and wealth are more likely when inheritance laws or social norms do not treat daughters and sons equally and/or when spouses have no provision for inheritance. Marital regimes determine spouses' ownership of assets during the marriage, when it is dissolved and on a spouse's death. Full and partial community property confers joint ownership of assets acquired during the marriage; full community property includes inherited assets and assets acquired prior to the union, whilst partial community property does not. Conversely, the separation of property regime means individual ownership of assets. Women are more likely to be asset owners when marital regimes provide for community property (Deere et al., 2013; Frémeaux and Leturcq, 2022; Gaddis et al., 2022) and when states implement joint-titling programmes of land and buildings giving equal rights to married partners (consensual unions may be recognised under the law in a similar way to marriage).

Unequal distribution of assets and wealth among household members can be a source of unequal power relations within the household. Women's asset ownership has implications for their agency and wellbeing. Decision-making is often considered an indicator of agency, and evidence suggests that a more egalitarian distribution of assets, or the wife owning property, correlates with the wife's participation in intra-household decision-making (Oduro et al., 2012; Twyman et al., 2015; Mishra and Sam, 2016). In Karnataka, India, property ownership by rural women was found to be positively associated with increased mobility and participation in household decisions regarding their employment, healthcare and use of income (Swaminathan et al., 2012b). There is also evidence of a protective effect of women's asset ownership against intimate partner violence (primarily moderated by the socio-economic context) (Panda and Agarwal, 2005; Oduro et al., 2015; Peterman et al., 2017). An increase in women's control over household resources has also been found to lead to increased spending on food, greater investment in health and education and improvements in children's wellbeing (Allendorf, 2007; Luke and Munshi, 2011; Menon et al., 2014).

Individualising measures of assets and wealth

In the global south, household surveys are the primary vehicle for obtaining information on various development parameters. While several demographic indicators are collected for all household members, information on asset ownership, particularly physical assets, is operationalised at the household level. A standard question would be: 'Does this household own a plot of land or the house you reside in?' When no further questions are fielded on which member(s) own(s) the asset(s), this has disadvantages, particularly from a gender perspective. Gender analysis of asset inequality is limited to comparing households classified by sex of household head (i.e. male-headed or female-headed). This results in women's asset ownership being likely to be incorrectly estimated because women asset owners residing in households headed by men are not counted. Deere et al. (2012) compare the share of landowning households that have women landowners, with the share of landowning households headed by women in Latin America and the Caribbean, finding the former exceeding the latter. A similar finding emerges for home and business ownership.

Furthermore, the measured inequality is distorted if household-level data are used, and household wealth simply divided by the number of household members to obtain a per capita value. Thus, the value of agricultural land owned by one household member is distributed across all adult members without any information on individual ownership. This method underestimates overall wealth inequality in the population and masks intra-household inequalities, making inequality appear much less severe (De Vreyer and Lambert, 2021). Based on a sample of couple respondents from Karnataka, India, Malghan and Swaminathan (2017) find high levels of wealth inequality using individual data (with a Gini coefficient of 0.86), as compared to distributing the total asset value equally between the partners (resulting in a Gini coefficient of 0.76). Overall inequality in a population can be decomposed into inequality between and within households. The same study finds 38 per cent of overall wealth inequality attributable to within-household inequality, thereby highlighting the importance of understanding intra-household resource allocation in overall inequality.

Data on individual-level assets also lend themselves to a gender analysis of asset poverty (Hillesland, 2019; Anglade et al., 2022). In addition, heterogeneity among women and men can be explored using individual-level data. In Ecuador, for example, women are more likely to be asset-poor than men, and asset poverty among cohabiting men and women is higher than among married individuals (Anglade et al., 2022).

In response to the shortcomings of household-level asset data, the Gender Asset Gap Project (GAGP) in 2010 pioneered the collection of individual-level asset and wealth data in Ecuador, Ghana and the state of Karnataka, India. There were several unique aspects to the GAGP surveys (in which the authors of this chapter were involved). First, qualitative research was conducted for six months in each country to understand the nuances of asset ownership. Second, the household questionnaire of the GAGP surveys included an inventory of all physical assets owned by household members and identified each asset's owner. Third, there was a conscious effort to move away from the 'household headship' concept (interviewing the person considered to be the 'head of the household'). In all three research sites, an attempt was made to interview two members in each household, preferably a couple. Households often comprised several generations residing together – older parents with married children, for example – necessitating a protocol for choosing a couple pair. In Ghana and Karnataka, the primary respondent was the adult who either self-identified or was identified by household members as the most knowledgeable about the household's assets. The second respondent was his/her spouse. This pair was termed the 'principal couple'. But in Ecuador the principal couple was defined as the one both responsible for supporting the household and the most knowledgeable regarding its assets. To obtain information about asset ownership and value in Ecuador, the principal couple were interviewed together whenever possible. Qualitative inquiry suggested that this enhanced the quality of information, as the couple could discuss their responses (Deere and Contreras Diaz, 2011). Interviewing the couple together was not an option in Ghana and India, however, due to gender norms that might have hindered women from speaking freely in men's presence. Thus, men and women were interviewed separately. Finally, a detailed individual questionnaire was administered separately to the two respondents in each country, collecting information on their financial assets and debts, the mode of asset acquisition (for large assets and immovable property), their rights of management and alienation (rights to sell or bequeath) and loss of assets due to adverse events such as natural disasters.

The GAGP provided evidence of the feasibility of collecting individual-level asset data and provided early estimates of gender gaps in asset ownership and wealth and their determinants (Deere and Contreras Diaz, 2011; Oduro et al., 2011; Swaminathan et al., 2012a; Hillesland, 2019) and the importance of property rights to women's accumulation of wealth (Deere et al., 2013) as well as modes of asset acquisition (Doss et al., 2019). The GAGP studies also examined methodological issues involved in collecting data on assets (Doss et al., 2011, 2018) and the relevance of assets for gauging women's wellbeing and decision-making (Swaminathan et al., 2012b; Oduro et al., 2015; Twyman et al., 2015) and for analysing individual-level poverty (Vijaya et al., 2014; Anglade et al., 2022). Drawing largely on the GAGP experience, the Evidence and Data for Gender Equality project also conducted asset surveys in seven countries in collaboration with national statistical offices, resulting in the United Nations *Guidelines for Producing Statistics on Asset Ownership from a Gender Perspective* (United Nations, 2019).

Conceptualising asset ownership

The GAGP identified several issues in measuring asset ownership. It distinguished between reported and documented ownership. Surveys that collect data on individual asset ownership typically pose questions such as: 'Who in the household owns this asset?' Reported owners are individuals identifying themselves as owners or identified as such by others. Surveys can also ask about documents regarding assets such as land and buildings and whose names appear on these – referred to as documented or legal ownership. Typically, however, the reported or 'documented' ownership claim is not verified against actual documentary evidence.

Identifying asset owners based solely on documentary evidence can underestimate the overall incidence of asset ownership, particularly for women (Oduro et al., 2011; Joshi et al., 2022). This is because it is not uncommon to find legal ownership differing from reported ownership. Registration of assets such as land, housing and businesses is still not widespread in the global south. Registration costs can create disincentives. Other factors may also play a role in understanding this difference; some individuals could lack awareness of their rights over their spouse's assets and, therefore, of their status as legal owner. In stable relationships, individuals perceive themselves as co-owners of their spouse's assets and report the situation as such. In the global north, however, one study showed that the length of their marital status, and/or whether the union is formalised or cohabitation, for example, can also affect individuals' perceptions of asset ownership versus its actual status in law (Joseph and Rowlingson, 2012).

The GAGP, therefore, needed to grapple with how to define ownership when documentation is not widespread. Ownership was initially defined as the relation between a person and a thing.[2] The current concept of ownership is that it is a bundle of rights (McCarty, 2002). Honore (1961), cited in Breakey (2012), identifies 11 rights defining ownership, including rights to possession, usage, management and income. Legal rules, customary laws and social norms, varying across different countries and societies, will determine the bundle of ownership rights.

Each right is distinct, and the owner's rights can include some and exclude others (see Schlager and Ostrom, 1992). Evidence from the GAGP (Swaminathan et al., 2012a; Oduro, 2015) and other studies (Slavchevska et al., 2021; Joshi et al., 2022) find differences in rights reported by female and male owners and by documented and reported owners. It is essential to know whether female and male asset owners have the same complement of rights, since this determines what they can do with the asset, as well as their economic rights or their claims over income it generates. These dimensions of ownership may be correlated, but they do not overlap perfectly.

In contexts in which formal legal systems and customary laws and traditions co-exist, and the scope of statutory laws and regulations does not have a meaningful impact on people's lives, reported ownership cannot be dismissed. However, when identifying asset owners, including legal or documented ownership for immovable property is also relevant. Alienation and economic rights (the rights to use income generated from the asset) may also be more significant in other contexts. This is relevant in the global south, especially for agricultural land, where documented ownership may not necessarily be the norm.

Someone may be the exclusive owner of an asset or own it jointly with others. There are also different permutations of joint ownership; for example, assets may be held jointly by a couple, all household members or with others who are not household members – with siblings, for example. To identify asset owners, any individual holding an asset exclusively or jointly must be counted. Joint asset ownership introduces challenges to the calculation of individual asset wealth. This will be discussed next.

Collecting data on assets and wealth

Individualising measures of assets and wealth poses unique challenges for data collection. The critical questions include which assets must be enumerated; who should be interviewed; and what indicators should be developed to derive meaningful measures of gaps at the group level.

Which assets matter?

In a comprehensive asset survey, there is usually complete coverage of all physical and financial assets. When the unit of data collection is the individual, decisions must be made on which assets to include or exclude because of the costs involved in collecting individual-level data.

Immovable property must be included, as this contributes a disproportionate share of total wealth. It is particularly relevant for countries in the global south, where financial assets may not be particularly prominent due to low levels of financial inclusion. However, if overall property ownership is low in the population of interest, then the data collected about assets must be broadened.

Depending on context, other assets may also affect intra-household dynamics. In rural areas livestock is a valuable resource, and there are likely to be gendered ownership patterns, with larger stock typically owned by men and smaller stock owned by women (Doss et al., 2014). Similarly, agricultural equipment can be valuable, with demarcated ownership. But it is also true that a sense of individual ownership may be lacking for smaller items of equipment. In Karnataka, India, for example, smaller items of agricultural equipment tend to be owned by all household members (83 per cent in rural areas), reflecting their low value and their everyday use among men and women (Swaminathan et al., 2012a).

In low-income settings, women's employment is often mainly in the informal sector and consists of seasonal and multiple activities. If such work involves the home production of goods or self-employment, capturing data on assets used in such activities is relevant. These could be household appliances, consumer durables and smaller vehicles (such as cycles or pushcarts used for transport). The GAGP identified consumer durables used in income-generating activities by asking whether items were used in a household business.

From the perspective of gender dynamics, collecting data on individual ownership of a broad range of assets is best. The context can shape the granularity of asset categories. For example, assets such as jewellery in Egypt and India may be owned primarily by women; excluding these from data collection may result in overestimating the gender asset gap.

Whom to talk to within the household?

Respondent selection and identity

There is a growing literature on respondent selection within the household and its impact on understanding measures of assets and wealth (Kilic and Moylan, 2016; Kilic et al., 2021; Joshi et al., 2022). When deciding on who and how many people to interview within a household, the main issues are the study's objective(s), the scale of the survey, the demographic structure of the population and financial and other resources for the study. If an intra-household analysis is the intention, at least two household members should be interviewed. Preferably, these should be the principal couple (see above), as bargaining and negotiation are most applicable to this dyad. Moreover, one can expect the two partners to be at a similar stage of life with respect to asset acquisition, making discussion of gaps in assets and wealth more meaningful. However, if the purpose is to estimate individual asset ownership, a third adult must be included where relevant. With only principal couple respondents, the levels of asset ownership in the population may be underestimated or overestimated. Analysing data from Georgia, Mongolia and the Philippines, for example, Joshi et al. (2022) find that a third respondent (a randomly chosen adult within the household, in addition to both partners in the principal couple as respondents) is much less likely to own the dwelling they live in compared to the principal couple also living there.

It is also important to be mindful of on whose behalf the respondent is providing information. Across several domains, it is established that when individuals give information about themselves (self-reporting), this gives different results from information provided by someone else (proxy reporting). Much of the evidence of differences between self- and proxy reporting relates to labour market participation and earnings for both adults and children (Bardasi et al., 2011; Janzen, 2018; Galdo et al., 2021). More recently, however, respondent identity has also gained traction in studies of asset ownership (Ambler et al., 2021; Joshi et al., 2022). The evidence suggests that self-reporting, on average, increases the probability of both men and women being found to own property, compared to proxy reporting. However, it is also true that self- and proxy reporting do not necessarily always diverge. The literature on respondent identity in relation to assets is still nascent, with many avenues for deepening our understanding.

The United Nations guidelines (2019) recommend collecting individual-level data via self-reporting. This is desirable if one is interested in intra-household analysis or correlating asset ownership with empowerment. Perceptions of ownership can be just as relevant for agency and a sense of self-worth and would be likely to enhance negotiating power within the household.

What measures are most relevant, and how do they affect data collection?

Incidence versus value

Measures of asset ownership can be obtained using two indicators. The first is the proportion of asset owners in the population or the incidence of asset ownership. Incidence reveals how widespread asset ownership is among men and women and estimates the gender asset gap. The second is the gender distribution of asset owners, i.e. the share of men and women within the class of asset owners. However, both the incidence and distribution of owners have limitations as measures. They do not consider the number of assets each owner possesses or capture the quality and other characteristics of the asset (such as size). These measures also count an individual as an asset owner irrespective of whether they are the exclusive owner.

The value of assets owned is used to calculate women's share of wealth and provides information on wealth distribution by gender. Comparing the mean value of assets owned by women and men also includes information on the gender gap in asset wealth. The advantage of the wealth measure over the incidence and distribution measures is that it captures the number of assets owned, the form of ownership (exclusive or joint) and the quality of the asset.

The different measures provide different perspectives on asset ownership. For example, the GAGP (Doss et al., 2014) found that women's share of asset owners was consistently higher than their share of gross housing, agricultural land and business wealth. This is because women's assets tended to be fewer and of lower quality. Ecuador was an exception, where women's share of homeownership was almost identical to their share of gross housing wealth.

Turning to efforts to measure individual wealth (i.e. the value of assets, rather than ownership of the assets alone), data collection must address four issues. These are: which assets to collect valuation data about; which valuation method to employ; how to assign the value of jointly owned assets to each owner; and how to reconcile differences in the valuation of an asset by several owners.

Ideally, information about the values of all assets should be collected. When there are resource constraints, the decision on which assets to collect valuation data about should be determined by what assets are essential for women and men in the locale (country or community) of data collection and the purpose(s) for which the data are being collected. Three methods exist for the valuation of immovable property, applied to the place of residence, agricultural land and other forms of real estate. These are the current potential sale value, purchase (or construction) value and rental value. The GAGP (Deere and Catanzarite, 2016; Doss et al., 2018) analysed the robustness of these valuation methods and recommended valuing assets using the potential sale value.

Joint ownership poses the challenge of assigning asset values to several owners. If the asset was purchased, each owner's share could be determined by their contribution to its acquisition. Thus, the survey must include questions on the purchase price of the asset and each owner's contribution. This disadvantages women, as in-kind contributions are not easily quantified. Where the marital regimes in force are either full or partial community property, all assets acquired during the marriage are considered to be jointly owned by the couple, and this may guide how asset values should be shared between partners in any study. Similarly, inheritance laws may specify how inherited assets should be shared. Without legal guides, the researcher may consider allocating the value of the asset equally between the owners.

When joint owners are interviewed separately, they are unlikely to provide identical valuations, with differences leading to concerns about reconciling the values suggested. Depending on the household circumstances, gender dynamics and the sensitivity of asset ownership, joint owners can be interviewed together. Deere and Catanzarite (2016) find that in Ecuador, interviewing couples together to obtain housing and land values reduces the likelihood of guessing and thus increases the reliability of the values provided. When joint interviews are not possible (due to social norms of interviewing men and women together, practical issues of availability and/or other reasons), it is recommended that valuation data should be obtained from the member who is most knowledgeable about the household's assets (United Nations, 2019).

New directions for analysis

There has been rapid progress in individualising measures of assets and wealth from the perspectives of data collection and analysis. As this field opens up, we identify research opportunities to advance the frontier of knowledge. We focus here on issues related to better measurement of asset and wealth patterns within a household.

First, we need more information on laws affecting women's ability to own property. For women in the global south, inheritance and marriage remain the primary means of acquiring high-value assets such as immovable property. However, beyond knowing the broad legislative framework of the country (see above), there is little information on how these laws intersect with people's lives in practice – via social norms, awareness of laws and their implementation in practice.

The marital regime is a crucial element of legislation but neglected in the collection of individual-level asset ownership data. Incorporating questions on awareness of the default marital regime could provide insights into ownership trends and how these may vary with the respondent's identity. Knowledge of these laws would be likely to influence how respondents perceive asset ownership, particularly for high-value assets. To effectively triangulate information on the marital regime with information on respondents' ownership of assets, it would also be necessary to collect data on when and how the asset was acquired; such data are rarely collected. Similarly, questions on how rights to sell or bequeath property would change on a spouse's death or marriage dissolution could be included. In cases in which couples cohabit, or marriages are not registered, the marital regime may not fully apply to the couple. Thus, it would be helpful to include questions in the survey instrument on whether marriages are registered or formally recognised.

Second, qualitative research can reveal nuances that can complement survey data. How men and women understand concepts of ownership, including use rights, documented rights and joint ownership, may play a significant role in answers to questions in a survey that seeks information on assets and wealth. Qualitative findings can also enrich knowledge about trends in social norms associated with marriage dissolution, women owning and managing property and the freedom they enjoy in accessing various spaces that can affect their employment, awareness of laws and broader acquisition of information.

Third, there is hardly any research on gendered patterns of asset ownership or wealth inequality using administrative data in countries from the global south. If such records exist, these could provide rich information on gendered ownership patterns and the effectiveness of pieces of legislation that promote women's property ownership. However, this line of inquiry is challenging. Records are usually not digitised; in addition, there may be bureaucratic red tape and inertia. The upside is that researching such data is relatively uncharted territory and could yield rich dividends. It may be easier to initially focus on urban areas – where digitisation may be more common – and explore various options.

Finally, intersectional research addressing women's heterogeneity would be a valuable contribution. Women are often treated as a homogeneous category, but their opportunities and constraints depend on where they are situated on different social axes. The data available thus far on individual asset ownership tend to be from large-scale surveys that do not necessarily answer questions about the interplay of social identities (class, race, ethnicity, caste, religion, etc.). All these developments in research methods and topics of investigation would further enrich knowledge about individual ownership of assets and wealth in the future.

Notes

1. The System of National Accounts is a joint production of the United Nations, European Commission, Organisation for Economic Co-operation and Development, World Bank and the International Monetary Fund: https://unstats .un.org/unsd/nationalaccount/sna2008.asp (accessed 24 September 2021).
2. See McCarty (2002) for a discussion on the conceptual history of ownership.

References

Allendorf, K. (2007). 'Women's Land Rights Promote Empowerment and Child Health in Nepal?' *World Development* 35(11), 1975–1988.

Ambler, K., Doss, C., Kieran, C. and Passarelli, S. (2021). 'He Says, She Says: Spousal Disagreement in Survey Measures of Bargaining Power'. *Economic Development and Cultural Change* 69(2), 765–788.

Anglade, B., Useche, P. and Deere, C.D. (2022). 'A Gendered Analysis of Individual-Level Asset Poverty in Ecuador'. *Feminist Economics* 28(1), 56–85.

Atta-Ankomah, R., Darko Osei, R., Osei-Akoto, I., Asante, F.A., Oduro, A.D., Owoo, N., Lambon-Quayefio, M. and Afranie, S. (2020). *Inequality Diagnostics for Ghana*. Cape Town: African Centre of Excellence for Inequality Research. https://webcms .uct.ac.za/sites/default/files/image_tool/images/560/Images/Publications/Country _reports/Diagnostic%20Report_Ghana_final-26Nov2020-for-web.pdf (accessed 23 April 2022).

Bardasi, E., Beegle, K., Dillon, A. and Serneels, P. (2011). 'Do Labor Statistics Depend on How and to Whom the Questions Are Asked? Results from a Survey Experiment in Tanzania'. *World Bank Economic Review* 25(3), 418–447.

Breakey, H. (2012). Property. *Internet Encyclopedia of Philosophy*. www.iep.utm.edu/prop-con/ (accessed 9 February 2022).

Carter, M.R. and Barrett, C.B. (2006). 'The Economics of Poverty Traps and Persistent Poverty: An Asset-Based Approach'. *Journal of Development Studies* 42(2), 178–199.

Chancel, L., Piketty, T., Saez, E. and Zucman, G. (eds) (2021). *World Inequality Report 2022*. https://wir2022.wid.world/site/uploads/2023/03/D_FINAL_WIL_RIM_RAPPORT_2303.pdf (accessed 22 February 2023).

De Vreyer, P. and Lambert, S. (2021). 'Inequality, Poverty, and the Intra-Household Allocation of Consumption in Senegal'. *World Bank Economic Review* 35(2), 414–435.

Deere, C.D. and Catanzarite, Z.B. (2016). 'Measuring the Intra-Household Distribution of Wealth in Ecuador: Qualitative Insights and Quantitative Outcomes'. In F.S. Lee and B. Cronin (eds), *Handbook of Research Methods and Applications in Heterodox Economics*. Cheltenham, UK and Northampton, MA, USA: Edward Elgar Publishing, 512–534.

Deere, C.D. and Contreras Diaz, J. (2011). *Asset Accumulation: The Challenge for Equity*. Quito: FLACSO. https://biblio.flacsoandes.edu.ec/libros/digital/43329.pdf (accessed 2 September 2017).

Deere, C.D. and Doss, C. (2006). 'The Gender Asset Gap: What Do We Know and Why Does It Matter?' *Feminist Economics* 12(1–2), 1–50.

Deere, C.D., Alvarado, G. and Twyman, J. (2012). 'Gender Inequality in Asset Ownership in Latin America: Female Owners vs Household Heads'. *Development and Change* 43(2), 505–530.

Deere, C.D., Oduro, A., Swaminathan, H. and Doss, C. (2013). 'Property Rights and the Gender Distribution of Wealth in Ecuador, Ghana and India'. *Journal of Economic Inequality* 11(2), 249–265.

Doss, C., Deere, C.D., Oduro, A.D. and Swaminathan, H. (2014). 'The Gender Asset and Wealth Gaps'. *Development* 57(3–4), 400–409.

Doss, C., Deere, C.D., Oduro, A.D., Swaminathan, H., Catanzarite, Z. and Suchitra, J.Y. (2019). 'Gendered Paths to Asset Accumulation? Savings, Markets and Credit in Developing Countries'. *Feminist Economics* 25(2), 36–66.

Doss, C., Catanzarite, Z., Baah-Boateng, W., Swaminathan, H., Deere, C.D., Boake-Yiadom, L. and Suchitra, J.Y. (2018). 'Do Men and Women Estimate Property Values Differently?' *World Development* 107, 75–86.

Doss, C., Deere, C.D., Oduro, A.D., Swaminathan, H., Suchitra, J.Y., Lahoti, R., Baah-Boateng, W., Boakye-Yiadom, L., Contreras, J., Twyman, J., Catanzarite, Z., Grown, C. and Hillesland, M. (2011). *The Gender Asset and Wealth Gaps: Evidence from Ecuador, Ghana and Karnataka, India*. Bangalore: Indian Institute of Management Bangalore. https://repository.iimb.ac.in/bitstream/2074/13750/1/Sen_DCMFA_2011.pdf (accessed 13 March 2017).

Frémeaux, N. and Leturcq, M. (2022). 'Wealth Accumulation and the Gender Wealth Gap across Couples' Legal Statuses and Matrimonial Property Regimes in France'. *European Journal of Population* 38(4), 643–679.

Gaddis, I., Lahoti, R. and Swaminathan, H. (2022). 'Women's Legal Rights and Gender Gaps in Property Ownership in Developing Countries'. *Population and Development Review* 48(2), 331–377.

Galdo, J., Dammert, A.C. and Abebaw, D. (2021). 'Gender Bias in Agricultural Child Labor: Evidence from Survey Design Experiments'. *World Bank Economic Review* 35(4), 872–891.

Hays, D. and Sullivan, B. (2022). 'The Wealth of Households: 2020'. Current Population Reports, P70BR-181. Washington, DC: United States Census Bureau. www.census .gov/content/dam/Census/library/publications/2022/demo/p70br-181.pdf (accessed 20 February 2023).

Hillesland, M. (2019). 'Investigating the Gender Wealth Gap in Ghana'. *Oxford Development Studies* 47(1), 63–78.

Honore, A. (1961). 'Ownership'. In A. Guest (ed.), *Oxford Essays in Jurisprudence*. Oxford: Oxford University Press, 107–147.

Janzen, S.A. (2018). 'Child Labour Measurement: Whom Should We Ask?' *International Labour Review* 157(2), 169–191.

Joseph, R. and Rowlingson, K. (2012). 'Her House, His Pension? The Division of Assets among (Ex)Couples and the Role of Policy'. *Social Policy and Society* 11(1), 69–80.

Joshi, K., Martinez, A.M., Addawe, M., Soco, C.F.M. and Swaminathan, H. (2022). 'Contextualising Individual-Level Asset Data Collection: Evidence from Household Surveys'. *Journal of Development Studies*, 58(6), 1259–1279.

Kenya National Bureau of Statistics. (2020). *Inequality Trends and Diagnostics in Kenya 2020*. Cape Town: African Centre of Excellence for Inequality Research. https:// webcms.uct.ac.za/sites/default/files/image_tool/images/560/Images/Publications/ Country_reports/Kenya_Inequality_Trends_Diagnostics_2020_Report-for_website -final.pdf (accessed 14 April 2022).

Kilic, T. and Moylan, H. (2016). 'Methodological Experiment on Measuring Asset Ownership from a Gender Perspective'. Washington, DC: World Bank. https://doi .org/10.1596/33653

Kilic, T., Moylan, H. and Koolwal, G. (2021). 'Getting the (Gender-Disaggregated) Lay of the Land: Impact of Survey Respondent Selection on Measuring Land Ownership and Rights'. *World Development* 146: 105545.

Lersch, P.M., Struffolino, E. and Vitali, A. (2022). 'Wealth in Couples: Introduction to the Special Issue'. *European Journal of Population* 38(4), 623–641.

Luke, N. and Munshi, K. (2011). 'Women as Agents of Change: Female Income and Mobility in India'. *Journal of Development Economics* 94(1), 1–17.

Malghan, D. and Swaminathan, H. (2017). 'Intra-Household Wealth Inequality and Economic Development: Evidence from Karnataka, India'. *IIM Bangalore Research Paper No. 487*. https://ssrn.com/abstract=2611889

McCarty, L.T. (2002). 'Ownership: A Case Study in the Representation of Legal Concepts'. *Artificial Intelligence and Law* 10(1–3), 135–161.

Menon, N., Van der Meulen Rodgers, Y. and Nguyen, H. (2014). 'Women's Land Rights and Children's Human Capital in Vietnam'. *World Development* 54: 18–31.

Mishra, K. and Sam, A.G. (2016). 'Does Women's Land Ownership Promote Their Empowerment? Empirical Evidence from Nepal'. *World Development* 78, 360–371.

Oduro, A.D. (2015). 'Ownership of the Place of Residence in Ghana: A Gender Analysis'. *Journal of African Development* 17(1), 17–44.

Oduro, A.D., Baah-Boateng, W. and Boakye-Yiadom, L. (2011). *Measuring the Gender Asset Gap in Ghana*. Accra: Woeli Publishing Services.

Oduro, A.D., Boakye-Yiadom, L. and Baah-Boateng, W. (2012). 'Asset Ownership and Egalitarian Decision-Making among Couples: Some Evidence from Ghana'. Gender Asset Gap Working Paper No. 14. Bangalore: Indian Institute of Management Bangalore.

Oduro, A.D., Deere, C.D. and Catanzarite, Z.B. (2015). 'Women's Wealth and Intimate Partner Violence: Insights from Ecuador and Ghana'. *Feminist Economics* 21(2), 1–29.

Office for National Statistics. (2022). 'Household Total Wealth in Great Britain: April 2018–March 2020'. Statistical Bulletin. United Kingdom: Office for National Statistics. www.ons.gov.uk/peoplepopulationandcommunity/personalandhouseholdfinances/ incomeandwealth/ bulletins/ totalw ealthingre atbritain/ april2018tomarch2020 (accessed 15 February 2023).

Panda, P. and Agarwal, B. (2005). 'Marital Violence, Human Development and Women's Property Status in India'. *World Development* 33(5), 823–850.

Peterman, A., Pereira, A., Bleck, J., Palermo, T.M. and Yount, K.M. (2017). 'Women's Individual Asset Ownership and Experience of Intimate Partner Violence: Evidence from 28 International Surveys'. *American Journal of Public Health* 107(5), 747–755.

Ponthieux, S. and Meurs, D. (2015). 'Gender Inequality'. In A.B. Atkinson and F. Bourguignon (eds), *Handbook of Income Distribution*, Vol. 2A. Amsterdam: Elsevier, North Holland, 981–1146.

Schlager, E. and Ostrom, E. (1992). 'Property-Rights Regimes and Natural Resources: A Conceptual Analysis'. *Land Economics* 68(3), 249–262.

Schneebaum, A., Rehm, M., Mader, K. and Hollan, K. (2018). 'The Gender Wealth Gap across European Countries'. *Review of Income and Wealth* 64(2), 295–331.

Slavchevska, V., Doss, C., De la O Campos, A.P. and Brunelli, C. (2021). 'Beyond Ownership: Women's and Men's Land Rights in Sub-Saharan Africa'. *Oxford Development Studies* 49(1), 2–22.

Swaminathan, H., Lahoti, R. and Suchitra, J.Y. (2012a). 'Gender Asset and Wealth Gaps: Evidence from Karnataka'. *Economic and Political Weekly* 47(35), 59–67.

Swaminathan, H., Lahoti, R. and Suchitra, J.Y. (2012b). 'Women's Property, Mobility, and Decisionmaking: Evidence from Rural Karnataka, India'. FPRI Discussion Paper 1188. Washington, DC: International Food Policy Research Institute.

Twyman, J., Useche, P. and Deere, C.D. (2015). 'Gendered Perceptions of Land Ownership and Agricultural Decision-Making in Ecuador: Who Are the Farm Managers?' *Land Economics* 91(3), 479–500.

United Nations. (2019). *Guidelines for Producing Statistics on Asset Ownership from a Gender Perspective.* New York: United Nations.

Vijaya, R.M., Lahoti, R. and Swaminathan, H. (2014). 'Moving from the Household to the Individual: Multidimensional Poverty Analysis'. *World Development* 59, 70–81.

8. Control 'of' resources or control 'over' individuals? Exploring the management and distribution of resources within the household and economic abuse

Marilyn Howard and Nicola Sharp-Jeffs

Introduction

This chapter considers research into economic abuse in relation to research into the management and distribution of resources within the household.[1] Both bodies of literature focus on power, structural factors, gender relations and decision-making. Hence there are links and overlaps between them which, until now, have been underexplored.

Literature on within-household resources includes exploration of the control 'of' such resources, and how this creates the potential for conflict and relationship damage, disadvantaging women in particular. The literature on economic abuse sits within broader research into domestic abuse, in which power is considered as a form of 'coercive control' (Stark, 2007) exerted 'over' a household member (Singh, 2022: 2) in order to create dependence and instability across several domains, including the economic. Control in this context is exerted deliberately with the intention of limiting freedom and/or preventing the abused partner from leaving and living independently. The two literatures – on domestic abuse and on resources within the household – have thus far evolved largely separately, although Sharp-Jeffs (2015b) recognises a 'meeting' of the two regarding men's perceptions of financial abuse (see below). Thus, we suggest directions for further developing a focus on economic abuse in wider research into within-household resources.

Defining and researching economic abuse

Economic abuse and financial abuse are both forms of domestic abuse; although sometimes used interchangeably, they are in fact distinct. Their definitions, in the context of domestic abuse, and some key research findings are outlined below.

Domestic abuse

Domestic abuse (like many other intra-household issues) is underpinned by power, including gender relations (discussed below). Although some 'victim-survivors' are male, most are female, so in this chapter we refer to 'victim-survivors' as women.

Over recent decades, in many countries, the understanding of 'domestic abuse' has moved beyond incidents of physical and sexual violence to encompass controlling tactics which include emotional, psychological and/or economic abuse (Council of Europe, 2011; Royal, 2022). Domestic abuse is also increasingly regarded as a 'course of conduct', i.e. a pattern of behaviour which includes combinations of these tactics (Kelly et al., 2014), alongside isolation; minimising, denying and blaming; intimidation and coercion; and threats. This creates a context in which the victim-survivor recognises that there will be negative consequences from non-compliance (Dutton and Goodman, 2005), so that refusing a demand is dangerous, compelling them to act in accordance with the abuser's wishes. Leaving the perpetrator – the ultimate challenge to control – may often be the time when abuse escalates, and women are most at risk of homicide. In the United Kingdom (UK), the concept of 'space for action' includes various dimensions of control, within which a perpetrator can set parameters (including economic) limiting the victim-survivor's freedom to act (Kelly et al., 2014; Sharp-Jeffs et al., 2018).

Primarily, this understanding is informed by research into heterosexual intimate partner relationships. However, many definitions of domestic abuse include other forms of relationship (including same-sex couples) and other household members beyond partners, discussed below and in Sharp-Jeffs (2022).

Economic, including financial, abuse

Historically, financial and economic abuse were conceptualised as forms of emotional abuse (e.g. Loring, 1994). Littwin (2012) argues that financial abuse refers only to control of money, not control over what money can buy (e.g. food or transport). Although money is central to both, and they involve similar behaviours (Singh, 2022), financial abuse is a 'sub-category' of economic abuse, with the latter recognising a broader range of economically controlling behaviours (Sharp-Jeffs, 2015a, 2022).

Economic abuse is the least researched area of domestic abuse and has been explored only relatively recently (Sharp-Jeffs, 2021, 2022) – which may explain why potential links and overlaps with wider research into within-household resources have been underexplored. For instance, a multi-country study identified just 46 peer-reviewed articles with a full or partial quantitative focus on economic abuse, a far smaller number than would be expected had this instead been a global review of physical or sexual violence (Postmus et al., 2020). The articles meeting the researchers' selection criteria were mainly from the United States (US) but also included four articles from South Africa, three each from Canada and Palestine and two each from the UK, Ivory Coast and the Philippines; one article was derived from a multi-country study in Asia and the Pacific. Although this shows increasing attention globally, much research is currently from countries such as the UK, US and Australia (Royal, 2022).

Economic, including financial, abuse was conceptualised within a seminal study undertaken by US researchers as involving 'behaviors that control a person's ability to acquire, use, or maintain economic resources, thus threatening their economic security and potential for self-sufficiency' (Adams et al., 2008: 564). Such behaviours can be organised into distinct constructs; building on this original research, Adams and Beeble (2019) identified these as economic restriction and economic exploitation.

Potentially an element of wider research into within-household resources, economic restriction refers to the limiting of access to, and use of, household resources. Tactics include limiting or denying access to income, bank accounts and financial information and limiting the use of property (Sharp, 2008; Howard and Skipp, 2015). However, such tactics are commonly used alongside other forms of abuse. Economic abuse is associated with both physical and psychological abuse (Adams et al., 2008; Postmus et al., 2012, 2016), reinforcing and overlapping with other coercively controlling tactics (Sharp, 2008). This makes challenging the abuser dangerous (Dutton and Goodman, 2005; Sharp-Jeffs, 2015b). Interfering with victim-survivors' ability to acquire and use economic resources is designed to create economic dependence, making it difficult for them to leave and rebuild their life safely. For example, 52 per cent (n = 126) of victim-survivors responding to one survey in England agreed with the statement that they had no money and therefore could not leave (Howard and Skipp, 2015).

Economic exploitation relates to abusers appropriating the victim-survivor's resources for their own benefit. Tactics include 'freeloading' (demanding that the victim-survivor is the only one to pay for household necessities, or that they buy goods for the abuser or pay their bills for them); stealing the victim-survivor's money and/or property; and/or generating debt in their name through fraud and/or coercion (Sharp, 2008; Howard and Skipp, 2015; Sharp-Jeffs, 2015b). These tactics are also underpinned by an abuse of power, potentially creating economic dependence and economic instability, diminishing what the victim-survivor has built up and compromising her economic wellbeing (Sharp-Jeffs, 2022).

A third construct is sabotage, initially relating to employment (Postmus et al., 2016). Yet UK research (Sharp, 2008; Sharp-Jeffs, 2021) identified other sabotage tactics to generate economic costs, including disconnecting utilities, which must then be reconnected, and/or destroying a partner's belongings, which must then be replaced; the same tactics were found in research from the US (Anderson et al., 2003) and Australia (Smallwood, 2015). Credit ratings can also be sabotaged (Littwin, 2012). This behaviour creates additional expenses which absorb available income – again creating economic instability. Thus, economic abuse is a multi-faceted and evolving concept (Sharp-Jeffs, 2021).

Determining the prevalence of economic, including financial, abuse is difficult, due to differing definitions and ambiguity in the wording of questions in research and official statistics, compounded by the difficulty in identifying when such behaviour has taken place (e.g. Home Office, 2021, concerning England and Wales).

In England and Wales, the term 'financial abuse' is used in official crime statistics, which focus on incidents rather than patterns of behaviour, thus broadly reflecting economic restriction and exploitation. However, financial abuse is not reported on separately, but instead is grouped with (other) 'non-physical' forms of domestic abuse, and so its prevalence is unknown (Office for National Statistics, 2020). The question about financial abuse in the survey underlying these official statistics asks respondents whether someone has prevented them from having their 'fair share' of the household money, though how this is interpreted depends on the context, and responses are subjective (Sharp-Jeffs, 2022). Using this question, Sharp-Jeffs (2015b) found that men and women were almost equally likely to state that this was the case; but the wording does not adequately capture the concept central to domestic abuse – misuse of power (in this case, through economic resources) by one household member to gain control over another and to reduce their space for action. This also highlights the importance of crafting survey and interview questions which relate to the specific concept being measured (see Myhill, 2017).

Research representative of the UK population, using more nuanced questions to explore economic control, suggested that around one in five adults had experienced economic abuse from a current or former partner (Sharp-Jeffs, 2015b). Another recent nationally representative survey updating Sharp-Jeffs (2015b) also found that 39 per cent of UK adults reported behaviours indicating that a current or former partner was preventing them from, or interfering with their ability to, acquire, use or maintain economic resources (Butt, 2020: 23).

Power is influenced by factors which may be structural (such as employment) and relational (e.g. discourses around parental roles and responsibilities) (Goode et al., 1999). These factors can be deliberately used by abusers to limit victim-survivors' freedoms, for example by preventing partners from working, sabotaging their employment and/or exploiting their employment status by refusing to work and contribute to household costs. The abuser may have a victim-survivor's benefits paid to them, or use benefit/immigration rules to control a victim-survivor (Howard and Skipp, 2015; Dudley, 2017). Or they may draw on discourses about male authority to justify using household allocation systems such as a housekeeping allowance (e.g. Pahl, 1989) as a tactic of financial abuse (Home Office, 2015; Howard and Skipp, 2015; Sharp-Jeffs, 2015b), including deliberately allocating an amount insufficient for household needs. Sharp-Jeffs' representative survey of UK adults on economic abuse (2015b) found that some men described economic abuse as their partner expecting too much for household expenses, leaving them with insufficient money to pursue hobbies or socialise. Whilst these men perceived this as disadvantaging them, challenging the situation was not dangerous for them in the same way as it was for women.

Wider research into within-household resources has found instances of women being left without income (Warburton Brown, 2011), for reasons that were unclear. This experience resonates with victim-survivors' descriptions within research on economic abuse. Some wider research into within-household resources has indicated that women may exercise more day-to-day management of household spending; however, this does not necessarily equate to controlling the amount of, or strategy for, that spending (Pahl, 1989; Goode et al., 1999; Bisdee et al., 2013). Control of money can also operate independently of how it is allocated (Bennett, 2013).

'Ecological models' of abuse (e.g. Heise, 1998) indicate that factors at a social, community and individual level are related to economic abuse (Corrie and McGuire, 2013). As indicated above, one aspect of these related factors includes gender, which also features prominently in wider research into within-household resources.

Gender

Like domestic abuse, economic abuse is regarded as both a cause and a consequence of gender inequality; gendered norms and stereotypes form the foundations of, and perpetuate, male violence against women (Women's Aid et al., 2021). One debate concerns 'gender symmetry' in the prevalence of abuse, as different definitions and methodologies affect results (e.g. Hester, 2010). 'Intimate partner violence', in which one partner is violent and controlling and the other is not, can be distinguished from other situations, such as 'situational couple violence', in which couple conflict escalates into violence (Johnson, 2006). Intimate partner violence, predominantly experienced by women, is reported in particular in studies involving participants from specialist domestic abuse services, but much less so in studies of the general population (this is also due to differences between patterns and incidents, discussed earlier). Thus men and women have qualitatively different experiences of domestic abuse. Men are more likely than women to report economic abuse as single, exploitative incidents, happening for short periods, whereas women are more likely to experience economic abuse within an ongoing pattern of intimate partner violence, for longer durations and also after separation (Sharp-Jeffs, 2015b).

Women's experiences of economic abuse have also been recognised within wider research into within-household resources – e.g. Pahl's reference to studies of violence in marriage and the ideology of male dominance, as expressed in both physical abuse and male control of the couple's money (1989: 117).

Although economic equality is crucial, there appears to be no simple link between increasing the economic security of women and decreasing violence. Sharp-Jeffs (2022) observes that abuser tactics have evolved as women's position in relation to that of men has improved. Whilst abusers continue to take advantage of women's inequality and dependence, they also forcibly create economic dependence and/or instability in cases in which women have acquired considerable resources. International literature concerning women's empowerment indicates that greater access to finances may reduce domestic abuse through expanding women's networks (thus increasing the likelihood of private matters becoming public) and/or reducing pressures on men as main breadwinners (discussed in Kabeer, 2017). However, there are also risks of retaliatory actions (Heath, 2014; Annan et al., 2021). Littwin (2012: 981) suggests that abusive men adapted their control tactics in the light of 'financial advances that women have made over the past forty years', therefore regarding economic abuse as a 'patriarchal phenomenon' intended to 'wage war on women's growing equality'.

Literature on domestic abuse has also focussed on Nordic countries which, although considered among the most gender equal across measures such as pay and employment, also experience high levels of violence against women (Kelly, 2011; Gracia and Merlo, 2016; Gracia et al., 2019). However, how abuse is defined and measured also affects whether and to what extent such a 'Nordic paradox' exists. Swedish research has questioned this paradox, highlighting factors such as willingness to disclose abuse and having economic resources to leave an abusive partner, as well as gender norms in private life lagging behind formal equality measures (Wemrell et al., 2021). Furthermore, cross-country analysis reveals that the 'Nordic paradox' disappears when the specific country context is considered (Humbert et al., 2019), highlighting the complexity of gender equality, which cannot be reduced to a simple formula.

Unequal relationships or abuse?

The constructs of control (restriction, exploitation and sabotage) discussed above occur and overlap with multiple behaviours, and can be regarded as one extreme of a continuum of the control, management and distribution of resources within the household. Corrie and McGuire (2013: 1) suggest that a particular financial arrangement may either be abusive or embedded within an 'unequal (but mutually agreed upon) economic relationship', though distinguishing between these is challenging. The complexity of economic abuse makes it difficult to identify the point at which uneven power relations (which may be evident in the findings of wider research into within-household resources) become abusive. Women's roles 'as wives and mothers involve a measure of unpaid servitude, even in otherwise egalitarian relationships', which can make 'oppression difficult to see' (Tolmie, 2018: 56).

There are additional reasons why economic/financial abuse can be hard to identify. Victim-survivors may not always realise that they have experienced it. For example, only 38 per cent (n = 275) of the one in five (n = 730) respondents who had experienced financial abuse out of a nationally representative UK survey of 4002 people said that they had recognised it from the outset

(Sharp-Jeffs, 2015b). Economic abuse can begin when life changes occur, thus making it more difficult to recognise; for 25 per cent of study respondents, the abuse began on moving in together (with women more likely to report this) and seven in ten women reported that abuse began when they stopped working (Sharp-Jeffs, 2015b). Wider research into within-household resources has also documented alterations in money arrangements triggered by life events (such as children's arrival) or women desiring to make changes (Bennett, 2013) – the latter reflected in studies showing that lone parents may prefer, and experience, greater financial control than remaining with an unreliable or controlling partner (e.g. Griffiths, 2017, and this volume).

In addition to gender, structural and economic inequalities such as those of ethnicity, sexuality, disability and age can be linked with economic abuse. Economic abuse can encompass a wide variety of behaviours that interfere with a victim-survivor's ability to acquire, use and maintain economic resources. This is important to remember, as otherwise responses to economic abuse can tend to 'other' women from different socio-economic and ethnic backgrounds through suggesting that their experiences are solely due to their culture (Thiara and Gill, 2010). When the intersection of multiple oppressions increases marginalisation, access to economic, social and personal resources decreases, restricting options to achieve safety and economic security (VonDeLinde and Sussman, 2017). Hence, individuals experiencing intersecting inequalities are at particular risk of economic abuse.

Households and relationships

As noted above – and consistent with wider research into within-household resources (Bennett, 2013) – research into economic abuse has begun to consider a more diverse range of relationships than (usually female/male) couples. Previously, there was a tendency to read across from what was known about economic abuse within heterosexual intimate partner relationships to other relationships (Kelly and Westmarland, 2014). Whilst LGBT+ victim-survivors can experience similar kinds of (economic) abuse similar to those experienced by opposite-sex couples, their experiences can be shaped by multiple risk factors, including discrimination (Magić and Kelley, 2018).

The dynamics underpinning the economic abuse of a partner differ from those involved in the economic/financial abuse of an older person or family member, and abuse by a partner taking on a caring role may constitute either elder abuse or ongoing coercive control. Approaches to adult family violence have tended to ignore gender and structural issues (Sharp-Jeffs, 2022). In addition, some perpetrators (categorised as 'schemers', unlike 'controllers' or 'exploiters') deliberately enter into a relationship with the aim of gaining resources (Cameron, 2014: iv). Nonetheless, all such patterns of behaviour will reflect the misuse of power.

Research exploring women's experiences of economic abuse across different national and cultural contexts has considered family and intimate partner violence in situations in which joint family living (i.e. in complex households) is the norm (see Moore and Hlabana; Burchardt and Karagiannaki; Oduro and Swaminathan, this volume). Such research has identified behaviours similar to those found by research in the US and UK. For example, in rural Bangladesh Yount et al. (2021) found instances of interference with the acquisition and use/maintenance of economic resources, including family money. Chowbey (2017) considered the experiences of South Asian women in India, Pakistan and Britain, identifying the exploitation of women's marriage gifts, such as a dowry, as one example of such behaviours, with husbands and sometimes mothers-in-law taking control of women's jewellery for their own use. South Asian women in Britain described how their long-term finances were jeopardised, with money (set aside for essential household expenses) being used to build properties 'back home' instead. This chimes with research by Singh (2022) into the experience of Anglo-Celtic and Indian women in Australia, which also contained examples of husbands demanding dowry, as well as sending all their earnings, and some of their wives' earnings, to their parents (see also Singh, this volume). In addition, Anitha's (2019) study of South Asian women in transnational marriages in the UK and India found examples of control over bank accounts, usually in the name of the male head of the household (often the father-in-law). Indeed, Singh (2020) suggests that although economic abuse takes different pathways – intimate partner or family violence – it will always instil fear, intimidation and degradation, such that women lose their sense of self. Intimate partner violence is characterised by a breach of trust in jointness and partnership, whilst the control of family money becomes abusive when the money is not used for the wellbeing of all members, and when it becomes dangerous to challenge.

Control of economic resources after separation

Another key feature of economic abuse is that it can occur after the victim-survivor has left the abuser, as it does not require physical proximity (Stark, 2007). Post-separation abuse thus extends the research emphasis beyond the immediate household. Economic abuse may continue, escalate or even start after separation (Sharp, 2008; Kelly et al., 2014; Howard and Skipp, 2015, in the UK; and Branigan, 2005; Camilleri et al., 2015; Smallwood, 2015, in Australia). Whilst the UK survey by Sharp-Jeffs (2015b) referenced above

found that one in five adults experienced economic abuse (n = 730), interestingly, a larger group reported financial abuse post-separation (n = 913):
one in four women (25 per cent, n = 513) and one in five men (21 per cent, n
= 400). This might be explained by the fact that finances are often contested
when relationships end. Hence the concept of 'space for action' (discussed
earlier) is especially useful for post-separation circumstances in highlighting
that, whilst victim-survivors may have more freedom on some measures, on
others their 'space for action' can be curtailed (Kelly et al., 2014; Sharp-Jeffs
et al., 2018), with perpetrators adopting new tactics made possible due to the
post-separation context. For example, in addition to continuing tactics (such as
damaging/stealing property, spending money from the joint account, running
up bills in their ex-partner's name and/or interfering with employment), the
abuser may prolong divorce proceedings, continuously take their ex-partner
to court (causing financial costs), lie about assets in financial settlements and
refuse to give spousal/child support or maintenance (Sharp-Jeffs, 2015b; see
also Kelly et al., 2014).

Research into economic abuse has shown how joint financial products such
as bank accounts and mortgages can facilitate ongoing control by an abuser.
One UK survey cited above found that three-quarters of adults who reported
economic abuse said that this had started when they opened a joint bank
account (Sharp-Jeffs, 2015b). In countries in which a joint bank account held
in the names of both partners is relatively common, the 'jointness' implied in
such accounts is based on trust (e.g. that joint ownership means equal access).
However, wider research into within-household resources has indicated that
a joint bank account does not guarantee equal access or equal power (e.g. for
qualitative research involving low-/moderate-income couples in the UK, see
Bennett and Sung, 2013). Ongoing control can be exercised by an ex-partner
as both parties must consent to close a joint account.

Economic exploitation can also appear within wider research into
within-household resources – for example, cases in which women's attempts to
budget were sabotaged by their partner borrowing beyond the family's means
(e.g. Goode, 2010). Economic abuse research has also found victim-survivors
being forced to obtain loans or items in their own name which were then used
solely by the perpetrator, described as 'coerced debt' (Sharp, 2008; Littwin,
2012).

Having explored the constructs used in research into economic abuse, and
considered some of the links with wider research into within-household
resources, we conclude this chapter with some suggested directions for further
research.

Future directions for research

The discussion above suggests three broad directions for future research into economic abuse in the context of wider research into within-household resources: strengthening the links with such research; filling the gaps identified in existing research on economic abuse; and exploring how to build an evidence base that can inform policy and practice.

Given the difficulties of identifying and disclosing economic abuse, research should be attentive to the impact of particular questions, measures and methods. Researchers investigating the management and distribution of within-household resources may interview each partner individually, and sometimes also the couple jointly (e.g. Griffiths et al., 2020); separate interviews may or may not describe situations closer to actual practice than joint ones do (Pahl, 1989). Such research may recruit from population samples and, whilst people who are currently experiencing or perpetrating abuse may be less likely to participate in research, some may do so (around one in ten adults in a recent UK survey were at the time experiencing ongoing economic abuse: Butt, 2020). Thus, such sampling should be alert to the possibility of economic abuse, even if it is not named. Research into economic abuse is more likely to recruit participants through specialist domestic abuse organisations to obtain a sample and to ensure that individuals have access to support services, reducing potential risks of participation (Women's Aid, 2020). When general population groups are asked about abusive experiences, clear guidance should be provided; for example, participants should be asked if it is safe for them to take information about available support and should not be expected to participate in the presence of someone else or when they could be interrupted/overheard (Women's Aid, 2020). These safeguards have important implications for research methods and funding.

Potential links between the issues explored within wider research into within-household resources and research into economic abuse could be further investigated and strengthened. As noted by Bennett (2013), control of money can operate independently of allocation systems, and so different types of money management may not automatically read across to control or abuse; however, research could explore the implications of different types of money management in the light of research into economic abuse. It could also explore nuances in the concept of control ('of' resources) and how this is experienced and perceived, and whether such control takes place within the context of coercive and controlling behaviour 'over' another person (see the title of this chapter).

Although research into economic abuse has developed in recent years, gaps remain. Further research could develop survey questions and indicators to measure its prevalence more accurately. More evidence from the global south could illuminate experiences of economic abuse within different social and cultural contexts, enriching our thinking about economic abuse as a concept, for example by testing the relevance of the current constructs.

Furthermore, the experiences of different groups of victim-survivors and the impact of various characteristics (e.g. age, race, disability, sexuality and gender), and their interrelationships, need further consideration. Studies concerning the Nordic paradox, discussed above, highlight the need for further research into the interaction between gender equality on the one hand and economic inequality and abuse on the other. States which have ratified the 2011 Istanbul Convention on action against violence against women and domestic violence must collect disaggregated data on all forms of violence, including economic abuse (Council of Europe, 2011). Criminal and civil legislation around domestic abuse is recognised as requiring better coordination, so it would be helpful to have additional research into aspects of economic control relating to financial proceedings and financial services policy, such as coerced debt (Sharp-Jeffs, 2022).

Economic abuse results from coercion and, as we have explored, can lead women in particular to live in fear – even after leaving a household. Consequently, growing the evidence base and evolving our understanding of related concepts will help to make clear what behaviour is unacceptable and ensure that abusers are held accountable.

Note

1.   In this chapter, this is abbreviated to 'wider research into within-household resources'.

References

Adams, A.E. and Beeble, M.L. (2019) 'Intimate partner violence and psychological well-being: Examining the effect of economic abuse on women's quality of life', *Psychology of Violence*, 9(5), pp. 517–525.

Adams, A.E., Sullivan, C., Bybee, D. and Greeson, M. (2008) 'Development of the scale of economic abuse', *Violence against Women*, 14(5), pp. 563–587.

Anderson, M.A., Gillig, P.M., Sitaker, M., McCloskey, K., Malloy, K. and Grigsby, N. (2003) '"Why doesn't she just leave?" A descriptive study of victim reported impediments to her safety', *Journal of Family Violence*, 18(3), pp. 151–155.

Anitha, S. (2019) 'Understanding economic abuse through an intersectional lens: Financial abuse, control, and exploitation of women's productive and reproductive labor', *Violence against Women*, 25(15), pp. 1854–1877.

Annan, J., Donald, A., Goldstein, M., Martinez, P.G. and Koolwal, G. (2021) 'Taking power: Women's empowerment and household well-being in sub-Saharan Africa', *World Development*, 140, 105292.

Bennett, F. (2013) 'Researching within-household distribution: Overview, developments, debates and methodological challenges', *Journal of Marriage and the Family*, 75(3), pp. 582–597.

Bennett, F. and Sung, S. (2013) 'Dimensions of financial autonomy in low-/moderate-income couples from a gender perspective and implications for welfare reform', *Journal of Social Policy*, 42(4), pp. 701–719.

Bisdee, D., Daly, T. and Price, D. (2013) 'Behind closed doors: Older couples and the gendered management of household money', *Social Policy and Society*, 12(1), pp. 163–174.

Branigan, E. (2005) *His Money or Our Money? Financial Abuse of Women in Intimate Partner Relationships*. Coburg: Coburg Brunswick Community Legal and Financial Counselling Centre.

Butt, E. (2020) *Know Economic Abuse*. London: Cooperative Bank/Refuge.

Cameron, P. (2014) *Relationship Problems and Money: Women Talk about Financial Abuse*. West Melbourne: WIRE Women's Information.

Camilleri, O., Corrie, T. and Moore, S. (2015) *Restoring Financial Safety: Legal Responses to Economic Abuse*. Melbourne: Good Shepherd and Wyndham Legal Service.

Chowbey, P. (2017) 'Women's narratives of economic abuse and financial strategies in Britain and South Asia', *Psychology of Violence*, 7(3), pp. 459–468.

Corrie, T. and McGuire, M. (2013) *Economic Abuse: Searching for Solutions*. A Spotlight on Economic Abuse Research Report. North Collingwood, Australia: Good Shepherd Youth & Family Service.

Council of Europe (2011) *Explanatory Report to the Council of Europe Convention on Preventing and Combating Violence against Women and Domestic Violence*. Available at: www.coe.int/en/web/istanbul-convention/basic-texts (accessed 3 August 2022).

Dudley, R.G. (2017) 'Domestic abuse and women with "No Recourse to Public Funds": The state's role in shaping and reinforcing coercive control', *Families, Relationships and Societies*, 6(2), pp. 201–217.

Dutton, M.A. and Goodman, L.A. (2005) 'Coercion in intimate partner violence: Toward a new conceptualization', *Sex Roles: A Journal of Research*, 52(11–12), pp. 743–756.

Goode, J. (2010) 'The role of gender dynamics in decisions on credit and debt in low income families', *Critical Social Policy*, 30(1), pp. 99–119.

Goode, J., Callender, J. and Lister, R. (1999) 'Household income distribution in a context of changing patterns of work and welfare', *Practice*, 11(1), pp. 15–22.

Gracia, E. and Merlo, J. (2016) 'Intimate partner violence against women and the Nordic paradox', *Social Science and Medicine*, 157, pp. 27–30.

Gracia, E., Martin-Fernandez, M., Lila, M., Merlo, J. and Ivert, A.-M. (2019) 'Prevalence of intimate partner violence against women in Sweden and Spain: A psychometric study of the "Nordic paradox"', *PLOS ONE*, 14(5), e0217015.

Griffiths, R. (2017) 'No love on the dole: The influence of the UK means-tested welfare system on partnering and family structure', *Journal of Social Policy*, 46(3), pp. 543–561.

Griffiths, R., Wood, M., Bennett, F. and Millar, J. (2020) *Uncharted Territory: Universal Credit, Couples and Money*. Bath: Institute for Policy Research, University of Bath.

Heath, R. (2014) 'Women's access to labor market opportunities, control of household resources, and domestic violence: Evidence from Bangladesh', *World Development*, 57, pp. 32–46.

Heise, L.L. (1998) 'Violence against women: An integrated, ecological framework', *Violence against Women*, 4(3), pp. 262–290.

Hester, M. (2010) 'Gender and sexuality', in C. Itzin, A. Taket and S. Barter-Godfey (eds), *Domestic and Sexual Violence and Abuse: Tackling the Health Effects of Abuse and Violence*. London: Routledge, pp. 99–113.

Home Office (2015) *Controlling or Coercive Behaviour in an Intimate or Family Relationship: Statutory Guidance Framework*. London: Home Office. Available at: https:// assets .publishing .service .gov .uk/ government/ uploads/ system/ uploads/ attachment _data/ file/ 482528/ Controlling _or _coercive _behaviour _ - _statutory _guidance.pdf (accessed 3 August 2022).

Home Office (2021) *Review of the Controlling or Coercive Behaviour Offence*. London: Home Office. Available at: www .gov .uk/ government/ publications/ review -of -the -controlling-or-coercive-behaviour-offence (accessed 3 August 2022).

Howard, M. and Skipp, A. (2015) *Unequal, Trapped and Controlled: Women's Experience of Financial Abuse and Potential Implications for Universal Credit*. London: Women's Aid/Trades Union Congress.

Humbert, A.L., Strid, S., Hearn, J. and Balkmar, J. (2019) 'Undoing the "Nordic paradox": Factors affecting rates of disclosed violence against women across the EU', *PLOS ONE*, 16(5), e0249693.

Johnson, M.P. (2006) 'Conflict and control: Gender symmetry and asymmetry in domestic violence', *Violence against Women*, 12(11), pp. 1003–1018.

Kabeer, N. (2017) 'Economic pathways to women's empowerment and active citizenship: What does the evidence from Bangladesh tell us?', *Journal of Development Studies*, 53(5), pp. 649–663.

Kelly, L. (2011) 'Standing the test of time? Reflections on the concept of the continuum of sexual violence', in J. Brown and S. Walklate (eds), *Handbook on Sexual Violence*. New York: Taylor and Francis, pp. xvii–xxvi.

Kelly, L. and Westmarland, N. (2014) 'Time for a rethink: Why the current government definition of domestic violence is a problem', *Trouble and Strife*. Available at: www .troubleandstrife .org/ 2014/ 04/ time -for -a -rethink -why -the -current -government -definition-of-domestic-violence-is-a-problem/ (accessed 3 August 2022).

Kelly, L., Sharp, N. and Klein, R. (2014) *Finding the Costs of Freedom: How Women and Children Rebuild Their Lives after Domestic Violence*. London: Solace Women's Aid and Child and Woman Abuse Studies Unit.

Littwin, A. (2012) 'Coerced debt: The role of consumer credit in domestic violence', *California Law Review*, 100(4), pp. 951–1026.

Loring, M.T. (1994) *Emotional Abuse*. New York: Lexington Books.

Magić, J. and Kelley, P. (2018) *LGBT+ People's Experiences of Domestic Abuse: A Report on Galop's Domestic Abuse Advocacy Service*. London: Galop.

Myhill, A. (2017) 'Measuring domestic violence: Context is everything', *Journal of Gender-Based Violence*, 1(1), pp. 33–44.

Office for National Statistics (2020) *Domestic Abuse Prevalence and Trends, England and Wales: Year Ending March 2020*. November. Available at: www.ons.gov.uk/peoplepop ulationand community/ crimeandjustice/ articles/ domestic abuseprevalenceandtrendsenglandandwales/yearendingmarch2020 (accessed 3 August 2022).

Pahl, J. (1989) *Money and Marriage*. Basingstoke: Macmillan Education.

Postmus, J.L., Plummer, S., McMahon, S., Shaanta Murshid, N. and Sung Kim, M. (2012) 'Understanding economic abuse in the lives of survivors', *Journal of Interpersonal Violence*, 27(3), pp. 411–430.

Postmus, J.L., Plummer, S.-B., and Stylianou, A.M. (2016) 'Measuring economic abuse in the lives of survivors: Revising the scale of economic abuse', *Violence against Women*, 22(6), pp. 692–703.

Postmus, J., Hoge, G., Breckenridge, J., Sharp-Jeffs, N. and Chung, D. (2020) 'Economic abuse as an invisible form of domestic violence: A multi-country review', *Trauma, Violence & Abuse*, 21(2), pp. 261–83.

Royal, K. (2022) *Economic Abuse: A Global Perspective*. London: Surviving Economic Abuse.

Sharp, N. (2008) '*What's Yours Is Mine': The Different Forms of Economic Abuse and Its Impact on Women and Children Experiencing Domestic Violence*. London: Refuge.

Sharp-Jeffs, N. (2015a) *A Review of Research and Policy on Financial Abuse within Intimate Partner Relationships*. London: Child and Woman Abuse Studies Unit, London Metropolitan University.

Sharp-Jeffs, N. (2015b) *Money Matters: Research into the Extent and Nature of Financial Abuse within Intimate Relationships in the UK*. London: Co-operative Bank/Refuge.

Sharp-Jeffs, N. (2021) 'Understanding the economics of abuse: An assessment of the economic abuse definition within the Domestic Abuse Bill', *Journal of Gender-Based Violence*, 5(1), pp. 163–173.

Sharp-Jeffs, N. (2022) *Understanding and Responding to Economic Abuse: Feminist Developments in Violence and Abuse*. Bingley: Emerald Publishing.

Sharp-Jeffs, N., Kelly, L. and Klein, R. (2018) 'Long journeys toward freedom: The relationship between coercive control and space for action – measurement and emerging evidence', *Violence against Women*, 24(2), pp. 163–185.

Singh, S. (2020) 'Economic abuse and family violence across cultures: Gendering money and assets through coercive control', in M. McMahon and P. McGorrery (eds), *Criminalizing Coercive Control: Family Violence and the Criminal Law*. Singapore: Springer, pp. 51–72.

Singh, S. (2022) *Domestic Economic Abuse: The Violence of Money*. New York: Routledge Focus.

Smallwood, E. (2015) *Stepping Stones: Legal Barriers to Economic Equality after Family Violence*. Victoria: Women's Legal Service.

Stark, E. (2007) *Coercive Control: How Men Entrap Women in Personal Life*. Oxford: Oxford University Press.

Thiara, R. and Gill, A. (2010) *Violence against Women in South Asian Communities: Issues for Policy and Practice*. London: Jessica Kingsley.

Tolmie, J.R. (2018) 'Coercive control: To criminalize or not to criminalize?', *Criminology & Criminal Justice*, 18(1), pp. 50–66.

VonDeLinde, K.C. and Sussman, E. (2017) 'Economic coercion and survivor-centered economic advocacy', in Center for Survivor Agency and Justice (ed.), *Guidebook on Consumer and Economic Civil Legal Advocacy for Survivors: A Comprehensive and Survivor-Centered Guide for Domestic Violence Attorneys and Legal Advocates*. Washington, DC: Center for Survivor Agency and Justice, pp. 1–17.

Warburton Brown, C. (2011) *Exploring BME Maternal Poverty: The Financial Lives of Ethnic Minority Mothers in Tyne and Wear*. Oxford: Oxfam GB.

Wemrell, M., Stjernlof, S., Lila, M., Gracia, E. and Ivert, A.-M. (2021) 'The Nordic paradox: Professionals' discussions about gender equality and intimate partner violence against women in Sweden', *Women and Criminal Justice*, 32(5), pp. 431–453.

Women's Aid (2020) *Research Integrity Framework on Domestic Violence and Abuse*. Available at: www .womensaid .org .uk/ wp -content/ uploads/ 2020/ 11/ Research -Integrity -Framework -RIF -on -Domestic -Violence -and -Abuse -DVA -November -2020.pdf (accessed 11 August 2022).

Women's Aid, Hester, M., Walker, S.-J., and Williamson, E. (2021) *Gendered Experiences of Justice and Domestic Abuse: Evidence for Policy and Practice*. Bristol: University of Bristol and Women's Aid.

Yount, K.M., Cheong, Y.F., Miedema, S. and Naved, R.T. (2021) 'Development and validation of the economic coercion scale 36 (ECS-36) in rural Bangladesh', *Journal of Interpersonal Violence*, 37(13–14), pp. NP10726–NP10757.

9. Intra-household resources in complex migrant households

Supriya Singh

A gap in the study of money: Complex migrant households

The study of money within the household was expanded and deepened through the work of Jan Pahl in the United Kingdom and Viviana Zelizer in the United States (Pahl, 1989; Zelizer, 1994). They went beyond thinking of the household as a 'black box' on the one hand and money as an undifferentiated unit of value and means of exchange on the other. Their work led to better understanding of money management and control; money, family and relationships; and power and decision-making in relation to intra-household resources.

However, much of the literature on money management and control focuses on the nuclear household in the west. Studies of intra-household resources have not often focused on multigenerational complex households, which are more prevalent in the global south.

In addition, the focus on the nuclear family household has also meant that the 'household' has often not been distinguished from the 'family'. Especially in the global south, the family can extend across different households. When money is shared in the family, the flow of money between households across life stages needs to be taken into account when studying intra-household resources in the global south in particular.

The literature on family also does not focus on money in migrant households. Migration studies as a discipline has also concentrated on money in recipient rather than migrant households. These are important gaps, as the intergenerational contract of care which shapes the use and distribution of resources within the family applies across all household types, within and across national boundaries.

Research on the management and distribution of resources within the household has tended not to focus on complex households

The nuclear family household in developed countries has been central in research on how money is handled within households. However, typologies of money management and control in nuclear family households in developed countries do not adequately explain how money operates across genders and generations in more complex households. This has been one factor leading in turn to sparse research on money within the household in the global south, as many households are multigenerational and complex (Moore and Hlabana, this volume). The United Nations notes that most older people in Africa, Asia and Latin America and the Caribbean live in extended family households, 'which may include relatives such as grandchildren, nieces and nephews' (United Nations, 2020: 13).

A study of money in the three-generational patrilineal joint family household in India shows that in extended family households money must be examined both within and across generations. Overall control and management of money at the parental level can be complemented by subsidiary management and control by the married children and their spouses. Money management and control are often shared by men across generations – by father and son, or by brothers – without women's involvement (Singh and Bhandari, 2012).

Money management patterns can also differ from those commonly identified in the west. Women in India in this study spoke of their 'irregular dole'; they often had to ask for money and justify the need to receive it from their husbands (Singh and Bhandari, 2012). In Kenya and Papua New Guinea, independent control and management are more common than joint control. Independent control, however, means men and women in the family managing and controlling separate heaps of money – these amounts may be unequal, leading to unequal power and agency for women (Macintyre, 2011; Singh and Nadarajah, 2011; Johnson, 2017).

The 'household' and 'family' are conflated in the nuclear family

The dominance of the nuclear family household in the west has meant that there is often no clear distinction between the 'household' and the 'family'.

This is not a problem for the study of intra-household resources when money flows are mainly within the nuclear family household. Among Anglo-Celtics in Australia[1] – the dominant community, accounting for 51.1 per cent of the population in 2021 (Australian Bureau of Statistics, 2022) – the couple is the standard domestic financial unit. Husband and wife, singly or together, manage and control money in the household/family. Money frequently flows in only one direction, from parents to dependent children (Singh, 1997). In the global south, however, money is seen as belonging to the family, variously defined. Money is morally expected to routinely flow two ways – from parents and grandparents to children and grandchildren, as well as from them to parents and grandparents (Singh, 2013).

The boundary of the family unit within which money is shared can also be wider than the nuclear family. It can include uncles and aunts, nephews and nieces, siblings and cousins and/or in-laws, or fluid kinship clusters and lineages, as with the Māori, indigenous Australians and the Dinka of South Sudan (Taiapa, 1994; Senior et al., 2002; Akuei, 2005). Sharing money across generations and households is accompanied by a morality of money, about being good parents or children and moral individuals. In India, good parents should help their children with money in a timely fashion, and children have a responsibility to care for parents and elders. This is also enshrined in religion and affirmed through court judgments and government sanctions (Ministry of Law and Justice, 2007). Not helping a wide network of kin makes a Dinka man feel that he is not a moral person (Akuei, 2005). Among the Māori, the moral obligation to gift money for a funeral meeting of the *whanau*, a descent group, takes priority over everyday household expenses (Taiapa, 1994).

The morality of money, and two-way sharing of money across generations, households and national borders in the transnational family, influences resources coming in and going out of migrant households. This has led to international remittances being one of the largest and most resilient international flows of funds. In 2022, formal international remittances to low- and middle-income countries were estimated to reach US$630 billion (Ratha et al., 2022). Informal remittances may add another estimated 45 per cent to remittances to developing countries (as argued by Buencamino and Gorbunov, 2002). Remittances are an important element of the gross domestic product in many low- and middle-income countries, and a major part of the budget in low-income households, helping to pay for food, education, health services, housing and emergencies (Hussain, 2014; Ratha, 2014).

The figures for remittances reflect money sent by migrants to their families in the source countries (from which they migrated). But money is also sent from middle- and high-income parents as reverse remittances to their migrant children, to help with the costs of education, housing and operating businesses in the country of destination (Mazzucato, 2011; Singh and Gatina, 2015).

Migration literature has tended to ignore money management and control in migrant households sending money home. As noted, the overarching focus in migration literature has instead been on the scale of international remittances. There is literature on the value of remittances for development (Iskander, 2010). Migration also changes the ways in which money is managed, controlled, used, owned and inherited in relation to gender in both source and destination countries (George, 2005; Rahman, 2008). However, migration literature has seldom examined how couples do or do not negotiate the sending of remittances.

Remittances can be a burden on the migrant household in countries where settlement (rather than return home after a temporary stay) is possible (Akuei, 2005). But there is little detail about how this works. This gap in migration research arises partly because attention has often been focused on the lone domestic or international migrant sending money back to their family, and on the influence of the migrant on the use of money in the recipient household (Gamburd, 1998; Rahman, 2008; Kurian et al., 2022). But when international migrants can settle in destination countries, decisions can be complicated as there are family members in both the destination and source countries.

Remittances are a currency of care. This is particularly relevant for 'taking care of' and 'caring about' the family left behind, as it does not depend on the face-to-face contact involved in 'care giving' and 'care receiving' (Fisher and Tronto, 1990). It feels difficult to get beyond this to ask: How are settlement needs balanced against the needs of the family in the source country? Can remittances be a medium of economic abuse? How often are remittances kept secret from the partners, or used to deny them money, appropriate their assets and/or sequester money in another jurisdiction (see Singh and Sidhu, 2022; Howard and Sharp-Jeffs, this volume)?

Migrant households, like others, change across life-course stages. There is some recent research on parents who migrate to join their already migrated children (termed the 'zero generation') in order to give and receive care. However, changes or tensions in terms of how money is handled are not usually at the centre. This literature mainly examines parent-migrants who are financially dependent on their migrant children in both source and destination countries. The research has focused on challenges for parents in adjusting to a foreign country and the loneliness and tensions of intergenerational living (Nedelcu and Wyss, 2020).

Indian parent-migrants in Australia

This case study of middle- and high-income Hindu and Sikh Indian parents who migrate to join their children in Australia helps to fill gaps in the literature on money in complex migrant households. It highlights key issues relevant to the study of intra-household resources by focusing on parent-migrants' experience of changes in money management and control in the newly formed extended households. Most Indian parent-migrants paid for their children – both sons and daughters – to be educated in Australia. They then chose to migrate to be with their children and grandchildren when most or all of their children had settled in Australia. After migration, most Indian parent-migrants become economically dependent on their children for housing and day-to-day expenses. This is because of migration-related expenses, migration policy, difficulties in finding paid work and parents' substantial gifts of money, mainly to their sons with whom they usually live. Some parents accept economic dependence as an anticipated shift in the extended family's development; for others, this is experienced as a troubling change.

The study (carried out from 2016 to 2019) focuses on 17 Indian parents (including one couple) who had migrated or were actively considering migration ('parent-migrants'). These parent-migrants' choice of living in an 'upside-down joint family household' (see below), and their management and control of money, are compared with those of eight parents who regularly visit their children in Australia but do not intend to migrate because of family and business obligations in India, and with 14 older Indian parents (including one couple) who migrated when they were younger and have aged in Australia.

The 39 participants were drawn from the researchers' networks. They had participated in a wider project on 'Money, Gender, and Family Violence' (2016–2017) [2] and a subsequent project on 'Money, Gender and Ageing' (2018–2019).[3] These examined how family violence was shaped by money, gender and life stage among Indian and Anglo-Celtic communities in Australia.

The participants were studied through conversation circles and open-ended interviews in English, Hindi and Punjabi, which were recorded with permission. The author carried these out singly or with colleagues and translated when necessary. The researchers used a grounded theory approach that moves predominantly from data to theory. The data were thematically coded and analysed using NVivo, a computer programme for analysing qualitative data.

The 'upside-down joint family household'

As noted above, Indian parent-migrants migrate to Australia when all or most of their children already live there,[4] primarily because they want to be with their children and grandchildren in a joint family (extended family), in order to give and receive hands-on care.

The joint family household was a lived experience in India for all 39 older Indians at some point. This is a traditional choice. In India, 81.7 per cent of people over 60 years old continue to live with their children and other relatives in multigenerational joint family households. The older persons predominantly (90.6 per cent) live in a house they own themselves or jointly with their spouse (National Statistical Office, 2021). The house is usually owned by the father, as more men (65 per cent) than women (37 per cent) aged 15–49 own a house (International Institute for Population Sciences and ICF, 2017).

There is a diversity of household and family types in India, but the patrilineal three- or four-generation joint family of grandparents/parents, married son(s) and their child/ren is the cultural norm (Uberoi, 2006). The joint family starts off with parents, married son(s) and their children in one household. However, as the joint family grows, and married son(s) form their own households, the family disperses across multiple households as part of its development process. The married son's separate household in turn becomes a joint family household when his son gets married (Shah, 2005).

Parent-migration to Australia, however, turns the joint family upside-down, as the parents join their children's (mainly son's) household, rather than the married son living with them in a house usually owned by the father. Sons are traditionally charged with the duty of care towards their parents; so parents' preference is to stay with the son if they have one. In this study in Australia, 13 of the 17 parent-migrants lived with their children, one lived in a house owned by the children and another planned to live in a house next to their son and daughter-in-law's home (with these parents contributing substantially to the home, although it would be in the son's name). The exception was a couple among the parent-migrants who jointly owned the house and business with their son and daughter-in-law. This was also the only case in which the parents were business migrants, rather than being sponsored by their children for parent visas.

In India, elderly coresidence is being reinterpreted and renegotiated to better meet mutual needs. Parents and children may establish nuclear households close to each other to form a 'network family' (Cheung, 2019; Kaur, 2022), to be 'embedded' or 'enwebbed' in order to be able to provide intergenerational care (Croll, 2006). A sole parent or parents may also join a child's household if all of the sons have separated or migrated away. But the upside-down joint family household is not usual.

In this Australian study, most parent-migrants lived in upside-down joint family households. The economic dependence of parent-migrants is the crucial factor behind this choice. The 14 older Indians who aged in Australia and were financially independent lived in their own homes, preferably 'enwebbed' households, in other words close to their children.

Migration results in economic dependence for most Indian parent-migrants

Migration leaves most Indian parent-migrants economically dependent on their children within the upside-down joint family household. This is partly due to migration-related expenses: the Permanent Residence (PR) visa for two parents can cost 110,000–128,000 Australian dollars. This can be the price of a modest house in regional cities and urban villages in India.

Migration leads to the selling of property in India to pay for visa expenses and travel costs and to satisfy a desire to migrate with money in hand. Parent-migrants who had already moved to Australia had sold most of or all their property in India. They gave all or most of their money to their son(s), to help with the mortgage and/or business. Some also put money into their children's account(s).

Parents' gifting of money to children (mainly sons) is part of the morality of money in India. These parents feel a moral imperative to help their children in a timely fashion. As Joginder,[5] in the 65- to 70-year-old band, said, 'We have lived our lives. Whatever we have is for the children. We can't take it with us.' Even visiting parents do not want to come empty-handed.

The PR visa gives parent-migrants immediate access to Medicare, the government health service. However, parent-migrants are not eligible for social welfare benefits for the first ten years.

As most parents have given all or most of their money to their children, the children manage and control money in the (now multigenerational) household for everyday expenses. They regularly deposit money into their parents' accounts or respond otherwise to parents' needs. One refrain in the study is parent-migrants saying 'the children are very good to us'.

Chetan, a widower in his early 70s, who still had a small flat and a pension in India, gave enough money to his son to buy a house. He said, 'We have a joint account between me, my son and daughter-in-law … Sometimes, I also withdraw money from my account in India.'

This shift of money management and control from parents to children is part of the joint family's development process. Eleven of the 17 parent-migrants in the study accepted this. Inder, in the 71- to 75-year-old band, came with his wife on a PR visa to Australia in 2015 to live with their only unmarried son. He sold all of his urban property in India. He said, 'We fulfilled our duty to look after and educate the children … Now my son looks after everything and is responsible for everything. We have no problems.'

Younger parent-migrants who were employed and/or ran their family businesses in India realised that getting paid work or starting a business in their 60s in a new country would be difficult. The probability of facing financial dependence in Australia after leaving a full and prosperous life in India was making at least two reconsider their decision to migrate. Chandana, in the 60- to 65-year-old age band, and her husband had applied for PR. She said that her husband was having second thoughts. He said, 'In India after so much difficulty I got property. How can I sell it immediately? Then we will be "empty".' Gita, also in the 60- to 65-year-old age band, was worried that she might lose her independence. Although Gita had lived happily in her husband's joint family for 15 years in India, she worried whether it would work with her son. She wondered, even if they sold all of their three or four properties in India, 'Will we have the finances to stay [live] separately?'

Economic dependence reduces parent-migrants' options for choosing other connected ways of living with their children. Indeed, if relationships begin to falter, this lack of choice can expose them to elder abuse. Only three of the 17 parent-migrants had enough money to both help their children financially and keep some to preserve their own independence and sense of place. This included the couple with the joint house. The other who had applied for PR was the one who planned to buy a house near their son. Interestingly, in both cases, the daughter-in-law was not Indian.

Living close to but not with the children was the preferred option for older Indian migrants who had aged in Australia, even if they had lived in joint families in India and Australia.

Colliding moralities of money

Migration adds another set of challenges to parent-migrants' morality of money in the family. When Indian parent-migrants give money to their son (most often) to pay the house deposit or contribute to the mortgage, they think of this money and property as belonging to the family, including parents, children and grandchildren. They do not anticipate the marital home being divided at separation or divorce.

India, other than Goa, is governed by the 'separation of property regime'. At separation or divorce a woman has a legal right to maintenance. She also has a right to property in her name and any money and goods she brought to the marriage. But she is not legally entitled to property acquired during the marriage if it is not in her name, even if she has contributed financially towards it (Singh, 2013).

In Australia, however, money and property are owned by the couple, most often through joint home ownership and joint bank accounts. Australia has the 'community of property regime'. The default at separation or divorce is that marital property is divided equally between the couple, depending on multiple factors. The wife's/partner's financial and non-financial contributions are recognised. Oral family agreements may not be sufficient (Australian Law Reform Commission, 2017) to prove that the parents' financial contribution was given in exchange for care in the family property.

In this study, it was unusual for Indian parents to document money transactions between themselves and their children. As described, some parent-migrants had deposited money in the son's account. As noted above, one parent-migrant is planning to substantially contribute to a house next to the son while putting it in the son's name. Another parent-migrant who migrated in 2001 – and lived with her daughter, as she had no son – even had her social welfare payments go into a joint account shared with her daughter.

Jasleen, aged 80, living in Australia since the 1980s, lent money to her son and daughter-in-law to build a house; but when they were getting divorced, she had to dispute her daughter-in-law's claim that this loan was part of the couple's marital property. The resulting physical, emotional and relational stress led Jasleen to warn three parents who were thinking of giving money to their children 'to record everything in writing. Let it be wholly transparent, for otherwise, in a divorce, you will get involved.'

New directions for analysis

The dominant narrative in research about intra-household resources developed around the management and control of money by a married couple in a western nuclear family household. It has four in-built assumptions. First, money is managed and controlled by the couple, separately, jointly and/or independently. Second, money flows one way, from parents to dependent children within the household. Third, the boundaries of the nuclear family and the household are the same. And fourth, the nuclear family household is within the nation-state. Studying complex migrant households questions all four of these assumptions.

First, in complex migrant households, it is important to study money management and control not only for one couple but for all constituent couples in the multigenerational household. It is also important to investigate the different contributions of these couples to managing and controlling money for the household. Gender as well as generation must be considered across different life stages.

This chapter analysed a case study of changes in middle- and high-income Indian parent-migrants' control and management of money after they joined their children in Australia. These Hindu and Sikh parent-migrants had all lived in patrilineal joint families at some point in their lives in India. In Australia, they joined their son's family, for it is the son who is traditionally held responsible for the care of parents. This changed their son's nuclear family household to an upside-down joint family household in Australia.

Money flows and household composition changed across life stages for the children as well as for the parent-migrants. In the beginning, money flowed across borders from parents to children for education and settlement in Australia. When the children started earning, money went to the parents to repay loans and for gifts. After the parents migrated, nearly all became economically dependent on their children even for everyday expenses. Most parent-migrants were comfortable with this change. They saw it as part of ageing and life-stage changes in the extended family household. Money belonged to the family rather than to the individual or the couple. However, a few parents who were economically active in India were uncomfortable about losing control and becoming dependent as they aged in a new country.

If the original study on which this chapter is based had been planned with intra-household resources rather than family violence at the centre, it would have included the perspectives of the son (usually) and daughter-in-law as well as those of the parent-migrants. Money management and control would be studied for each couple. We would want to know how each couple dealt with the money they earned/owned. Who controlled and managed the household finances?

Taking a life-course perspective, an important question would be: How had the management and control of money changed for each couple when parent-migrants joined them in their now complex migrant household? The study would need to deal with gender issues more broadly, not only in relation to the parents' preference to stay with the son. It would have asked: How differently did the son and daughter-in-law, the mother and the father experience the changes? This is a complex question, for the values associated with financial resilience and economic dependence can differ across gender, cultures and generations. It would be important to have individual as well as joint interviews with each member of the constituent couples in the household, in order to gauge differences in perspectives.

Second, this chapter also shows the centrality of the two-way flow of money, from parents to children and from children to parents. This morality of money defines good parents, filial children and moral persons. Parents in this study gave all or most of their money to their children when they migrated, with more money going to the son. They argued that this was the time when their child(ren) needed the money, and that the money would go to them in any case. Most parents were comfortable in their expectation that the children would look after them in turn in a new country. The younger parents were conflicted, however, for they wondered whether they would be comfortable receiving money from their children. Older Indians who had aged in Australia had worked out ways of keeping to the traditional morality by gifting money to their children, as well as upholding Australian values by retaining their financial resilience.

The study of migrant households, particularly from the global south, needs to detail the resources that flow in and out of the household. This is a more complex exercise than charting the different sources of income of a couple, for there could be substantial resources that flow from the parents who may be in households across state borders. Similarly, it is crucial to detail the money that is spent on household expenses and the money that flows out of the household for parents who may or may not be within national borders.

In addition, complex migrant households upend the third and fourth assumptions of the traditional narrative around intra-household resources. This chapter details money flows between households in the family and across national borders. The family rather than the household is the boundary. These money flows are substantial and can comprise a large percentage of the household budget, as well as contributing to the building of assets and wealth. This is why international remittances to low- and middle-income countries are one of the largest international flows of money. The amount and direction of these flows of money change across life stages as migrant households form, disperse and re-form.

The study of migrant households needs to investigate these inflows and outflows of resources across generations and borders, for they can be seen as defining family values. This means that in migrant households interhousehold flows have to be investigated to gauge interhousehold resources. The questions that need to be asked are: Does each partner have similar information about these inflows and outflows? How does each partner interpret these family values, as against the settlement needs of the couple and children in the country of destination? What does this say about earlier investigations regarding the management and control of money within the household? How have these flows of resources changed across life stages, especially when the need for care increases? How have the moralities of money changed for the children and parents? Has the migration of parents changed not only the form of the household but also the nature of relationships within the family?

Qualitative research involving open-ended interviews, participant observation and thick description is essential to understand the generational and cultural shifts related to money flows in migrant households. It will also help to discover what other questions need to be asked. Longitudinal quantitative research, such as the National Family Health Survey in India and the Household, Income and Labour Dynamics in Australia survey, has been useful to discover how the flow, management and control of intra-household resources have changed over the years across gender, age and socio-economic divides. This macro picture provides an important context to the fine-grained qualitative research and could be extended.

Questioning the assumptions of the dominant narrative around intra-household resources goes beyond rethinking how we collect and analyse data. It involves reworking our concepts of a 'household' and a 'family', for these assumptions inform our everyday evaluation of the 'normal' management of intra-household resources (Moore and Hlabana, this volume). They are also built into census data collection and presentation, which in turn inform policy.

Studying diverse households across cultures, we need to be 'attentive to complexity, context and culture' (Smart and Shipman, 2004: 507). This means going beyond 'methodological nationalism', which sees 'the nation-state and its boundaries as a given in social analysis' (Levitt and Schiller, 2004: 1007). It also means questioning the majority social group that may claim 'universal validity' for their institutions (Beck and Beck-Gernsheim, 2010: 401).

This attentiveness to context and culture will become even more important to avoid sweeping generalisations as migrant family households and other forms of complex households increase in the global north (Burchardt and Karagiannaki, this volume).

Notes

1. The ancestry of the Anglo-Celtic group in Australia is predominantly English, Irish and Scottish (Australian Bureau of Statistics, 1995).
2. The other research colleagues in this project were Marg Liddell, RMIT University, and Jasvinder Sidhu, Federation University of Australia.
3. The team was joined by Rachna Bowman of South East Community Links.
4. Having all or most children living in Australia is a requirement for the parent visa which offers permanent residence.
5. The names of the participants are pseudonyms. Ages may be given in bands.

References

Akuei, S.R. (2005). *Remittances as Unforeseen Burdens: The Livelihoods and Social Obligations of Sudanese Refugees*. Geneva: Global Commission on International Migration.

Australian Bureau of Statistics 1995. *1301.0 – Year Book Australia, 1995: Ethnic and Cultural Diversity in Australia*. Canberra: Australian Bureau of Statistics.

Australian Bureau of Statistics 2022. *2021 Australia, Census All persons QuickStats*. Canberra: Australian Bureau of Statistics.

Australian Law Reform Commission 2017. *Elder Abuse: A National Legal Response*. Sydney: Australian Law Reform Commission.

Beck, U., and Beck-Gernsheim, E. (2010). 'Passage to Hope: Marriage, Migration, and the Need for a Cosmopolitan Turn in Family Research'. *Journal of Family Theory & Review*, 2(4), 401–414. https://doi.org/10.1111/j.1756-2589.2010.00069.x

Buencamino, L. and Gorbunov, S. (2002). *Informal Money Transfer Systems: Opportunities and Challenges for Development Finance*. Geneva: United Nations. www.un.org/esa/desa/papers/2002/esa02dp26.pdf (accessed 27 September 2021).

Cheung, P.L.A. (2019). 'Changing Perception of the Rights and Responsibilities in Family Care for Older People in Urban China'. *Journal of Aging & Social Policy*, 31(4), 298–320.

Croll, E.J. (2006). 'The Intergenerational Contract in the Changing Asian Family'. *Oxford Development Studies*, 34(4), 473–491.

Fisher, B. and Tronto, J. (1990). 'Toward a feminist theory of caring'. In: E. K. Abel and M. Nelson (eds) *Circles of Care*. Albany, NY: State University of New York, 35–62.

Gamburd, M.R. (1998). 'Absent Women and Their Extended Families: Sri Lanka's Migrant Housemaids'. In: C. Risseeuw and K. Ganesh (eds) *Negotiation and Social Space: A Gendered Analysis of Changing Kin and Security Networks in South Asia and Sub-Saharan Africa*. Walnut Creek, CA: AltaMira Press, 276–291.

George, S.M. (2005). *When Women Come First: Gender and Class in Transnational Migration*. Berkeley, CA: University of California Press.

Hussain, Z. (2014). 'The Bangladesh Remittance Story Reaffirmed'. *End Poverty in South Asia*. http://blogs.worldbank.org/endpovertyinsouthasia/bangladesh-remittance-story-reaffirmed

International Institute for Population Sciences and ICF 2017. *National Family Health Survey (NFHS-4), 2015–16: India*. Mumbai: International Institute for Population Sciences.

Iskander, N. (2010). *Creative State: Forty Years of Migration and Development Policy in Morocco and Mexico*. Ithaca, NY: ILR Press.

Johnson, S. (2017). 'We Don't Have This Is Mine and This Is His': Managing Money and the Character of Conjugality in Kenya. *Journal of Development Studies*, 53(5), 755–768.

Kaur, R. (20220. 'Gendered Parenting and Returns from Children in Contemporary India: A Study of IIT Students and Their Parents'. *Current Sociology*, 70(4), 578–597.

Kurian, V., Sreddharan, S. and Valenti, F. (2022). 'Calling the Shots: Determinants of Financial Decision-Making and Behavior in Domestic Migrant Households in India'. *Journal of Emerging Market Finance*, 21(3), 317–342.

Levitt, P., and Schiller, N. G. (2004). 'Conceptualizing Simultaneity: A Transnational Social Field Perspective on Society'. *International Migration Review*, 38(3), 1002–1039. http://www3.interscience.wiley.com/cgi-bin/fulltext/119921755/PDFSTART

Macintyre, M. (2011). 'Money Changes Everything: Papua New Guinean Women in the Modern Economy'. In: M. Patterson and M. Macintyre (eds) *Managing Modernity in the Western Pacific*. St Lucia: University of Queensland Press, 90–120.

Mazzucato, V. (2011). 'Reverse Remittances in the Migration–Development Nexus: Two-Way Flows between Ghana and the Netherlands'. *Population, Space and Place*, 17(5), 454–468.

Ministry of Law and Justice 2007. *The Maintenance and Welfare of Parents and Senior Citizens Act, 2007: No 56 of 2007*. New Delhi: Ministry of Law and Justice.

National Statistical Office 2021. *Elderly in India*. New Delhi: National Statistical Office, Ministry of Statistics and Programme Implementation, Government of India.

Nedelcu, M. and Wyss, M. (2020). 'Transnational Grandparenting: An Introduction'. *Global Networks*, 20(2), 292–307.

Pahl, J. (1989). *Money and Marriage*. London: Macmillan.

Rahman, M. (2008). *Gender Dimensions of Remittances: A Study of Indonesian Domestic Workers in East and Southeast Asia*. Bangkok: UNIFEM.

Ratha, D. (2014). *The Hidden Force in Global Economics: Sending Money Home*. Rio De Janeiro: TED Talks. www.ted.com/talks/dilip_ratha_the_hidden_force_in_global _economics _sending _money _home/ transcript ?language = en (accessed 27 April 2023).

Ratha, D., Kim, E.J., Plaza, S., Riordan, E.J., Kebbah, J. and Chandra, V. (2022). *Migration and Development Brief 36: A War in a Pandemic: Implications of the Russian Invasion of Ukraine and the COVID-19 Crisis on Global Governance of Migration and Remittance Flows*. Washington, DC: KNOMAD-World Bank.

Senior, K., Perkins, D. and Bern, J. (2002). *Variation in Material Wellbeing in a Welfare Based Economy*. Wollongong: South East Arnhem Land Collaborative Research Project, University of Wollongong.

Shah, A.M. (2005). 'The Phase of Dispersal in the Indian Family Process'. In: T. Patel (ed.) *The Family in India: Structure and Practice*. New Delhi: Sage Publications, 214–228.

Singh, K. (2013). *Separated and Divorced Women in India: Economic Rights and Entitlements*. New Delhi: Sage.

Singh, S. (1997). *Marriage Money: The Social Shaping of Money in Marriage and Banking*. St Leonards, NSW: Allen & Unwin.

Singh, S. (2013). *Globalization and Money: A Global South Perspective*. Lanham, MD: Rowman & Littlefield.

Singh, S. and Bhandari, M. (2012). 'Money Management and Control in the Indian Joint Family across Generations'. *The Sociological Review*, 60(1), 46–67.

Singh, S. and Gatina, L. (2015). 'Money Flows Two-Ways between Transnational Families in Australia and India'. *South Asian Diaspora*, 7(1), 33–47.

Singh, S. and Nadarajah, Y. (2011). *School Fees, Beer and 'Meri': Gender, Cash and the Mobile in the Morobe Province of Papua New Guinea*. Irvine: Institute for Money, Technology and Financial Inclusion. https://www.imtfi.uci.edu/files/blog_working _papers/working_paper_singh.pdf (accessed 22 November 2023).

Singh, S. and Sidhu, J. (2022). 'Remittances, Migration and Economic Abuse: "Invisible in Plain Sight"'. In: N. Ribas-Mateo and S. Sassen (eds) *The Elgar Companion to Gender and Global Migration: Beyond Western Research*. Cheltenham, UK and Northampton, MA, USA: Edward Elgar Publishing, 233–239.

Smart, C. and Shipman, B. (2004). 'Visions in Monochrome: Families, Marriage and the Individualization Thesis'. *British Journal of Sociology*, 55(4), 491–509.

Taiapa, J. (1994). *'Ta Te Whanau Ohanga': The Economics of the Whanau – the Maori Component of the Intra Family Income Study*. Palmerston North: Department of Maori Studies, Massey University.

Uberoi, P. (2006). *Freedom and Destiny: Gender, Family, and Popular Culture in India*. New Delhi: Oxford University Press.

United Nations 2020. *World Population Ageing 2020 Highlights: Living Arrangements of Older Persons (ST/ESA/SER.A/451)*. New York: United Nations. www .un .org/ development/ desa/ pd/ sites/ www .un .org .development .desa .pd/ files/ undesa _pd -2020_world_population_ageing_highlights.pdf (accessed 30 December 2022).

Zelizer, V. (1994). *The Social Meaning of Money*. New York: Basic Books.

10. Who counts in intra-household sharing? Children as active agents in the household economy

Gill Main

Introduction

There exist various different conceptualisations and experiences of childhood within and between countries, cultures and contexts (James and Prout, 2015). Nevertheless, childhood is typically recognised as a distinct phase of life with specific needs and rights, as evidenced by international treaties such as the United Nations Convention on the Rights of the Child (UNCRC) (1989). Despite this, research into intra-household management and distribution of resources (here called intra-household sharing) – following broader studies of poverty and inequality – often overlooks children or treats them as passive adjuncts to parents or consumers of household resources (Ridge, 2002). This restricts knowledge of intra-household processes and outcomes related to the management and distribution of resources. Furthermore, it is at odds with the motivation behind efforts to open up the 'black box' of the household – a central motivation for early research in this area (Maruyama, this volume).

This chapter intends to draw attention to children as active participants in intra-household and intra-family sharing, moving beyond positioning children as consumers of household resources, or (in some economics literature) 'public goods'. We contend that this is vital to developing a holistic understanding of intra-household sharing practices and outcomes. We begin by reviewing the underpinning theoretical bases in the field and then turn to three case studies, across varied international contexts, to illustrate different ways of including children in research on intra-household sharing. We focus here on children who depend on parental economic resources (but see Burchardt and Karagiannaki, this volume, for complex households, including non-dependent young people). Our conclusions outline recommendations for future study, policy and practice.

The ultimate goal of this field of study is to augment knowledge that can then be used to improve children's and families' lives. This chapter posits that embracing the complexity of intra-household sharing is necessary not only to deepen academic understanding but also to contribute to that goal. As Lanau and Fifita (2020: 1954) highlight, 'ignoring intra-household deprivation dynamics can ... potentially result in a misdirection of resources, as in order to effectively direct resources to the most vulnerable, policy makers rely on the correct identification of the poor'.

Poverty, inequality and the 'black box' of the household

There is a range of reasons for concern about the management and distribution of resources within the household. This chapter focuses on one of these – poverty, especially child poverty. Poverty is a complex and contested concept (Lister, 2021). Nevertheless, there is growing consensus that it is multidimensional, and can be experienced at different levels, for example at the individual, household or community level (Townsend, 1979). It is also fundamentally associated with shame and stigma (Walker, 2014). Despite the convincing case made by Lister (2021) for clearly articulating (and differentiating between) how poverty is conceptualised, defined and measured, income-based measures of poverty – the dominant approach in the field – are usually narrower than a comprehensive conceptualisation of poverty. Moreover, when making policy recommendations, insufficient attention is paid to the limitations of a focus on household income without considering intra-household inequalities.

A comprehensive appraisal of income-based poverty measurement is beyond the scope of this chapter (see, e.g., Atkinson et al., 2019). Here, we acknowledge that income-based poverty measures are often extremely useful, but focus upon one key limitation to their application, sometimes shared with other measures based on material circumstances: the restrictions on the ability to make inferences about children's living standards, given their heterogeneous needs and experiences. This limitation arises from underpinning theoretical assumptions about household resources.

Popular and academic discussions of poverty focus on access to resources, and debates over the nature of the resources needed to avoid poverty are extensive (Lister, 2021). Academic discussion often also emphasises *control* over how resources are acquired and used. Townsend (1979) references 'command over' resources within relative deprivation theory and Sen (1999: 285) underscores in his capability theory the importance of the 'freedom' to live a 'life [people] have reason to value'. Meanwhile, moving beyond the individual or household level, control is also implicit in political power and the ability to inform societal agenda setting within relational theories of poverty (Mosse, 2010).

A focus on control is not unwarranted; empirical studies demonstrate that having a degree of power or control over resources can contribute to rejecting the stigmatising and shaming experiences of poverty (Narayan-Parker and Patel, 2000). However, fully understanding control over resources means taking an intersectional approach, such as that taken in the literature on the gendered nature of poverty and intra-household sharing. Research, dating from the emergence of the field (e.g. Millar and Glendinning, 1987) to citations in Bennett's (2013) more recent review, confirms that living in a higher-income household is no guarantee of increased autonomy in using resources – at least for women in female/male couples.

An intersectional lens also challenges the conceptualisation of 'autonomy' in the use of resources – given the weight of social, cultural and even legal norms, the range of 'choices' available to those responsible for household budgets can result in such 'control' being experienced as a burden rather than a privilege (Bennett, 2013). Families in poverty in particular face impossible dilemmas in balancing the needs for social acceptance that conspicuous consumption can fulfil with the requirements for performative frugality, which are established by narratives pitting the 'deserving' against the 'undeserving' poor (e.g. Golightley and Holloway, 2016).

Given the complexity involved in controlling household budgets, and the potential impact of decisions on household members, it is unsurprising that these have tended to be seen as belonging firmly to the 'adult' domain. However, as we now discuss, the maintenance of child/adult distinctions in managing life in poverty, including money in the household, is not reflected in the lived experiences of children and families.

Childhood studies: Needs, rights and agency

The previous five decades have seen a step change in attitudes towards children and childhood, including in academic, policy and practice settings (James and James, 2008). Sociological approaches have challenged influential assumptions of developmental psychology, particularly that childhood is primarily important as a (linear and universal) preparatory phase for adulthood (James et al., 1998). Whilst acknowledging children's biological immaturity, sociologists highlight their active participation in the social world: making sense of their own lives, participating in relationships and holding valuable knowledge. This change in perspective has contributed to children being positioned as bearers of human needs and in particular human rights, important in shaping present wellbeing and future well-becoming (Biggeri, 2020) – although these needs may be an addition to, and different from, those of adults.

Arguably, the most powerful reflection of this approach is the 1989 UNCRC. The most widely ratified international treaty, the UNCRC asserts children's rights to conditions that allow progression towards adulthood alongside rights to take an active part in the world during childhood. As noted above, the UNCRC acknowledges childhood as a unique life stage with concomitant needs and rights, reflecting childhood's social, legal and biological realities. In contrast to previous approaches, which delegated children's 'political' rights to parents or deferred them to the future self, it established that children's views should carry weight in decision-making. As a normative document, the UNCRC is debated and criticised; nevertheless, it presents a powerful statement on what childhood should be.

These academic and legislative shifts have important implications for research on intra-household and intra-family sharing. Whilst the complexities introduced are frequently put beyond the scope or capacity of inquiry, a burgeoning literature highlights the importance of considering children's presence and active participation in the household. Following Bessell (2022), we contend that this is central to methodological validity, as well as to human rights and social justice: neglecting to consider children's experiences or views contravenes their rights as outlined in the UNCRC and renders any policy measures based on such a restricted perspective suboptimal. This is not to say that including children is a simple task; even within a rights-based approach, tensions exist between participation, provision and protection. We consider some such tensions – which often mirror those in gender-based studies – throughout this chapter.

Child poverty and intra-household sharing

Studies of poverty and social studies of childhood often share a focus on agency. However, these have not yet been fully reconciled in studies of *child poverty*, which primarily position children as passive consumers. As Redmond (2009: 544) notes, a focus on agency is important because 'poverty both facilitates and constrains children's agency': children are actively engaged in making decisions – relating to what happens within, as well as outside, their households and families – but the structure of poverty bounds these decisions.

Incorporating children's agency demands attention at the level of measuring and documenting intra-household sharing but also at the level of conceptualising it. More than two decades ago, Millar and Glendinning (1989: 369) wrote that 'women's access to, use of, and attitudes towards material resources of all kinds are radically different from, and cannot be equated with, those of men'. Early in the second decade of the twenty-first century, academics are on the brink (and some in the process) of acknowledging the same principle regarding differences between children and adults.

However, children's status precludes adoption of the logic applied by Millar and Glendinning to women – that the avoidance of poverty depends on an 'individual right to a minimum degree of potential economic independence' (Millar and Glendinning, 1992: 464). Exerting autonomy over some resources during childhood is important, but *economic independence* is neither possible nor desirable for most children. The agency of children in poverty is constrained by both economic conditions and their social status as children – but is nonetheless agency (Skattebol et al., 2017).

Recognising children as interdependent individuals within complex networks, we must revisit conceptualisations, definitions and measures of poverty in order to elucidate their position in family and household environments. In the next three sections, we draw on three case studies – in Pakistan, Tonga and the United Kingdom (UK) – to demonstrate and critically appraise different approaches to including children in considerations of intra-household sharing in relation to poverty in particular. We use the distinction emphasised by Lister (2021) between concepts, definitions and measures of poverty, with concepts being the broadest idea of what poverty is and how it is experienced; definitions being what divides those living in poverty from those not doing so; and measures being necessarily the narrowest of the three, because of the strictures imposed by counting and comparability. Here we begin with measures, proceed to consider definitions and end with reflections on conceptualisations.

Child-specific poverty measures: The case of Pakistan

Internationally, knowledge about child poverty is primarily produced using pre-existing data collected through national surveys, typically official statistics. These data are useful but have their limitations. Key among these is a conservative approach to procedure and content, adapting only slowly to advances in knowledge. For example, this affects decisions about who to include as respondent(s): relying on a 'head of household' to provide data about all household members and retaining existing survey questions both minimise expenditure on the survey – a critical factor in the context of limited resources – as well as maintaining the continuity essential for longitudinal research. However, it excludes children as respondents and precludes advances in methods (for example, measures to reflect updated concepts or mixed-methods approaches).

Through creatively analysing available data, however, it is possible to develop child-level indicators of poverty that draw attention to intra-household sharing and children's needs. Indeed, following the adoption of the 2015 Sustainable Development Goals (SDGs) – especially SDG1, which commits countries to eradicate poverty 'in all its forms' – many countries began using existing data to do so. This can produce important information for research, policy and practice, as illustrated in the following case study of UNICEF in Pakistan.

Following a rights-based approach, UNICEF Pakistan examined children's living standards independent of household income, based on UNICEF's Multiple Overlapping Deprivation Analysis (MODA) (Chaudhry et al., 2021).[1] MODA is a child-centred approach, examining the nature and depth of deprivations across multiple domains and linked to the UNCRC (de Neubourg et al., 2012a). The approach can examine children's experiences within a country but also compare deprivations across multiple countries (de Neubourg et al., 2012b). A key strength of MODA is its flexibility, and it has been validated in diverse contexts, including comparative studies within sub-Saharan Africa (de Milliano and Plavgo, 2014) and the European Union (Chzhen et al., 2014). In Pakistan, it has been applied to examine the strength of the association between household income poverty and child deprivation (Chaudhry et al., 2021).

Novel use of existing data can meet the dual aims of producing analysis quickly whilst generating compelling evidence on the need for better quality data – an important first step in highlighting the importance of child-specific poverty measures. Chaudhry et al. (2021) achieved this in Pakistan through using pre-existing Multiple Indicator Cluster Survey data, alongside other national sources, to illustrate children's experiences of poverty. Combining this with a rights-based framework, they developed indicators of child deprivation and its severity, shown in Table 10.1, to match the methodology used in MODA. Their deprivation measures include several dimensions of children's needs beyond the material (e.g. 'education' and 'health') and are also sensitive to differing needs throughout childhood (e.g. '5–7 years', '8–17 years').

Table 10.1   Pakistan child deprivation indicators

Dimension	Age range	Moderate deprivation measure	Severe deprivation measure
Shelter	<18 years	Dwelling has >2 people per room	Dwelling has >4 people per room
Sanitation	<18 years	Unimproved sanitation facilities	Open defecation use
Water	<18 years	Unimproved water facilities	Surface water use
Nutrition	<6 years	Stunting at two standard deviations below international reference population	Stunting at three standard deviations below international reference population
Education	5–7 years	Not currently in school	Never attended school
	8–17 years	Two classes or more behind age in school	Not attending school
Health	15–59 months	Not fully immunised	Not fully immunised for polio, measles and penta
	15–17 years	Only traditional contraception available	No access to contraception
Information	10–17 years	Mobile phone or internet but not both	Neither mobile phone nor internet

Source: Chaudhry et al., 2021.

The authors examined associations between child-specific deprivations and more traditional, income-based household poverty. As shown in Table 10.2, whilst non-poor children (not experiencing at least one severe deprivation) were more likely to be in a non-poor household (monetary poverty, or measured by income) than in a poor household, poor children (experiencing at least one severe deprivation) were less likely to be in a poor than a non-poor household (measured by income). This has implications for our understanding of the nature and (in)adequacy of existing poverty measures and processes of intra-household sharing.

Further analysis facilitated insights concerning the intra-household distribution of resources by gender and age. Overall, girls were 3.7 times more likely to be severely deprived on at least one dimension compared to boys; girls aged 0–9 were 1.5 times more likely to be deprived than boys, while girls aged 10–17 were 7.3 times more likely to be severely deprived (Chaudhry et al., 2021). This

Table 10.2   Child deprivation and household monetary poverty status in Pakistan

	Poor household (monetary)	Non-poor household (monetary)
Poor child (deprivation)	21%	36%
Non-poor child (deprivation)	6%	37%

Source: Chaudhry et al., 2021.

demonstrates the importance of the intersectional approach discussed in the preceding section.

Child-focused analysis, such as that described above, enables us to hypothesise about intra-household processes and outcomes. An interesting avenue to explore concerns child labour: literature from other contexts suggests that unpaid household work (traditionally considered 'women's work') is valued less than income-generating work. Therefore, power to negotiate access to personal resources tends to be greater for household members receiving money for their labour (Bennett, 2013). In Pakistan, child labour is highly gendered: girls are more likely to be engaged in unpaid (household) work, with boys more likely to be in paid work (Batool and Bilal, 2022; see also Bessell, 2022). This suggests that boys not only benefit from sexist attitudes, prevalent to varying extents internationally, but also may accrue greater power to negotiate access to intra-household resources.

However, this approach has important limitations. The hypothesis above is just that – these data cannot confirm or refute it, because how access to resources is gained is unobserved. One well-known risk here is that the robustness of findings is compromised when developing concepts based on available data, rather than generating data based on concepts (Bessell, 2022). Additionally, girls, especially older girls, appear more exposed to poverty than boys but, without data on whether the adults in the household have access to necessities, this may suggest the need for an income greater than the threshold used to fulfil all household members' needs. Addressing this limitation, the next case study utilises comparable deprivation measures for both adults and children.

Child-specific poverty definitions: The case of Tonga

Evidence consistently shows that different poverty measures – such as income poverty and deprivation – may be weakly related (Bradshaw and Finch, 2003). This lack of 'fit' may exist irrespective of household sharing practices, posing a key challenge to the analysis discussed above, which utilised different poverty measures at the child level (deprivation) and household level (income). This example illustrates why definitions of poverty are important: income-based and material-based measures, both imperfect measures, may also operationalise slightly different definitions (and concepts) (Bradshaw and Finch, 2003). A consistent approach to measuring child and adult poverty, based on deprivation of child- and adult-specific necessities, is argued here to be a more robust approach to understanding experiences within the household (see Main and Bradshaw, 2016). Rather than including income, this approach prioritises deprivation as the key definition of poverty (what separates those living in poverty from those who are not) and applies this within the household.

A recent study in Tonga utilises such a consistent approach (Lanau and Fifita, 2020). In line with previous research, it found that 80–88 per cent (depending on the threshold selected) of parents and children within the same household shared the same deprivation status. However, in contrast to the findings of Main and Bradshaw (2016), and with much research using other methods indicating that parents prioritise children's needs in a context of poverty, they find that roughly similar percentages of children are not poor whilst the adults in the household are in poverty (7–11 per cent) compared to those who are poor whilst the adults are not (5–10 per cent). However, the latter were more likely to have parents reporting experiences related to poverty (e.g. difficulty paying bills). The analysis further indicated that the likelihood of children being exposed to deprivation did not differ by gender of household head.

These findings offer food for thought: they are inconsistent with other studies demonstrating adults' – especially women's – protective behaviours; yet an exploration of deprivation patterns reveals that needs typically considered more 'fundamental' by adults – such as nutrition – tend to be prioritised over resources more relevant to children's own social worlds. This reflects findings in the UK study by Main (2013), based on focus groups with children, who perceive adults as dismissive of certain needs they consider important. Lanau and Fifita (2020) suggest that this may occur because decisions about fulfilling household members' needs relate not only to who is prioritised in principle but also to what resources are readily available: for remote households in

Tonga, parents are constrained in what they can provide, irrespective of their preferences.

This example highlights the importance of a structural perspective on poverty. That is, focusing on individuals' and households' choices about their use of resources must not detract attention from whether infrastructure, policy and economic conditions permit needs to be met. 'Drilling down' into the specific domains of deprivation (Lanau and Fifita, 2020) helps to illuminate the differing constraints on individuals and their families and the strategies they employ to cope in conditions in which their needs cannot be met.

It is important to note some methodological and theoretical limitations. Firstly, most data on child deprivation are provided by adults, and surveys commonly ask for responses which do not distinguish between individual children within the household. This is the approach taken in Lanau and Fifita (2020) and Main and Bradshaw (2016). It enabled a generalised and valuable comparison of deprivation based on generation and life stage. However, it cannot offer insight into dynamics within the household relating to other dimensions of disadvantage, including children's age and gender (highlighted in the Pakistan case study above) and children's biological or kinship relations with the adults they live with (e.g. in the context of parental repartnering).

Another important limitation (Bessell, 2022) is that defining poverty as deprivation is solely material, neglecting to explicitly measure poverty's social domains. The centrality of shame and stigma relating to poverty across time and space resulting from the inability to fully participate in society were discussed briefly above in the introduction. In this way, measures of poverty can be linked to intra-household sharing. For example, *control over* resources, rather than the lack of resources per se, forms the basis of most theories of poverty; yet poverty is almost universally measured in terms of *access to*, not *control over*, resources. A materially based definition of poverty, implicitly adopted in most empirical studies, neglects the socially negotiated aspects of control.

We do not argue that resources are not important; ample evidence confirms that they are crucial (Lister, 2021). However, to comprehensively understand poverty and its effects – and, by extension, how to design and implement interventions to tackle these – it is vital to incorporate the role of shame and stigma in shaping a life in poverty and determine whether interventions are genuinely helpful in combating these. This includes poverty measurement: despite conditions of anonymity, the emotional cost of reporting an inability to provide for children may lead to less than accurate accounts of actual living standards. Therefore, to understand the direct impact on children of lacking resources, as well as their own active roles in managing their material needs and wants, researchers must revisit what we measure and how, and the key factor defining poverty and distinguishing it from other states of being, but also how we conceptualise 'poverty' and 'family', and the implications of reconceptualising these.

Child-specific poverty conceptualisations: The case of the UK

Reconceptualising poverty to account for children's own positions within households and families is a monumental task. It requires underlying (typically unquestioned) concepts common to poverty studies to be unpacked. Without this, we risk failing to identify those children most in need of assistance. This is most evident in relation to assumptions about autonomy and parental responsibility. As the two previous case studies illustrate, parents – and wider social structures – differ in their treatment of children based on a range of factors, including gender.

To understand what forms of autonomy and ranges of choice are needed for children to avoid poverty during childhood – which are different from those for adults – we also need to understand their experiences of the relationship between poverty, shame and stigma, as well as their own approaches to negotiating autonomy, especially when it is constrained by both 'childhood' and 'poverty'.

Over two decades of research into children's experiences of poverty demonstrate that they are much more aware of the constraints on their lives than adults often assume (Ridge, 2002; Main and Bradshaw, 2016). Children's experiences, like those of adults, are diverse, but unified by the shame and stigma of poverty (Ridge, 2002; Walker, 2014; Bray et al., 2019). In response, children often hide needs from their parents, other adults and other children; and, while their aspirations may remain high, their expectations – of what resources they can access, and of fair treatment by the wider society – can be damaged irreparably.

The impacts on children's wellbeing and well-becoming are vast but are entirely obscured in adult-centred approaches to poverty conceptualisation, definition and measurement. Research has, however, sought to integrate children's own perspectives and experiences. For example, Main and Mahony

(2018) draw on iterative waves of ethnographic and survey research with children (aged 10–17) and their families in England. They found that networks need to be conceptualised for children more broadly than the people within their family home, including but not limited to children living across multiple households; children should be understood as active participants in shaping family processes and norms about fairness and the distribution of resources, sensitive to several factors including age and gender. Children and their families were also active participants in narratives around what poverty is – narratives which can reproduce, or challenge, shame and stigma. Within the UK context (but necessarily elsewhere, as discussed in the previous case study) they found that poverty constrained what families shared, but not how families went about sharing their resources.

These findings have important implications for future research. Focusing on children's active roles in intra-household sharing, the findings of Main and Mahony (2018) imply that greater ethical individualism (Burchardt et al., 2013) – with an individual moral compass as a guide, rather than societally dictated obligations – is needed to understand children's experiences of poverty. This must, however, be done alongside a structural, relational approach to theorising poverty, which places responsibility for addressing poverty with powerful social and political actors, rather than with the 'poor' changing their behaviours in response to policy interventions designed to achieve this.

There is a tension in advocating for greater individualism in understanding experiences of poverty and greater collectivism in efforts to address poverty. Yet this mirrors rights-based theories which position individual entitlements as flowing upwards from the least powerful to the most powerful, whilst collective responsibilities flow from the most powerful in society to the least powerful.[2] Critically, in the context of this chapter, this relates to processes within households, in which differential levels of power are accorded to parents compared with children; to different children, based on age and gender; and to non-household members who can exert power over household dynamics through the provision or withholding of resources.

This power of non-household members in household dynamics is evidenced by Main and Mahony (2018). Monetary contributions from outside the household were important to families across the income distribution. These could be experienced positively – for example, one family received a large sum of money from a grandmother to fund a holiday. But they were experienced negatively in others – for example, one young woman was aware that her father proactively policed the maintenance payments he made to her mother, and that this created great stress in the management of 'household' resources in one of her two homes. These issues problematise the nature of the 'household' (Singh, this volume). Whilst the household is a valuable unit of measurement, it must not be conflated with the reality of children's and families' lives, which are often lived across multiple households, with their meaning varying depending on multiple factors (Ridge, 2002; Redmond, 2009).

Similar complexity is important in conceptualising children as vulnerable to, but not entirely passive in the face of, adult power. Main and Mahony (2018) suggest that children who earn money (formally or informally) are seen by themselves and adults as entitled to greater influence in decisions about household resources. While practices regarding this were similar across the income distribution, better-off families frequently positioned child participation in work as an educational and developmental tool; by contrast, it was a practical necessity for managing life in poverty in families with lower incomes. These findings are mirrored in international studies on children's active contributions and roles within and outside the household (e.g. see Skattebol et al., 2017).

This perspective on children as active agents in negotiating life in poverty is unusual in the global north. A hegemonic belief that child poverty is fundamentally different in the global south follows colonial thinking on the nature of poverty and childhood. This encourages thinking of children in the global north world as privileged 'others', free from the 'burden' of autonomy; meanwhile, children in the global south are hyper-visible in their 'otherness' and in their 'unchildlike' capacities to exercise autonomy.

Children may emphasise their agency in providing for themselves and their families, their enthusiasm at being able to engage in paid work and their emphasis on peer networks and fitting in with friends to avoid shame and stigma. These were the findings of several UK-based studies (see Main, 2013; Main and Mahony, 2018; Main and McCartney, 2019), as well as studies based in the global south (e.g. Bessell, 2009). Older children's economic participation may be seen as a societal threat, while younger children's efforts can often be greeted with sympathy. Main and Mahony (2018) demonstrated this in their findings on the intersection of age and gender in the UK: one 13-year-old girl reported being praised by her mother's colleagues for helping out at home by selling her baked cupcakes; in contrast, a 17-year-old boy was seen as avoiding the responsibilities of adulthood because he was raising money via informal means rather than formal employment. This links with the observation by Punch (2002) that household 'boundaries' are often more permeable in the global south: obligations span households and are overtly placed on children as well as adults. The findings above show that dichotomies of 'dependent child' and 'independent adult' in the global north obscure more complex realities.

Recapitulating one of the core points underlying this chapter, many theories of poverty highlight *command over* resources as being at the core of poverty. Bessell (2009: 531–532), for example, found that many children in that context preferred 'a life on the streets, characterised by periodic violence, economic hardship, exclusion from public services *and independence*, to a life at home, characterised by periodic violence and economic hardship *and a lack of independence* and choice'. The household is a key concept in children's lives – but without acknowledging their interdependence and active contributions to negotiating intra-household distribution, influencing central conceptualisations about what goes on within households in relation to resources, we cannot fully understand or address child poverty.

Discussion and conclusion

This chapter outlined the theoretical basis for considering children as active participants in intra-household management and distribution of resources, with a focus on child poverty. We illustrated methods for incorporating children's independent experiences of access to resources using three case studies in varying contexts. How far children are included in research is bound to be determined by the research questions and pragmatic considerations. But more efforts to include children and awareness of the limitations of not doing so (completely or partially) are required.

We made the case that greater inclusion of children is necessary for academic rigour and the validity of findings, but also because of the ethics of including children's perspectives in matters which affect their lives, in line with the UNCRC. We introduced a range of ways in which children can contribute, and have contributed, to understanding child poverty and intra-household sharing practices. Undoubtedly, there is much more that needs to be done to understand how children exercise autonomy – and navigate its constraints – in acquiring and using resources and how they experience their lives in poverty and in relation to household sharing. There is also significant potential in challenging dichotomous thinking about experiences in the global north and global south in this context. We hope that this chapter provides researchers in this field with some conceptual and methodological tools which may be useful in continuing its development.

Notes

1. See www.unicef-irc.org/research/multidimensional-child-poverty/ (accessed 27 May 2023).
2. See www.un.org/en/global-issues/human-rights (accessed 26 May 2023).

References

Atkinson, A.B., Micklewright, J. and Brandolini, A. (2019) 'Inequality within the household', in Atkinson, A.B. (ed.) *Measuring Poverty around the World*, Princeton, NJ: Princeton University Press, 73–76.

Batool, S.A. and Bilal, M. (2022) 'Understanding child labour: The debate of children's mental and physical health in Pakistan', *Journal of Humanities, Social and Management Sciences* 3(1): 217–231.

Bennett, F. (2013) 'Researching within-household distribution: Overview, developments, debates and methodological challenges', *Journal of Marriage and Family* 75(3): 582–597.

Bessell, S. (2009) 'Indonesian children's views and experiences of work and poverty', *Social Policy and Society* 8(4): 527–540.

Bessell, S. (2022) 'Rethinking child poverty', *Journal of Human Development and Capabilities* 23(4): 539–561.

Biggeri, M. (2020) 'Capability approach to children's wellbeing and well-becoming', in Chiappero-Martinetti, E., Osmani, S. and Qizilbash, M. (eds) *The Cambridge Handbook of the Capability Approach, Part III: Issues in Public Policy*, Cambridge: Cambridge University Press: 523–543.

Bradshaw, J.R. and Finch, N. (2003) 'Overlaps in dimensions of poverty', *Journal of Social Policy* 32(4): 513–525.

Bray, R., De Laat, M., Godinot, X., Ugarte, A. and Walker, R. (2019) *The Hidden Dimensions of Poverty*, Montreuil: Fourth World Publications.

Burchardt, T., Evans, M. and Holder, H. (2013) 'Public policy and inequalities of choice and autonomy', *CASEPaper 174*, London: Centre for Analysis of Social Exclusion, London School of Economics and Political Science.

Chaudhry, O., Raza, M.A., Gorjon, L., Delamónica, E., Espinoza-Delgado, J., Giacoponello, M. and Obaidy, M. (2021) *Technical Note: Pakistan Child Poverty National and Subnational Trends*, New York: UNICEF, available at www.unicef.org/ pakistan/ media/ 4431/ file/ Technical %20Note %20 - %20Pakistan %20Child %20Poverty.pdf; and *Overview*, New York: UNICEF, available at www.unicef.org/ pakistan/ media/ 4426/ file/ Overview %20 - %20Pakistan %20Child %20Poverty .pdf (both accessed 27 May 2023).

Chzhen, Y., de Neubourg, C., Plavgo, I. and de Milliano, M. (2014) 'Understanding child deprivation in the European Union: The Multiple Overlapping Deprivation Analysis (EU-MODA) approach, Innocenti Working Paper 2014-18, Florence: UNICEF Office of Research.

de Milliano, M. and Plavgo, I. (2014) 'Analysing child poverty and deprivation in sub-Saharan Africa: cross country Multiple Overlapping Deprivation Analysis', Innocenti Working Paper 2014-19, Florence: UNICEF Office of Research.

de Neubourg, C., Chai, J., de Milliano, M., Plavog, I. and Wei, Z. (2012a) 'Step-by-step guidelines to the Multiple Overlapping Deprivation Analysis (MODA)', Working Paper 2012-10, Florence: UNICEF Office of Research.

de Neubourg, C., Bradshaw, J., Chzhen, Y., Main, G., Martorano, B. and Menchini, L. (2012b) 'Child deprivation, multidimensional poverty and monetary poverty in Europe', Innocenti Working Paper 2012-02, Florence: UNICEF Innocenti Research Centre.

Golightley, M. and Holloway, M. (2016) 'Editorial', *British Journal of Social Work* 46(1): 1–7.

James, A. and James, A. (2008) *Key Concepts in Childhood Studies*, London: Sage Publications.

James, A. and Prout, A. (eds) (2015) *Constructing and Reconstructing Childhood: Contemporary Issues in the Sociological Study of Childhood*, London: Routledge.

James, A., Jenks, C. and Prout, A. (1998) *Theorising Childhood*, Cambridge: Polity.

Lanau, A. and Fifita, V. (2020) 'Do households prioritise children? Intra-household deprivation: A case study of the South Pacific', *Child Indicators Research* 13(6): 1953–1973.

Lister, R. (2021) *Poverty*, 2nd edition, Oxford: Wiley.

Main, G. (2013) *A Child-derived Material Deprivation Index*, unpublished PhD thesis, University of York.

Main, G. and Bradshaw, J.R. (2016) 'Child poverty in the UK: Measures, prevalence and intra-household sharing', *Critical Social Policy* 36(1): 38–61.

Main, G. and Mahony, S. (2018) *Fair Shares and Families: Rhetoric and Reality in the Lives of Children and Families in Poverty*, London: Children's Society.

Main, G. and McCartney, C. (2019) *More Snakes than Ladders: A Report from the A Different Take Leeds Panel*, Leeds: Leeds City Council and University of Leeds.

Millar, J. and Glendinning, C. (1987) *Women and Poverty in Britain*, Brighton: Wheatsheaf.

Millar, J. and Glendinning, C. (1989) 'Gender and poverty', *Journal of Social Policy* 18(3): 363–381.

Millar, J. and Glendinning, C. (1992) *Women and Poverty in Britain: The 1990s*, London: Harvester Wheatsheaf.

Mosse, D. (2010) 'A relational approach to durable poverty, inequality and power', *Journal of Development Studies* 46(7): 1156–1178.

Narayan-Parker, D. and Patel, R. (2000) *Voices of the Poor: Can Anyone Hear Us?*, Oxford: Oxford University Press.

Punch, S. (2002) 'Research with children: The same or different from research with adults?', *Childhood* 9(3): 321–341.

Redmond, G. (2009) 'Children as actors: How does the child perspectives literature treat agency in the context of poverty?', *Social Policy and Society* 8(4): 541–550.

Ridge, T. (2002) *Childhood Poverty and Social Exclusion*, Bristol: Policy Press.

Sen, A. (1999) *Development as Freedom*, Oxford: Oxford University Press.

Skattebol, J., Redmond, G. and Zizzo, G. (2017) 'Expanding children's agency: Cases of young people experiencing economic adversity', *Children and Society* 31(4): 315–329.

Townsend, P. (1979) *Poverty in the United Kingdom*, London: Allen Lane and Penguin Books.

Walker, R. (2014) *The Shame of Poverty*, Oxford: Oxford University Press.

PART III

The inter-relationship between resources within the household and policy

11. Understanding the role of social grants as resources in multi-generational households: Examples from South Africa and Lesotho

Elena Moore and Thandie Hlabana

Introduction: Literature on money in the global south and multi-generational households

In the global south, high levels of poverty, inequality and unemployment are coupled with relatively weaker social protection systems and higher levels of vulnerability when compared to the global north. In such contexts, cash transfers play a critical role in supporting individuals, households and families. In the Southern African context, vulnerability is also shaped by the HIV/AIDS crisis, low rates of marriage (in some countries), high levels of multi-generational living and specific cultural obligations to care for others. In this context, we see that multi-generational households are often female dominated;[1] such households tend to be larger and poorer and have fewer resources, including cash transfers, spread more thinly across many family members.

Cash transfers – or social grants, as they are known in Southern Africa in particular – have transformed the lives of people across the global south (Hanlon et al., 2010) and have proved successful in recent years in reducing poverty in South Africa and Lesotho, the two countries in focus in this chapter (Garcia and Moore, 2012). These two countries offer interesting examples of a middle- and a low-income country with social protection systems including cash grants for children and pensioners. However, South Africa has a more generous range and higher value of social assistance supports than Lesotho, which has low-value social pensions and cash transfers. In South Africa, social grants reach approximately 50 per cent of all households (Seekings and Moore, 2014).

But there has been limited investigation into how these grants are shared within and between households (Moore and Seekings, 2019). Moreover, there is little understanding of the norms of sharing 'public transfers' in situations in which some people within the household receive a social grant and others do not. Given the increase in cash transfers across the global south (Hanlon et al., 2010), understanding how public transfers are distributed within families and wider households is essential. To date, critical approaches to understanding how money is handled in households in the global south have often focused on gender relations, specifically in relation to the command over land in largely agrarian economies (Agarwal, 1997; Doss, 2005). This chapter focuses instead on intergenerational aspects.

It is unclear whether social grants are distributed differently from other forms of income between recipients and others. This gap in our understanding is notable, as much of the research on money and families is located in (comparatively) well-established welfare contexts with relatively low levels of poverty and unemployment. In such contexts, welfare coverage and support tend to be more evenly spread, with fewer holes in the safety net. For example, in most high-income countries there is some form of unemployment insurance and/ or assistance and there are social grants (cash transfers paid regularly) that support caregivers. In contexts across the global south, where unemployment is high, welfare provision is not only limited in coverage but also uneven, with more resources targeted at the elderly and children and fewer at working-age able-bodied men and women (Moore and Seekings, 2019). Given the gaps in the safety net (the absence in particular of any benefit for unemployed people) and poor employment opportunities, many working-age able-bodied adults *have to* rely on the social grants that older persons and those with children receive. Thus, grants targeted to particular situations are shared within households and used to sustain the livelihoods of all family members through the purchase of necessities such as food.

Furthermore, research on money in households in the global north has tended to focus on gendered dynamics within fairly small families – often couples, including married couples (e.g. Nyman, 1999; Heimdal and Houseknecht, 2003; Burgoyne, 2004; Smock et al., 2005; Nyman and Dema, 2007; Yodanis and Lauer, 2007; Hamplova et al., 2014), and there is less emphasis on the dynamics within multi-generational households – although this is changing. Literature from the global north also provides little insight into how monies, specifically social grants, are redistributed within households in high-dependence contexts, in which a proportion of the middle generation is absent due to HIV/AIDS and/or labour migration. In Southern Africa, many households not only rely on social grants as the primary (or only) source of income but also do so in situations in which the caregiver for a child (probably an older person) and the grant recipient (e.g. the biological parent) may not live in the same household (Kearabetswe and Khunou, 2019). These issues are also important (beyond the intrahousehold ones) and remind us to foreground the fluidity of the boundaries of 'the household' in these and other contexts.

For example, the literature has shown how social grants influence living arrangements and kin support. Klasen and Woolard (2009) argue that many unemployed working-age adults may have little choice but to reside with kin who have stable income from social grants. Furthermore, research shows how child support grants may be used by adults to support themselves financially whilst looking for work in cities (Kearabetswe and Khunou, 2019). Other studies have shown how older women use their pension to support unemployed adult children and grandchildren, while other adult children seek employment elsewhere (Mosoetsa, 2011; Button and Ncapai, 2019). While old age pensions may be described as support to older people, studies have highlighted their positive impacts on child outcomes in Lesotho (Parker and Short, 2009; Harrison et al., 2014; Ansell et al., 2019). And Kelly (2019: 555) argued that high levels of structural unemployment leave many family members dependent on beneficiaries of disability benefits – which may have 'negative consequences for the health, wellbeing and social and economic inclusion of people with disabilities and chronic illness'.

This chapter contributes to analysis of the generational and gendered dynamics of sharing social grants in households, in contexts with many dependants in a wider kin group. The sections below examine how social policies can shape families' and household living arrangements. For example, households receiving disability and/or old age grants tend to be larger and attract more unemployed working-age adults, who may seek support from, and come to reside in, households with a stable income source (Klasen and Woolard, 2009). The chapter then considers the impact of social grants and policies targeted at individuals on other household and family members. Finally, the authors suggest ways forward for future research in this area.

Social grants and households in South Africa and Lesotho

Social grants are direct payments to poor and/or vulnerable individuals/ households. These have become a critical source of income in the majority of households in South Africa and Lesotho. In both settings, social grants have been massively expanded in recent years. In South Africa, this was a response to independence and the transition to democracy in 1994, whereas in Lesotho it was a response to the impact of the HIV/AIDS pandemic in the early 2000s. In 2021 in South Africa, approximately 18.4 million grants were paid monthly, benefiting 11.45 million individuals (Parliamentary Budget Office, 2021). In South Africa, the older person's grant and child support grant are means tested and targeted at the individual. In Lesotho, the history and volume of payments are very different. A universal old age pension for those aged 70 or over was introduced in 2004, while means-tested child grants only began in 2009 (Besnier at al., 2023). In both countries, an application for social grants needs to be made.

There is a great deal of variation in social grants within and across the region. For example, the major social assistance programmes in South Africa include social grants for older people, people living with disabilities, children and caregivers who have fostered children. However, grants for older people are almost four times the value of those for children. Lesotho, although a smaller economy, also offers a generous old age pension, albeit restricted to individuals aged 70 or older. Child grants in Lesotho are means tested, targeted at households in poverty with children. The old age pension is paid monthly, while child grants are paid quarterly. A grant for disabled individuals has also been introduced recently. Public assistance was introduced in the 1980s, however, targeted at individuals deemed destitute.

Social grants and social protection more generally in Southern Africa have received much scholarly attention, particularly due to their impact on alleviating poverty (Posel and Rogan, 2012), improving child educational outcomes (Heinrich et al., 2012), the dignity of older people (Sagner and Mtati, 1999) and outcomes for mothers and children (Wright et al., 2015; Zembe-Mkabile et al., 2015). Ansell and colleagues (2019) have also indicated positive spill-over impacts of these grants in communities in Lesotho. However, there remains endemic poverty, largely due to gaps in the coverage of social grants (value and reach of payments), as well as large-scale unemployment and landlessness. In South Africa, the unemployment rate continues to hover around 35 per cent and in Lesotho it is 25 per cent. Thus, with the ongoing unemployment crisis in the region, and in the absence of any benefit for unemployed people,[2] social grants are often the primary source of income in households.

In this context of high unemployment and poverty, economic interdependence both within and between households becomes more important. The redistribution of social grants within and between households could thus be expected to be significant. In South Africa, the large majority of social grants are paid to women (mostly for the benefit of children) (Moore and Seekings, 2019).

The gendered reliance on social grants is particularly significant given that most children live with women, and that women's access to employment and earnings is less secure than men's. Moreover, older women tend to redistribute their income within and between households (Schatz and Ogunmefun, 2007; Mosoetsa, 2011; Sidloyi, 2016; Ansell et al., 2019). Beneficiaries receiving a disability grant are also likely to be older (Mitra, 2010) and it is argued that this makes it probable that, much like older people's grants, disability grants are also used to support grandchildren and unemployed adults (Kelly, 2019).

Households and kin relations in South Africa and Lesotho

Households in Southern Africa have been characterised as 'porous' and 'fluid' (Spiegel et al., 1996; Young and Ansell, 2003). The household composition and individuals' relationships with household units can change over time and space, as members of connected households move from place to place and families choose who can best provide care for older people and/or children, based on adult employment options, labour migration and limited child care and elder care, as well as other opportunities and obstacles. As resources and people circulate between connected households over space and time, it is important to provide context to intrahousehold issues. In this way, too, therefore, individuals may receive or provide practical, personal or financial care from individuals outside the household.

Current patterns in family and living arrangements in the two countries have several important features. In both contexts, multi-generational households are very common, with (for example) some two-thirds of households in which children live being multi-generational in South Africa (Harrison et al., 2014; Hall and Mokomane, 2018: 34).

Multi-generational household living arises due to high rates of parental absence. In both countries, this is largely due to female labour migration rather than the death of a biological mother (Hall and Mokomane, 2018: 39), whilst high levels of orphanhood due to the HIV/AIDS pandemic still explain much parental absence in today's Lesotho (Harrison et al., 2014). In South Africa, the decline in marriage, meaning that almost two out of three adult women have never married or lived with a partner (Mhongo and Budlender, 2013), as well as the prevalence of female-dominated households (Posel and Hall, 2021), have been accompanied by maternal kin playing key roles in both financing social reproduction and providing practical care (Hatch and Posel, 2018; Moore, 2020). Boehm (2006: 153) has also added that Lesotho is experiencing a significant decrease in marriage rates and an increase in non-marital childbearing, with the children from these relationships often cared for by maternal grandparents. The care and financial support of maternal grandmothers (Ansell and Van Blerk, 2004; Parker and Short, 2009) and maternal grandfathers (Hlabana, 2007) have been highlighted as leading to improved child outcomes. In such instances, it is the intersection of generation and gender – rather than gender alone – that becomes another important axis of social division and critical to understanding how social grants shape household and family dynamics.

Social grants in multi-generational households: Examples from South Africa and Lesotho

To explore the role of social grants in multi-generational households in the chosen countries of South Africa and Lesotho, the chapter draws on the findings from two qualitative programmes of research: a study on intergenerational relationships in South Africa (Moore, 2020), with over 120 individuals in 76 households as research participants; and studies on the experiences of, and challenges facing, older people in Lesotho, as well as a study of social cash transfers in (Malawi and) Lesotho (Ansell et al., 2019).

The qualitative study on intergenerational relationships (Moore, 2020) was conducted in Johannesburg and Cape Town in 2018 and 2019. The sample was made up of individuals from diverse ethnic backgrounds and generations, largely from lower- or middle-income families. It included both men and women in middle-class occupations, such as teachers, police officers and nurses, and those earning lower monthly salaries, who typically work in lower-paid administrative positions but are members of larger households. The study consisted of at least two interviews with each participant, which included a mapping of the participant's family tree and a monthly budget, as highlighted in the findings below. All names from this study used in this chapter are pseudonyms chosen by the participants.

The data from Lesotho are from a study on 'Social cash transfers, generational relations and youth poverty trajectories in Lesotho and Malawi' conducted between 2016 and 2018 (Ansell et al., 2019). In-depth interviews were conducted with multiple members of 24 households receiving grants. Participatory workshops were also conducted with 64 young people (18 to 34 year olds). The objective was to understand how cash transfers were affecting relationships within and between households, as well as within the community.

Below we outline two examples, one each from South Africa and Lesotho, which depict different experiences of women in low-income multi-generational households who combine different sources of income to secure their family's livelihood. The main findings show how social grants are a critical source of regular and reliable income when other forms of income from employment (formal or informal) are less regular or simply not enough. Whilst social grants are vital, they are not enough to sustain livelihoods and, in the two examples below, we see that they need to be combined with other income sources. This occurs in contexts in which adults are responsible not only for biological children or parents but also frequently for nieces, nephews and grandchildren.

Example 1: Itumeleng's household

Itumeleng is a 58-year-old grandmother living in Soweto, South Africa. She is a widow and receives a pension of US$138 per month from her deceased husband's previous employer, though she has no right to a social transfer from the state. She lives with three of her adult children and seven grandchildren. Two of her adult children are employed. One of her adult children, Nonozi, passed away and Itumeleng took on the primary caregiving role for her two grandchildren (Nonozi's children), who are now 19 and 12 years old. Her other adult child, Dudu, does not live in the household, but Itumeleng is responsible for Dudu's children, Ayanda and Lonwabo. As part of this arrangement, Itumeleng is listed as the main caregiver and receives the child support grant to help meet the costs of each of the four grandchildren directly.

In addition, Itumeleng looks after children for neighbours and receives on average US$38 per month for minding two children during the week. She also uses the house to earn an income, renting out a garage and a room, and obtains US$88 each month for this. She describes herself as unemployed and explained that one of her adult children who lives with her, Ntomizodwa, is employed but receives only US$200 per month, from which she has to pay one third for transport to get to work. She does not ask Ntomizodwa to contribute to the household costs but does expect her to cover the costs of her child (who also lives in the household), such as nappies and milk. Zandile, her other adult child in employment also living in the household, moves in and out of contract work. Zandile participated in an interview and elaborated on her work situation, explaining that she had had six contract jobs in the last eight years, with regular periods in between contracts in which she had no income.

Example 2: 'Mathabo

As noted above, Lesotho has similar living and income arrangements, but households have much more limited resources than in the South African example above. For instance, 'Mathabo is 68 years old, an elderly woman (by

Lesotho's definition) with three generations in her household. She lives with her partner Teboho (aged 74), her disabled son Thabo (46) and her grand-daughter Lineo (13). Teboho receives an old age pension (US$53 per month), which is the main source of income for the household. He has been living with 'Mathabo for two years and the couple is not married. Teboho proudly reported that he was supporting his own grandchildren in the city with his pension. Thabo does not receive any income support from the state for his disability (there was no disability grant at the time of the interview). However, he is able to do odd jobs with wood in the village and earns some money to share with the household. 'Mathabo also receives a child grant for Lineo (US$17.60 per month), which she sometimes has to share with Lineo's mother (Palesa). Palesa is her daughter, a domestic worker in the city; but her employment is irregular, so she rarely sends money home, but often asks for financial support from 'Mathabo, who explained: 'Palesa feels entitled to her child's money [child grant], so that is what I share with her'.

'Mathabo also owns a field, but has been unable to plant anything due to the high cost of agricultural inputs. When she is lucky, her neighbours will rent the field and give her a third of the produce in return. In a nutshell, 'Mathabo's household is mainly dependent on government grants that are being shared not just within her household but also between several households (Teboho's grandchildren and Palesa), despite the small amounts. When asked about how the money is spent, she said: 'Teboho gives me money for papa [staple food] and soap ... Lineo's money mainly buys her school uniform, shoes, books, because that is what we were told ... but we also buy important things in the house like oil with it'.

The two scenarios of Itumeleng's and 'Mathabo's households described above depict complex flows of money both within and between households in Southern Africa. The examples indicate how care needs are high in contexts of co-existing crises such as high unemployment, the gendered consequences of HIV/AIDS and poverty. Whilst some grants are means tested and targeted at particular individuals (older people and the primary caregivers of children), individuals live within households where there are fewer resources and some people (able-bodied working-age adults) receive no grant. As a result, grants are redistributed within and between households, resulting in them being stretched thin, far beyond the targeted recipients.

Policy implications

When we consider the ways in which public provision has reshaped relationships within households and between kin in these examples, there are several implications for policy. Firstly, the findings in our research indicate the ways in which grants are used, consumed and redistributed in contexts of high unemployment and poverty. This research adds to previous studies (Klasen and Woolard, 2009; Mosoetsa, 2011; Button and Ncapai, 2019; Kearabetswe and Khunou, 2019) showing that the payment of social grants shapes family dynamics.

The examples indicate how income from pensions and child support grants are mostly managed by the older persons (the pension) and the primary caregiver for a child (the child support grant), but how complications may arise when a biological parent, who is not the primary caregiver, makes a claim on the child support grant to use for their own consumption, often at the cost of the wider needs of the household. Furthermore, whilst a pension makes a great difference for the security of a household, if it is not used/consumed within the household but instead distributed beyond the household, the household members can suffer, given the absence or low value of other social grants.

Incomes from social grants are managed in ways that provide reassurance, when income from employment can be haphazard and unreliable. Social grant income covers the cost of food for everyone in the household; it is therefore redistributed in ways determined by collective priorities. The necessities in most low-income households are food and electricity (and transport costs for some children to get to school and/or for anyone in employment). At a time of rising energy and food costs, social grants must be stretched in this way to cover these essentials and are often not enough. Although social grants are intended for the child or older person, in reality they support the necessities of many others in the same household and even beyond the household. Income from employment that is irregular and low and generated by the younger generation, especially if they have a child, is not expected to be shared in the same way that the older person's income, from employment or a pension, is shared within the household.

Public provision gives resources to some family members but not others, and meets the care needs of some people within some families but not others (at least not directly). Those whose needs are not met by public provision must instead look to the family for support. In this way, the economic conditions of high unemployment, coupled with the structure of (limited) public provision, shape practices of family care and the management and distribution of money within and between households.

The structure of public provision is shaping care practices in the sense that the responsibility for taking care of multiple dependants falls on women, and especially older women such as Itumeleng and 'Mathabo, in the examples above, who receive social grants. The presence of the pension has made it a vital source of household income. In this way, support for households is focused on older people and, in the absence of support for working-age adults who are unemployed, this can cause tensions (Button and Ncapai, 2019). We recognise and applaud the impact that social grants in the form of pensions have on older people and their households in enhancing the dignity of the elderly and reducing poverty (Sagner and Mtati, 1999). Women, and older women specifically, are critical financial providers in a context in which many unemployed able-bodied working-age adults are not supported by any social grants and are unable to obtain employment. In allocating resources within and between families/households, older women are making decisions and negotiating tensions around who should receive support. In doing so, not only do they carry an unequal burden in terms of responsibilities, but this also allows the state to be inattentive to the needs of other household members and oblivious to the challenges faced by older people in redistributing resources (Button and Ncpai, 2019).

A number of other studies have shown that the burden of financial and practical care has resulted in caregivers, especially older women, experiencing more strain (Schatz and Ogunmefun, 2007; Mosoetsa, 2011; Button and Ncapai, 2019). For example, in Lesotho, it is common to hear how pension beneficiaries are forced to pay off their 'local shop' credit, that has been accumulated by members of the younger generation without adequate consultation or agreement with the older person. The social grant in this case acts as collateral or security for spending by the younger generation. Shop owners who accept younger adults' indirect use/abuse of the state pension (by putting items on their grandmother's account) contribute to shaping relations in the household, including tensions such as these.

As our case studies show, and as other studies have demonstrated, given the often low value of social grants, these can only be part of the livelihood strategies pursued by individuals and families (Mosoetsa, 2011). Akin to Zelizer's work on the social meaning of money, and how 'special monies' are incorporated into webs of relationships among friends and family (Zelizer, 1989), evidence based on research indicates that culture and social processes affect the value of money in South African households, meaning that it is easier for members of the household or other kin to make a claim on social grants which are 'money that you have not worked for', compared to income earned from employment (Dawson and Fouksman, 2016). Similarly, in Lesotho, social grants are referred to as *seoa holimo* (money falling from the sky), suggesting entitlement for all, not just the intended beneficiaries (Ansell et al., 2019).

Implications for future research

In this section we consider the implications for future research. Firstly, there is very little comparative work on the redistribution of social grants in the global south or across different countries within the Southern Africa region. We would urge more regional comparative work to examine the specifics of each context, especially in the light of the variations in public provision across the region. Secondly, there are big gaps in our understanding of men's practices and priorities (specifically relating to older men and their use of pensions) not only in South Africa and Lesotho but also across the region more generally. Consequently, our knowledge about how pensions (and social grants more broadly) are redistributed in households relies heavily on women's experience and we lack understanding of the control, management and distribution of social grants – as well as other sources of income – from a male perspective.

Furthermore, the expenditure of social grants at the household level is unclear in contexts in which the beneficiary has considerable impairment(s). How do the specific health needs of the individual shape decision-making about household needs and costs when a pension or disability grant is being shared? More research on the ways in which social grants are controlled, managed and distributed is critical to highlighting how social policies shape forms of care and the ways in which any tensions within the wider household (as well as between households) are managed.

In contexts in which income is limited, research on the exchange of non-material as well as material resources is required in order to fully understand the process of redistribution of resources within households. More generally, a better understanding of normative attitudes and values underpinning the sharing of money, and how this may vary between different sources of income, is required. Finally, it is important to examine the policy-making process that lies behind the introduction of certain social grants and the ideologies that underpin such policies.

Notes

1. Posel and Hall (2021: 806–807) outline how household formation has become more gendered in South Africa in recent years, stating 'by 2018, almost half (46 per cent) of all households had resident adults of only one gender (25 per cent were female-dominated, and 21 per cent were male-dominated). Female-dominated households are far larger, and they are much more likely to include children (under 18 years) and adults of pensionable age (over 59 years)'.
2. A Social Relief Distress Grant was introduced in South Africa during the COVID-19 pandemic, which has a function similar to that of a benefit for unemployment; it was extended to March 2024, but is not necessarily a permanent feature of the social security system.

References

Agarwal, B. (1997) '"Bargaining" and gender relations: Within and beyond the household', *Feminist Economics*, 3(1), 1–51.

Ansell, N. and Van Blerk, L. (2004) 'Children's migration as a household/family strategy: coping with AIDS in Lesotho and Malawi'. *Journal of Southern African Studies*, 30(3), 673–690.

Ansell, N., van Blerk, L., Robson, E., Hajdu, F., Mwathunga, E., Hlabana, T. and Hemsteede, R. (2019) *Social grants, generational relations and youth poverty trajectories in rural Lesotho and Malawi*. London: Brunel University.

Besnier, E., Hlabana, T., Kotzias, V., Beck, K., Sieu, C. and Muthengi, K. (2023) 'Exploring economic empowerment and gender in Lesotho's Child Grants Program: A qualitative study'. *Health Policy and Planning*: https:// doi.org/ 10 .1093/ heapol/ czad009

Boehm, C. (2006) 'Industrial labour, marital strategy and changing livelihood trajectories among young women in Lesotho'. In C. Christiansen, H.E. Vigh and M. Utas (eds) *Navigating youth, generating adulthood: Social becoming in an African context*. Uppsala: Nordiska Afrikainstitutet, 153–182.

Burgoyne, C. (2004) 'Heartstrings and purse strings: Money in heterosexual marriage'. *Feminism and Psychology*, 14(1), 165–172.

Button, K. and Ncapai, T. (2019) 'Conflict and negotiation in intergenerational care: Older women's experiences of caring with the Old Age Grant in South Africa'. *Critical Social Policy*, 39(4), 560–581.

Dawson, H. and Fouksman, E. (2016) 'Don't give money to the lazy': The moral functions of wage labour and the rejection of social grants, from above and below, in South Africa. Presented at UK Development Studies Association conference, 12–14 September, University of Oxford.

Doss, C. (2005) 'The effects of intrahousehold property ownership on expenditure patterns in Ghana'. *Journal of African Economies*, 15(1), 149–180.

Garcia, M. and Moore, C. (2012) *The cash dividend: The rise of cash transfer programs in Sub-Saharan Africa*. Washington, DC: World Bank.

Hall, K. and Mokomane, Z. (2018) 'The shape of children's families and households: A demographic overview'. In K. Hall, L. Richter, Z. Mokomane and L. Lake (eds)

South African Child Gauge 2018. Cape Town: Children's Institute, University of Cape Town, 32–45.

Hamplova, D., Le Bourdais, C. and Lapierre-Adamcyk, É. (2014) 'Is the cohabitation marriage gap in money pooling universal?' *Journal of Marriage and Family*, 76(5), 983–997.

Hanlon, J., Hulme, D. and Barrientos, A. (2010) *Just give money to the poor*. Sterling, VA: Kumarian Press.

Harrison, A., Short, S.E. and Tuoane-Nkhasi, M. (2014) 'Re-focusing the gender lens: Caregiving women, family roles and HIV/AIDS vulnerability in Lesotho'. *Aids and Behavior*, 18(3), 595–604.

Hatch, M. and Posel, D. (2018) 'Who cares for children? A quantitative study of child-care in South Africa', *Development Southern Africa*, 35(2), 267–282.

Heimdal, K.R. and Houseknecht, S.K. (2003) 'Cohabiting and married couples' income organization: Approaches in Sweden and the United States'. *Journal of Marriage and Family*, 65(3), 525–538.

Heinrich, C., Hoddinott, J., Samson, M., MacQuene, K., van Niekerk, I. and Renaud, B. (2012) *The South African child support grant impact assessment: Evidence from a survey of children, adolescents and their households*. Pretoria: UNICEF South Africa.

Hlabana, T.K. (2007) 'The context of fatherhood in Lesotho: Effects of child-father co-residence on children's nutritional status'. Working paper, Brown University.

Kearabetswe, M.Z. and Khunou, G. (2019) 'Parental absence: Intergenerational tensions and contestations of social grants in South Africa'. *Critical Social Policy*, 39(4), 525–540.

Kelly, G. (2019) 'Disability, social grants and family practices in South Africa'. *Critical Social Policy*, 39(4), 541–559.

Klasen, S. and Woolard, I. (2009). 'Surviving unemployment without state support: Unemployment and household formation in South Africa'. *Journal of African Economies*, 18(1), 1–51.

Mhongo, C. and Budlender, D. (2013) 'Declining rates of marriage in South Africa: What do the numbers and analysts say?' In A. Claassens and D. Smythe (eds) *Marriage, land and custom: essays on law and social change in South Africa*. Cape Town: Juta and Company, 181–196.

Mitra, S. (2010) 'Disability social grants in the context of poverty and unemployment: The case of South Africa'. *World Development*, 38(12), 1692–1709.

Moore, E. (2020) 'Financing social reproduction: Women's responsibilities in financing and undertaking household social reproduction in multi-generational households in South Africa'. *Revue Internationale des Etudes du Développement* (Special Issue on Care, Inequalities and Policies in the Global South), 242(2), 37–62.

Moore, E. and Seekings, J. (2019) 'Consequences of social protection on intergenerational relationships in South Africa'. *Critical Social Policy*, 39(4), 513–524.

Mosoetsa, S. (2011) *Eating from one pot: The dynamics of survival in poor South African households*. Johannesburg: Witwatersrand University Press.

Nyman, C. (1999) 'Gender equality in the "most equal country in the world"? Money and marriage in Sweden'. *The Sociological Review*, 47(4), 766–793.

Nyman, C. and Dema, S. (2007) 'Research on couples and money'. In J. Stocks, C. Diaz and B. Hallerod (eds) *Modern couples sharing money, sharing life*. London: Palgrave Macmillan, 7–29.

Parker, E.M. and Short, S.E. (2009) 'Grandmother coresidence, maternal orphans, and school enrolment in Sub-Saharan Africa'. *Journal of Family Issues*, 30(6), 813–836.

Parliamentary Budget Office (2021) 'Social grant performance as end of March 2021'. Ref. no. 21/1/3 (March): www.parliament.gov.za/storage/app/media/PBO/National _Development_Plan_Analysis/ 2021/ june/ 03 -06 -2021/ May _2021 _Social _Grant _fact_sheet.pdf (accessed 19 April 2022).

Posel, D. and Hall, K. (2021) 'The economics of households in South Africa'. In F. Tregenna, I. Valodia and A. Oqubay (eds) *The Oxford handbook of the South African economy*. Oxford: Oxford University Press, 800–822.

Posel, D. and Rogan, M. (2012) 'Gendered trends in poverty in the post-apartheid period, 1995–2006'. *Development Southern Africa*, 29(1), 97–113.

Sagner, A. and Mtati, R.Z. (1999) 'Politics of pension sharing in urban South Africa'. *Ageing and Society*, 19(4), 393–416.

Schatz, E. and Ogunmefun, C. (2007) 'Caring and contributing: The role of older women in rural South African multi-generational households in the HIV/AIDS era'. *World Development*, 35(8), 1390–1403.

Seekings, J. and Moore, E. (2014) 'Kinship, market and state in the provision of care in South Africa'. *Soziale Welt*, 20, 435–450.

Sidloyi, S. (2016) 'Elderly, poor and resilient: Survival strategies of elderly women in female-headed households: An intersectionality perspective'. *Journal of Comparative Family Studies*, 47(3), 379–396.

Smock, P.J., Manning, W.D. and Porter, M. (2005) '"Everything's there except money": How money shapes decisions to marry among cohabitors'. *Journal of Marriage and Family*, 67(3), 680–696.

Spiegel, A., Watson, V. and Wilkinson, P. (1996) 'Domestic diversity and fluidity among some African households in Greater Cape Town'. *Social Dynamics*, 22(1), 7–30.

Wright, G., Neves, D., Ntshongwana, P. and Noble, M. (2015) 'Social assistance and dignity: South African women's experiences of the child support grant'. *Development Southern Africa*, 32(4), 443–457.

Yodanis, C. and Lauer, S. (2007) 'Managing money in marriage: Multilevel and cross-national effects of the breadwinner role'. *Journal of Marriage and Family*, 69(5), 1307–1325.

Young, L. and Ansell, N. (2003) 'Fluid households, complex families: The impacts of children's migration as a response to HIV/AIDS in Southern Africa'. *The Professional Geographer*, 55(4), 464–476.

Zelizer, V.A. (1989) 'The social meaning of money: "Special monies"'. *American Journal of Sociology*, 95(2), 342–377.

Zembe-Mkabile, W., Surender, R., Sanders, D., Jackson, D. and Doherty, T. (2015) 'The experience of social grants in alleviating childhood poverty in South Africa: Mothers' experiences of the child support grant'. *Global Public Health*, 10(7), 834–851.

12. Ageing populations, financial capability and household financial decision-making in the context of neoliberal social policy systems

Debora Price

Introduction

The now substantial global body of academic work on couples and money theorises access to household money as a product of gendered power relations, and demonstrates that women broadly speaking have less access to money and less financial power within households than men. With only a handful of exceptions, ageing is invisible in these studies. The degree to which this invisibility *matters* is related in part to the extent to which the wider financial, political and policy environment has a tendency to individualise rather than socialise late-life financial decision-making (Austen et al., this volume). This is because socialised risks do not require private discussion or agreement over investments, decumulation and consumption of household financial resources in the same way as privatised/individualised systems. The greater the need for individual financial decision-making in later life, the more we might be concerned to understand the gendered dynamics of the households in which older people live.

This chapter focuses on issues arising in financial management for older female/male couples living together in couple-only households (see Burchardt and Karagiannaki, and Moore and Hlabana, this volume, for consideration of complex households). For later-life couples this remains by far the dominant living arrangement, in higher-income countries at least. For example, in the 2021 Census for England and Wales, 87 per cent of the approximately 7.5 million people over 65 who lived with others in private households were living only with an opposite-sex partner, less than 1 per cent with a same-sex partner and 12 per cent in other household configurations (ONS, 2023).

The issue of how finances are managed in later life is growing in sociological and policy importance. With increases in longevity, especially for men, many more people are surviving into old age and coupledom is extending further into later life. Late life may also bring ill health and cognitive decline. Policy attention is largely focused on health, long-term care and pension systems. However, over the last two decades there has been mounting interest world-wide, from policymakers and academics, in the financial capability of populations, with increasing interest in financial capability at older ages (Choi and Cude, 2021).

This interest in financial capability in old age is principally due to four factors. First, populations are ageing and the oldest-old are growing at the fastest rate. The United Kingdom (UK), for example, anticipates the population of those aged 75 and above to grow from 5.8 million (8.6 per cent of the population) in 2020 to 9.7 million (13.7 per cent) by 2045 (ONS, 2022). Second, the incidence of cognitive impairment and dementia is increasing the world over as the numbers of people over 75 increase. Third, as policy changes across the world have exhibited a tendency to shift the burden for pensions, housing, long-term care and healthcare from collective solutions provided by the state and employers to individualised solutions involving personal risk, the necessity for older people to interact with financial products and financial services at later ages is continually increasing. While these shifts may differ in detail and extent between countries, this has been most evident in those that privilege market solutions for welfare. In the UK, for example, policy trends towards individualising financial welfare in later life have included housing policies, deregulation of financial markets, privatisation of utility companies, privatisation of part of the state pension, a new ability to liberate pension funds in mid-life (from age 55) without annuitisation and a largely marketised, and financially complex, adult social care system. Fourth, there have been substantial changes in the last 20 years in how financial services are presented and sold to consumers and how people are expected to interact with and use them (Greene, 2022). These changes include, amongst other things, telephone and online methods of communication, digital banking, digital management of pensions, investments, savings and loans and the increased use of websites and digital apps on smartphones and mobile devices.

The result of these directions of change in the political economy of welfare states is that individuals and families are increasingly expected to manage their finances in sophisticated ways for many years, sometimes in very complex circumstances. However, while the need for financial decision-making, and for financial collaboration, discussion and action, persist ever later in everyday life, in current conceptualisations of the problem of financial capability the internal financial workings of older people's households are mostly rendered invisible. Indeed, how money relations within such households are or might be affected by financial capability, declining cognition and lack of formal capacity for financial decision-making are matters largely unexplored in research or academic literature.

This chapter connects three so far disparate bodies of research to expose significant research gaps and raise important issues for those interested in how couples and families manage and distribute money, namely financial capability, declining cognition and money management among older couples. The chapter begins with a discussion of how neoliberal economic and political agendas change the role of finance and money in daily life for older people. It then reviews what is known about financial capability, cognitive change and money management and discusses limitations in using legal instruments for loss of capacity (such as powers of attorney). The discussion then turns to what is known about money management within older-couple households. Finally, the sociological and policy implications of these bodies of work for our understanding of the intra-household management and distribution of resources is considered, with suggestions as to how a future research agenda might be framed.

Financial capability and the policy context

The financial capabilities that we need to deal with money throughout our lives, including in late life, depend on how finance for later life is structured by government and the markets. If people need to accrue and manage their own housing, pensions, savings and health expenditure, they require far more financial competencies throughout their lives than if social housing is an option, or defined benefit pensions are provided by the government and/ or former employers, or there is a national health service free at the point of delivery. Experiences of money management in daily life for older people are therefore a product of a multiplicity of policy and industry responses over time across policy domains.

The issues discussed in this chapter will differ, but be present, for older people across high-, middle- and low-income countries. Their relative saliency will depend on the degree of financialisation of later life, especially across pension and benefit receipt, housing, healthcare, social care and daily consumption. As detailed below (and also in Austen et al., this volume), we know almost nothing about gender issues in intra-household distribution of resources among older couples in any part of the world. However, we do know that financialised products are becoming more central to daily life everywhere. For example, China now has one of the highest home ownership rates in the world (Huang et al., 2021), credit is increasingly available to households across the world (Léon, 2018) and health insurance in countries with less access to healthcare is a rapidly growing market (Hunter and Murray, 2019). Micro-decisions relating to consumption, saving and money transfers are arguably even more relationally complex in tightly resource-constrained environments. For example, grandparents in receipt of state or employer-sponsored pensions might be balancing essential financial support for grandchildren or adult children with their own increasing needs for health and social care, in countries with little to no state infrastructure (Moore and Hlabana, this volume).

While gender issues arising for older couples negotiating in these spheres have barely been researched, age brings with it another important and hidden domain. Largely unspoken, financial capability is highly sensitive to changes in cognitive abilities that can occur through natural ageing or illness, and older people are more vulnerable than younger age groups to financial scams and abuse. But changes to cognition and being a victim of abuse are stigmatised, and are often kept secret by older individuals, couples and families.

Financial capability across the life course

There is now a body of evidence from numerous countries around the world showing that financial knowledge and literacy matter for financial behaviours and financial outcomes in later life (see the review in Choi and Cude, 2021). However, research has shown that financial capability in the population at large varies greatly and so, as people age, they are not all starting from the same base. Even in countries with high levels of education, only about 30 per cent of the population demonstrate even minimal understanding of interest rates, inflation and investment risk (Lusardi and Mitchell, 2011a, 2011b). There is some variation, but a lack of this basic understanding is widespread across all countries, even where financial markets are well developed, such as in Germany, the Netherlands, Sweden, Italy, Japan, New Zealand and the UK. Although this finding is possibly unexpected, the financial competency profiles of older groups are only a little worse than those of younger age groups, but there is a greater problem of overconfidence in older age groups (Finney and Hayes, 2015; Money Advice Service, 2015).

These issues of financial competencies and resultant wise or poor financial decision-making have not been conceptualised within the intra-household money management literature, whether at younger or older ages. In addition, we have not yet sought to understand dyadic differences within couples nor how these may influence power dynamics relating to access to money across age and time.

Ageing and declining cognition in later life

Ageing populations, however, raise further questions about the impact of declining cognition on financial competencies. Even in the absence of disease, cognitive functions important for making sound financial decisions decline across the adult life course, but especially after age 60 (Salthouse, 2009; Boyle et al., 2012; Finke et al., 2016). Psychologists have shown that, although people also develop compensatory skills as they grow older, age-related cognitive declines worsen the ability to make sound financial decisions, on average after about age 70 (Strough et al., 2020). Scholars have also identified declining cognition as a key risk factor for vulnerability to financial abuse and financial scams (Gamble et al., 2014; Lichtenberg et al., 2018; Choi and Cude, 2021).

Apart from such age-related issues, as populations age across the world the incidence of dementias in late life is expected to markedly increase. There are currently estimated to be about 57 million people living with dementia, projected to triple to about 150 million by 2050. The largest increases (of more than 350 per cent) are anticipated in North Africa, the Middle East and eastern sub-Saharan Africa (Nichols et al., 2022). Even in countries with advanced social care systems, most people with dementia live at home. In the UK, for example, about 7 per cent of the population over 65 lives with diagnosed dementia (about 1 million people), about 60 per cent of whom live in the community (Wittenberg et al., 2019). However, and notably, the National Health Service (NHS) also estimates that 40 per cent of people living with dementia remain undiagnosed in the community (NHS Digital, 2022), i.e. in the region of a further half a million people in the UK.

The loss of cognitive abilities in the presence of age-related brain diseases in particular is especially important for financial decision-making. Marson, a leading United States (US) researcher in this field, has shown increasing incapacity in all financial domains as Alzheimer's disease advances. But importantly, he also showed substantial variation in financial functioning, especially with mild and moderate dementia (Marson, 2001). In the early stages of the disease, financial capabilities vary substantially (Sudo and Laks, 2017).

From the perspective of households, problems in financial domains in daily life are often early indicators of disease (Triebel and Marson, 2012). Indeed, using retrospective analysis of consumer credit data linked to Medicare claims in the US for over 80,000 people, Nicholas et al. (2021) showed that people who had an 'Alzheimer's disease or related dementias' diagnosis (ADRD) had begun to experience difficulties managing finances and adverse financial events up to six years before their diagnoses, patterns unique to ADRD. In a ten-year study of couples in the US in which one partner was living with cognitive decline, Hsu and Willis (2013) showed that money management problems long preceded giving up control of finances, and that in their sample 33 per cent of people living with dementia remained the primary financial decision-maker. Li et al. (2022), using US population data, showed that most individuals with mild cognitive impairment and diagnosed dementias (which they estimated at 20 per cent of the population over 65) reported continuing to manage finances within the household, and that one third of respondents with cognitive problems owned risky assets (such as stocks, retirement savings accounts and assets carrying a loan).

Importantly for considering the situation of couples, Okonkwo et al. (2008) showed that people with a diagnosis of mild cognitive impairment tend to overestimate their financial abilities; but that informants (loved ones, caregivers) overestimate them even more. Indeed, Angrisani and Lee (2019), using the large-scale longitudinal Health and Retirement Study of older people in the US, found that changes in cognitive abilities over time have little impact on changing the primary household financial decision-maker. Importantly, they found significant reductions in wealth among households whose financial decision-maker experienced such declines, as did the retrospective study by Gresenz et al. (2020). Mazzonna and Peracchi (2021) further demonstrated that this was a result of bad financial decisions, rather than rational disinvestment strategies. Cognitive difficulties with ageing and disease may of course also interact with other health problems associated with ageing, such as illness, mobility problems, pain, and loss of vision and hearing.

What this means, for the purposes of thinking about the everyday lives of couples, is that most people with a dementia diagnosis live at home; only a small proportion have severe dementia, with most having a mild form; but also that very substantial numbers living with cognitive decline are undiagnosed. Assessments and diagnoses about cognitive function are usually made long after individuals and their close kin are first worried about problems, and it is also a complex emotional space – often a closely guarded and stigmatised family secret. The body of research outlined above unwittingly tells a story of a lengthy period when the relational aspects of money management might become very challenging, and for which there is no ready script or narrative – a grey area between public and private worlds, stigmatised, hidden and privately managed within the household. Like the consideration of financial capability, our conceptualisation of couples' money management does not imagine how these issues, likely to be affecting somewhere between 7 and 20 per cent of the population aged over 65, affect gendered financial relations.

Mental capacity and instruments for financial management of another's affairs

Countries around the world have frameworks of legislation and practice to deal with lack of capacity for decision-making. When proxy decision-making powers are given to another person, these are often via instruments called durable or enduring or lasting powers of attorney, or the appointment of deputies or guardians by the courts. In the UK, for example, the legislative regime covering these matters is the Mental Capacity Act 2005 (MCA). This framework is (rightly) focused on the preservation of autonomy and independence, rather than on protecting people from making potentially terrible decisions about their money in the course of losing executive function to make optimal decisions (Hall et al., 2023).

In practice, the legal requirement of competence to make decisions under the MCA for older people is strongly related to formal diagnoses of mild cognitive impairment and dementia, although a diagnosis does not make someone incapable under the Act. Because an assessment that a person lacks capacity has major implications for their liberty, health and wellbeing, these are not decisions taken lightly. People are assumed to have capacity, and must not be treated as unable to make a decision unless all practicable steps to help them to do so have been taken without success, and must not be treated as unable to make a decision merely because they make an unwise decision. Research on the operation of the MCA has shown that capacity is mostly assessed in patients in making healthcare decisions or admission to residential or nursing care. It is used much less in the context of financial decisions, where there is little guidance and a reluctance by professionals to intervene in family and private life (Hall et al., 2023). It is of little to no assistance to families trying to get by in the long grey shadow of slowly declining capacity.

In the UK, the main legal instrument for others to exercise proxy power over decisions for a person who lacks capacity is the execution of Lasting Powers of Attorney (LPoA), whereby one person with full capacity gives enduring legal decision-making power to another. LPoAs are most often granted to a family member (e.g. a spouse, sibling or adult child) and can only lawfully be used once a person has lost capacity to make decisions. Once secured, however, the complexity for family members trying to exercise these powers is little recognised. The need for negotiation of day-to-day decisions does not end when a spouse or adult child decides that their partner or parent can no longer deal with their own money. There may be disagreement and denial, as well as potentially feelings of conspiracy and lack of trust perhaps engendered by the disease itself which sometimes manifests with delusions, aggression and anger. Exploratory research by Hall et al. (2023) has shown that the emotional space around family members using, or trying to use, powers of attorney for financial decisions is layered with tensions, complexity and difficulty. Sherman and Bauer (2008) have similarly emphasised the intergenerational tensions, and associated financial and psychological risks, that arise regarding financial decisions for remarried couples associated with the onset of Alzheimer's disease. In their small study in the US, remarried wives caring for a husband with dementia reported that financial decision-making resulted in them feeling diminished, distressed and embattled in their roles as wife and caregiver, often because of financial conflicts, diminished trust and financial exploitation by stepchildren.

What this means is that laws giving proxy decision-making powers are often of little help in the everyday lives of couples while people live with mild or moderate problems yet still have capacity under the law for decision-making. Moreover, the principal instruments under which people operate when things have progressed further, legal powers of attorney or similar, introduce yet further complexity into the dyadic space of coupledom. This is due to the relational, emotional and practical complexities of exercising such powers. Furthermore, once capacity is lost, legal systems will conceptualise the assets and income of an individual as necessarily being applied by proxies for the benefit of that individual. This may well hinder the kind of daily redistribution of financial resources or joint-lives planning that in normal circumstances takes place continuously within many couple households to optimally use combined resources for the benefit of both. Although precise rules can be complex, making proxy decisions in the best interests of the owner of those resources may no longer permit such redistribution. This may be especially problematic when legal ownership and perceived ownership of money and assets diverge (Ashby and Burgoyne, 2008).

Money management among couples in later life

Almost all research on money management and distribution within couples is conducted with those of working age. Research on coupledom in later life almost all relates to practices of intimate care in the face of ill health, with much less on understanding the everyday, including money management; and there is almost no literature on financial management within households in the face of failing health, declining cognition or the transition to the need for home care or admission to residential care.

Studies in the UK, Sweden, Canada and Australia suggest that financial inequalities long established earlier in the life course persist into later life and that, among older cohorts, money management arrangements are likely to have been highly gendered for a long time (Bisdee et al., 2013; Price et al., 2016; Austen et al., 2022). Pugliese and Belleau (2021), Kridahl and Duvander (2020, 2023) and Austen et al. (this volume) have shown that assumptions cannot be made that older couples share their retirement savings evenly, especially in the face of unequal power and unevenly accumulated wealth and income, and that financial conflicts persist into late life. Older couples, now highly unlikely to separate or divorce, may be resigned to this inequality; and this can be especially complicated in the context of remarriage or repartnering, with first and second families potentially competing (Bisdee et al., 2013; Price et al., 2016; Pugliese and Belleau, 2021). Price et al. (2016) found an unanticipated 'stickiness' about financial practices even in the face of major financial transitions such as retirement and pension receipt, with patterns established early on in the relationship persisting often through thick and thin.

The research reviewed above about practices in the face of a dementia diagnosis suggest a similar stickiness and, in an incentivised 'lab-in-the-field' experiment with Australian couples over 60, Hohn et al. (2022) suggest that men showed a low propensity to delegate financial decisions to their wives, even when it would be efficient to do so. Price et al. (2016) observed that failing health seems to be the main catalyst for change in gendered household money management within older-couple relationships; but, in long relationships, this is often accompanied by distress associated with a partner's potentially devastating ill health or cognitive decline. This was illustrated in the study of money practices in the face of cognitive decline by Bisdee et al. (2013), which found that if a man's ability to fulfil a money management role was threatened, their wives engaged in complex emotional work to maintain the breadwinner role identity in their partners. Scholars in this field therefore caution policymakers to beware of complacency and the underestimation of financial vulnerabilities within older people's households. The long-term vulnerabilities of those women who have lived with unequal access to money and material resources, with little power to influence change, are repeated themes in the literature.

Furthermore, Hancock and Wright (1999) long ago raised the potential importance of considering the intra-household allocation of resources for understanding the financial implications of one spouse requiring residential or nursing care, arguing that the financial complexities and consequences for couples in this situation deserve to be more widely recognised. They demonstrated under rules then prevailing that, on average, wives whose husbands enter residential care are best off financially when their combined income and savings are shared equally, but unequal distribution in men's favour was better for husbands if their wives entered care. The implications of intra-household ownership and distribution of money for access to adequate care within long-term care systems remains yet another little understood area.

Policy implications

In the policy sphere there is certainly increasing concern about issues of 'financial vulnerability' associated with the ageing of populations, but little concern with the inner workings of the household. The focus is squarely on the regulation of financial services and utilities tasked with supporting 'vulnerable customers' under their statutory consumer duties, and protecting people from financial scams and fraud.

Yet governments interested in the welfare of citizens should be concerned beyond these issues. Importantly, we should ask how we might protect a person against legal, but poor (and declining), financial management by their spouse or partner, especially when there are imbalances of power; and how we do, or should, protect individuals if the person with control of money becomes more vulnerable to financial scams. We should be concerned at how the daily reality of financial powers of attorney work, and for whose benefit, beyond the often limited reach of court oversight. It is a matter of public interest how we should identify problems of financial negligence, incompetence, neglect, exploitation and abuse behind closed doors, including the potential failure or inability to commit resources for the professional care of a person who needs it.

The issues discussed in this chapter therefore raise wider and currently unresolved difficulties of risk management for regulators, relevant industries and social care professionals, disclosure risks for vulnerable customers to fraudsters and scammers and moral hazards for governments in the financing of later life. All these domains would benefit from a multi-disciplinary collaborative strategy for money management in old age that puts the experiences and financial struggles of individuals, couples and families at the centre. But this chapter also raises specific concerns for the welfare of people within the household, and especially for couples, as financial decision-making that optimises welfare for individuals may be quite different when viewed from an individual's, partner's, couple's or family's perspective. From a policy viewpoint, we have not resolved the questions that arise from a relational view of coupledom, of who needs to be protected, against what and from whose point of view. In the face of changes in competencies or cognition, we do not currently have an answer as to what appropriate access to financial resources for each household member might look like. How we protect such access, and how we ensure that combined financial resources are being deployed for the benefit of someone needing them, but also manage future risks, perhaps for the other partner, remain important questions.

Directions for future research

The sociological research agenda therefore seems substantial. In the context of ageing and older couples, how do couple and family dynamics unfold in financial spheres in the face of poor financial capability and emerging cognitive decline? How (if at all) does the balance of power shift?

Numerous research gaps have been revealed by this analysis. Most married and cohabiting women will still become widows, often living in widowhood for a long time, and possibly in ill health and disability, before they die. Not only are the resources of the couple sometimes diminished by the lifelong unequal access to financial resources, leaving less for their later years of life, but in addition women have often had less say in decisions that may affect their widowhood severely, such as pension annuitisation and housing. Furthermore, we know that spouses may sacrifice their own consumption to help maintain the identity of their partner as breadwinner and money manager, but we know little about how this affects their own financial wellbeing and their future finances. Many women will also have little experience of taking control of financial decisions and may be ill-equipped, in terms of human and social capital, to begin this in later life. How couples' financial resources are managed for the period 'beyond' when frailty and cognition become part of the joint picture, and an individual's own care needs might become profound, is currently a question to which we do not have an answer.

We also do not currently have insight into whether there are long-term financial implications for those who might need care in late life if they lacked autonomy and control over finances over the course of their relationship and become reliant on their partner committing his or her own, or joint, resources for their care. Nor do we know anything about how access to money and resources is managed when the capacity of a partner who controlled money – perhaps physically and emotionally – begins to waver; nor what happens when a partner controlling money might begin making bad or unwise decisions, or begins to squander assets that could otherwise have been used to provide resources for their remaining joint lives. We should find out more about the challenges of accessing funds not held in joint names as the cognition and health of the party with individual assets deteriorates, and about the day-to-day challenges of exercising financial powers of attorney. We also know too little about what happens, either between partners or in relationships with the wider family, when *both* partners might start finding managing money difficult or impossible, and be vulnerable to bad financial decision-making and financial exploitation.

Importantly, this analysis has shown that almost no scholarly attention has been paid to the day-to-day management of household money in the liminal space of declining health, nor to the relational and dyadic issues heralded by issues of financial literacy and competence and/or declining cognitive function to manage financial affairs. In particular, scholars of gendered household dynamics, especially those focused on women lacking autonomy and control, or living with abusive partners who use financial resources as a means of coercive control (Howard and Sharp-Jeffs, this volume), might be concerned to understand how access to financial and material resources evolves over time in these circumstances.

Feminist scholars have long argued that the issues that arise from the individualisation of financial decision-making, financial responsibility and financial risk for families behind closed doors are little talked about, since the neoliberal welfare system depends on discourses of autonomy and choice which are at odds with interdependent lives and the need for less individualised state solutions. As this chapter has shown, in addition to other issues, gendered questions of resource distribution, autonomy and control have the potential to become ever more complex as people age, with substantial resulting challenges for those with an interest in the intra-household management and distribution of resources.

References

Angrisani, M. and Lee, J. (2019) 'Cognitive decline and household financial decisions at older ages', *Journal of the Economics of Ageing*, 13, pp. 86–101.

Ashby, K.J. and Burgoyne, C.B. (2008) 'Separate financial entities? Beyond categories of money management', *Journal of Socio-Economics*, 37(2), pp. 458–480.

Austen, S., Broomhill, R., Costa, M. and Sharp, R. (2022) 'Living with risk: Retired couples' experiences of a financialised retirement income system', *Economic and Labour Relations Review*, 33(4), pp. 737–753.

Bisdee, D., Daly, T. and Price, D. (2013) 'Behind closed doors: Older couples and the gendered management of household money', *Social Policy and Society*, 12(1), pp. 163–174.

Boyle, P.A., Yu, L., Wilson, R.S., Gamble, K., Buchman, A.S. and Bennett, D.A. (2012) 'Poor decision making is a consequence of cognitive decline among older persons without Alzheimer's disease or mild cognitive impairment', *PLOS ONE*, 7(8), e43647.

Choi, S.L. and Cude, B.J. (2021) 'Financial literacy among older adults', in G. Nicolini and B.J. Cude (eds) *The Routledge handbook of financial literacy*. Abingdon: Routledge, pp. 48–60.

Finke, M.S., Howe, J.S. and Huston, S.J. (2016) 'Old age and the decline in financial literacy', *Management Science*, 63(1), pp. 213–230.

Finney, A. and Hayes, D. (2015) *Financial capability in Great Britain, 2010 to 2012*. London: Office for National Statistics. www.bris.ac.uk/ media -library/ sites/ geography/ pfrc/ pfrc1504 -financial -capability -in -gb -2010 -2012 .pdf (accessed 30 January 2023).

Gamble, K.J., Boyle, P., Yu, L. and Bennett, D. (2014) *The causes and consequences of financial fraud among older Americans*. Boston: Boston College Center for Retirement Research WP 2014-13.

Greene, A.J. (2022) 'Elder financial abuse and electronic financial instruments: Present and future considerations for financial capacity assessments', *American Journal of Geriatric Psychiatry*, 30(1), pp. 90–106.

Gresenz, C.R., Mitchell, J.M., Marrone, J. and Federoff, H.J. (2020) 'Effect of early-stage Alzheimer's disease on household financial outcomes', *Health Economics*, 29(1), pp. 18–29.

Hall, A., Straub, C., Price, D. and Glover-Thomas, N. (2023) *Managing money in later life: Mental capacity assessment and support*. Manchester: University of Manchester. https://documents.manchester.ac.uk/display.aspx?DocID=65801 (accessed 27 July 2023).

Hancock, R. and Wright, F. (1999) 'Older couples and long-term care: The financial implications of one spouse entering private or voluntary residential or nursing home care', *Ageing and Society*, 19(2), pp. 209–237.

Hohn, S., Basu, A.K., Dulleck, U., Henry, J. and Cherbuin, N. (2022) 'Delegating financial decisions to the spouse: Experimental evidence in older couples', *SSRN Electronic Journal*. https://papers.ssrn.com/abstract=4231186 (accessed 27 July, 2023).

Hsu, J.W. and Willis, R. (2013) 'Dementia risk and financial decision making by older households: The impact of information', *Journal of Human Capital*, 7(4), pp. 340–377.

Huang, Y., He, S. and Gan, L. (2021) 'Introduction to SI: Homeownership and housing divide in China', *Cities*, 108, 102967.

Hunter, B.M. and Murray, S.F. (2019) 'Deconstructing the financialization of health-care', *Development and Change*, 50(5), pp. 1263–1287.

Kridahl, L. and Duvander, A.-Z. (2020) '"Why did you spend money on that?": Older partners' economic conflicts and management of household money in Sweden', *Stockholm Research Reports in Demography*. Stockholm: Stockholm University Demography Unit.

Kridahl, L. and Duvander, A.Z. (2023) 'Financial disagreements and money manage-ment among older married and cohabiting couples in Sweden', *Journal of Family and Economic Issues*, 44(2), pp. 394–411.

Léon, F. (2018) 'Convergence of credit structure around the world', *Economic Modelling*, 68, pp. 306–317.

Li, J., Wang, S. and Nicholas, L.H. (2022) 'Management of financial assets by older adults with and without dementia or other cognitive impairments', *JAMA Network Open*, 5(9), doi:10.1001/jamanetworkopen.2022.31436.

Lichtenberg, P.A., Gross, E. and Ficker, L.J. (2018) 'Quantifying risk of financial incapacity and financial exploitation in community-dwelling older adults: Utility of a scoring system for the Lichtenberg Financial Decision-Making Rating Scale', *Clinical Gerontologist*, 43(3), pp. 266–280.

Lusardi, A. and Mitchell, O.S. (2011a) 'Financial literacy and retirement planning in the United States', *Journal of Pension Economics and Finance*, 10(4), pp. 509–525.

Lusardi, A. and Mitchell, O.S. (2011b) 'Financial literacy around the world: An over-view', *Journal of Pension Economics and Finance*, 10(4), pp. 497–508.

Marson, D.C. (2001) 'Loss of financial competency in dementia: Conceptual and empirical approaches', *Aging, Neuropsychology, and Cognition*, 8(3), pp. 164–181.

Mazzonna, F. and Peracchi, F. (2021) 'Are older people aware of their cognitive decline? Misperception and financial decision making', *IZA Discussion Paper No. 13725*. https://papers.ssrn.com/sol3/papers.cfm?abstract_id=3699842 (accessed 30 January 2023).

Money Advice Service (2015) *The financial capability of the UK*. London: Money Advice Service.

NHS Digital (2022) *Recorded dementia diagnoses – NHS Digital*. https:// digital .nhs .uk/ data -and -information/ publications/ statistical/ recorded -dementia -diagnoses (accessed 30 January 2023).

Nicholas, L.H., Langa, K.M. and Bynum, J.P.W. (2021) 'Financial presentation of Alzheimer disease and related dementias', *JAMA Internal Medicine*, 181(2), pp. 220–227.

Nichols, E. and GBD 2019 Dementia Forecasting Collaborators (2022) 'Estimation of the global prevalence of dementia in 2019 and forecasted prevalence in 2050: An analysis for the Global Burden of Disease Study 2019', *The Lancet Public Health*, 7(2), e105–e125.

Okonkwo, O.C., Wadley, V.G., Griffith, H.R., Belue, K., Lanza, S., Zamrini, E.Y., Harrell, L.E., Brockington, J.C., Clark, D., Raman, R. and Marson, D.C. (2008) 'Awareness of deficits in financial abilities in patients with mild cognitive impair-ment: Going beyond self-informant discrepancy', *American Journal of Geriatric Psychiatry*, 16(8), pp. 650–659.

ONS (Office for National Statistics) (2022) *National population projections*. www.ons .gov .uk/ peoplepop ulationand community/ pop ulationand migration/ po pulationpr ojections/ bulletins/ nationalpo pulationpr ojections/ 2020basedinterim (accessed 27 July 2023).

ONS (Office for National Statistics) (2023) *England and Wales Census 2021 custom dataset downloaded from Office for National Statistics*. London: Office for National Statistics. www.ons.gov.uk/datasets/create/filter-outputs/8b109a6b-cde9-4dda-9901 -79ebda96a8c2#get-data (accessed 27 July 2023).

Price, D., Bisdee, D. and Daly, T. (2016) 'Money practices among older couples: Patterns of continuity, change, conflict and resistance', in S. Wong and S. Millns (eds) *Wealth and poverty in close personal relationships: Money matters*. Farnham: Ashgate Publishing, 58–73.

Pugliese, M. and Belleau, H. (2021) 'The management of retirement savings among financially heterogamous couples', *Social Policy and Society*, 20(4), pp. 580–598.

Salthouse, T.A. (2009) 'When does age-related cognitive decline begin?', *Neurobiology of Aging*, 30(4), pp. 507–514.

Sherman, C.W. and Bauer, J.W. (2008) 'Financial conflicts facing late-life remarried Alzheimer's disease caregivers', *Family Relations*, 57(4), pp. 492–503.

Strough, J., Wilson, J. and Bruine de Bruin, W. (2020) 'Aging and financial decision making', in T. Zaleskiewicz and J. Traczyk (eds) *Psychological perspectives on financial decision making*. Edinburgh: Springer, pp. 167–186.

Sudo, F.K. and Laks, J. (2017) 'Financial capacity in dementia: a systematic review', *Aging and Mental Health*, 21(7), pp. 677–683.

Triebel, K. and Marson, D. (2012) 'The warning signs of diminished financial capacity in older adults', *Generations*, 36(2), pp. 39–45.

Wittenberg, R., Hu, B., Barraza-Araiza, L. and Rehill, A. (2019) *Projections of older people with dementia and costs of dementia care in the United Kingdom, 2019–2040*. CPEC Working Paper 5. London: Care Policy and Evaluation Centre, London School of Economics.

13. Negotiating assets in a financialised retirement income system: Evidence from older mixed-sex couple households in Australia

Siobhan Austen, Susan Himmelweit, Rhonda Sharp and Monica Costa

Introduction

In households containing older people, generally more so than in those with working-age members, accumulated financial assets, including the balance on any retirement savings accounts, are key resources. However, currently we know very little about how members of older households manage their financial assets in retirement.

This is an issue of growing policy significance, not only because of the increasing share of older people but crucially also due to the financialisation of retirement, which tasks individuals with decisions about how to invest their savings and when to draw down their assets in retirement. In such a system people end up with assets rather than income or services (though they may receive these in addition), on the presumption that they have the financial motivation and ability to manage assets to meet their needs in retirement. However, the fact that decisions about retirement assets are often made within households and have implications for both gender and intra-household inequality has, to date, been poorly recognised (also see Price, this volume).

In many countries, including Australia, the United Kingdom (UK) and the Netherlands, the financialisation of retirement has been associated with a shift towards defined contribution pension schemes/superannuation, and away from defined benefit schemes and/or state old age pensions.[1] In a defined contribution system, individuals' retirement saving account balances grow over their working life through employer and employee contributions, together with any government contributions and subsidies, plus (or minus) investment returns.

In such systems, individuals have to make decisions about how their assets are invested even if by default, and how and when they will use these assets in retirement. This contrasts with defined benefit schemes and state pensions, where there is little need, or scope beyond earning more, for individuals to influence their retirement income. Defined benefit schemes generate an income stream in retirement based on prior earnings, not a pool of assets that needs to be monitored and managed. State pension systems also generate income in retirement rather than assets, and have more ability, by varying their design, to break or modify the link between prior earnings and retirement income.

Australia was an early adopter of defined contribution superannuation and now has a relatively mature system with a large share of retirees owning assets (OECD, 2021a: 25); but, with the country's care norms and labour market still highly gendered, women in general accumulate far fewer of those assets than men. This makes it a good place to study how decisions about unequal financial assets are negotiated in older couple households.

This chapter presents results from a qualitative study of decision-making on financial assets in older Australian female/male couple households, aiming to help fill important gaps in the literature on the intra-household distribution of assets, households with older members and pension financialisation. The implications of the study's results for policy on retirement, older households and gender equity are also evaluated, and suggestions are made for future research agendas.

Literature review

Perhaps reflecting how recent the trend towards defined contribution superannuation is, research on how household members navigate decisions about the management and use of retirement saving assets is relatively scarce, especially in the global north. Most research on intra-household resources is focused on income. A qualitative study by Joseph and Rowlingson (2012), examining the distribution of pension and other assets within UK couple households and how couples make decisions about assets, is an important exception. However, like other studies of intra-household differences in retirement savings, it focused only on working-age couples and on decisions about the accumulation, rather than use, of such assets (see Gibson et al., 2006). In the global south there is a growing body of work on the intra-household distribution of assets and its impacts on women's participation in household decision-making (Oduro and Swaminathan, this volume). However, much of this work is concerned with the ownership and use of physical assets, such as land and other agricultural assets, and it also tends to be limited to working-age households.

Research on the behaviour of households with older members in relation to their finances is also generally scarce. The work of Bisdee et al. (2013) on the gendered management of money in older couple households in the UK was pathbreaking. However, because this study was conducted in a context in which defined benefit pensions were still common, it was mainly concerned with how couples manage reduced household *income* in retirement, and had little to say about the management of financial *assets*. In the United States (US), where defined contribution accounts are more significant, Lim et al. (2022) examined the distribution of very broad financial decision-making roles (such as who decides about savings) in older couple (aged 50+) households. However, this study focused on how decision-making roles varied with income gaps between partners and had little to say about decisions made about assets specifically. Tennyson et al. (2022) take a similar approach in their study of the purchase of long-term care insurance by older (aged 50–75) couple households. In earlier work, Lundberg and Stillman (2003) found relatively large drops in consumption on retirement in married- versus single-person households in the US, and took this as evidence of women's greater preference to preserve financial resources (due to their greater longevity) and an increase in their bargaining power in retirement.

There is a growing literature on the consequences of pension financialisation, including risks posed to individuals' retirement savings by labour market absence and poor investment returns (De Deken, 2017). This literature has highlighted the negative impacts on gender equality stemming from women's greater unpaid care roles, which undercuts their capacity to accumulate retirement assets (James and Agunsoye, 2022). However, it has examined neither the challenges facing retirees confronting the need to make decisions about drawing down their retirement assets nor the issues facing older individuals attempting to negotiate such decisions within their households.

Our own research helps to fill these gaps in understanding how households, in particular those with older members, manage financial resources. In 2019, we conducted in-depth interviews with 36 older Australians living in female/male couple households to gain insights into the impacts of the financialisation of retirement. In earlier analysis (Austen et al., 2022; Broomhill et al., 2021), we identified many retirees' concerns about the financial risks to which they were exposed. In this chapter, we examine how older female/male couple households in Australia monitor and manage their superannuation and other assets, especially the apparent level of cooperation between the partners in undertaking these tasks.

Our study

The policy context

Studies of pension financialisation in Australia are important because the country is far ahead of others in its adoption of defined contribution super-annuation. In 2021, around 86 per cent of money in retirement income funds in Australia was in such accounts, compared to 19 per cent in the UK, 5 per cent in Japan and the Netherlands and 40 per cent in Canada (Thinking Ahead Institute, 2021). However, as noted, the trend towards defined con-tribution superannuation is occurring across the Organisation for Economic Co-operation and Development (OECD) countries, and Australia's experi-ences are, thus, a guide to issues that might become widespread.

Australia was an early adopter of defined contribution superannuation. Since 1992, Australian employers have been required to direct a share of wages and salaries to superannuation accounts in their employees' names.[2] Initially this share was 3 per cent; currently (in 2023) it is 10 per cent. Prior to 1992, super-annuation was an occupational benefit limited largely to public-sector and professional employees and most retirees depended on the state age pension, which is means tested on household income.

In the Australian system, individuals can also make additional, voluntary contributions to superannuation. Generous tax concessions apply to these (and employer contributions) and to the returns on superannuation funds, making investing in superannuation financially rewarding for those with a high income/wealth. Over age 60, neither the returns on superannuation nor withdrawals are taxed, nor generally is a survivor's receipt of their spouse's superannuation funds;[3] and there is no inheritance tax. Thus, taxation of superannuation is heavily regressive; and there is no balancing redistribution by the state, apart from its limited matching of superannuation contribu-tions made by low-paid employees. Many people do still receive a partial state age pension on low (household) income grounds; however, there is no non-means-tested state pension.

Defined contribution superannuation has had a large adverse impact on gender equality in Australia. Forty-one per cent of women aged 65+, compared to 24 per cent of men, have no superannuation assets. Among those with such assets, a 23.4 per cent gender gap in median account balances favours men, reflecting women's relatively low wage rates, typically interrupted work patterns and high rate of part-time work (Clare, 2022).

The intra-household effects are also likely to be significant. There are some tax/benefit incentives for individuals to share their superannuation wealth with their partners (married or *de facto* married – treated similarly under superannuation law). For example, a man entitled to a state age pension can boost his payments by transferring superannuation assets to his younger partner, because she will only be assessed under the pension means test once she reaches pension age. However, the evidence suggests that such incentives are rarely used.[4] Women thus remain dependent on their partner's superannuation in many older households in Australia.

Intra-household effects also arise because decisions about superannuation are individualised in the Australian system. Such decisions span choices about, for example, whether to make a lump sum withdrawal from one's superannuation account,[5] create a regular income stream (e.g. through a programmed series of withdrawals or a purchased annuity) or barely use superannuation assets at all. Although these decisions will, most often, affect the person's partner, there are no legal rights for individuals to participate in (or be informed about) their partner's decisions about superannuation, and this raises questions about how decisions about superannuation assets are negotiated within older couple households, and whose interests are best served.

Research approach

We collected data from a purposive sample spanning different demographic and economic groups to assess how financial assets are negotiated in older Australian couple households. Aware of the risk of recruiting only willing narrators who felt comfortable in placing their relationship and financial arrangements under our microscope, we used professional and social networks to identify potential interviewees. We interviewed partners separately to hear both partners' accounts of the management of money in their household, and to allow us to assess each partner's knowledge of its income and assets. The interviews, typically lasting 45 minutes, were recorded (with permission) and transcribed for thematic analysis via reading and discussion of each transcript by research team members.

Almost all the 36 retirees in the study were Australian-born and white. The oldest participant was aged 92 and the youngest 59. Most were in a long-term relationship (the longest being 69 years and the shortest 18 years). Many had been in only one relationship (either married or *de facto* married); however, others were in their second or third relationship and some had children from previous relationships. Several households were financially 'well off'. In such households, the man had experienced stable and well-paid employment and his superannuation assets were considerable. In some well-off households there were also substantial property and other financial assets. Other households had been affected, to varying degrees, by unemployment, ill health, low wages and/or financial decisions that turned out poorly. In some households super-annuation assets were minimal and, thus, reliance on the state age pension was high. In the following paragraphs we distinguish between these different household types, using 'W', 'C' and 'M' to denote, respectively, well-off, com-fortable and modest financial positions. We also distinguish between those households where, for most of their lives prior to retirement, both partners had been in paid work (labelling these 'former dual-earner households') and those where only the male partner had been employed ('former male-breadwinner households').

Decisions about the use of financial assets

In each household, decisions had had to be made about the use of assets in the form of superannuation balances – and in addition, in some cases, share-holdings, bank deposits and the proceeds from property investments. In some instances, decisions had also been made about the use of equity in the 'family' home. Superannuation was, however, the main asset used to meet household needs. Only a few households had other financial assets, and none was actively contemplating drawing down the equity in their home to support their needs, although some had already moved to a smaller home and transferred the proceeds to their superannuation account(s).

In each household, the rate at which superannuation assets were drawn down was a major concern. Some participants were anxious about longevity risk – whether their financial resources would last. Only one had bought an annuity and this was due to expire soon. Others expressed concerns about their ability to meet possible future care and health costs, in the context of a partially priva-tised system in which those with limited means can only access basic services (Myer, 2022, reports similar findings). Yet others were wanting to preserve their resources to avoid being reliant on the means-tested state age pension, understanding that it affords only a very basic standard of living.

Several participants seemed to be reluctant to see a reduction in their superannuation and other assets by using them. In contrast to the findings of Lundberg and Stillman (2003), such reluctance was more commonly reported in this study by men than women. Unprompted, a number of men described themselves as frugal, linking this to behaviours and habits learned in childhood. Several women explained that their partner 'doesn't like to spend'. A number of the male participants watched their accounts closely – sometimes on a daily basis – and were quite sensitive to negative changes in their superannuation accounts or share portfolios. Some engaged in risky investment behaviour to try to recoup past losses. For some, their superannuation balances were a source of pride, and thus something they were unwilling to relinquish.

Approaches to managing household finances: Former dual-earner versus former male-breadwinner households

Most of the financial assets of the households, including all superannuation assets, were individually owned. However, the level of cooperation within the households in managing such assets tended to vary in systematic ways across former dual-earner and former male-breadwinner households, with implications for the gendered distribution of resources. We identify cooperation in the management of superannuation and other financial assets as having the following key elements: a jointly devised plan for the drawdown of such assets; an agreed set of rules to govern access to the assets; the ability for each partner to veto decisions on their use; and a sharing between the partners of the tasks associated with monitoring household expenditure and finances. Together these elements are akin to Fleming's (1997) model of 'common ownership and responsibility' of/for income in working-age couple households. The elements were often apparent in the former dual-earner households in our sample. However, in many former male-breadwinner households, a 'plan' for the use of financial assets (whereby a budget was allocated for specific purposes) was imposed by the man and he typically had the final say in how such assets were used.

As an example of a cooperative approach to managing financial assets in retirement, the woman in former dual-earner household W3 said they had a 'family budget', and a monthly 'sit-down' when they would evaluate their financial position. Her partner took charge of monitoring their assets and income, and reporting this to her; she took charge of tracking their expenses and checking credit card receipts, and reporting this to him. He said that this gives a 'double check' that they are not spending too much. When it came to investment decisions, a similar cooperative approach was evident: changes only happened with both partners' consent. She described how her partner had proposed a change that she was unhappy about; so in one of their sit-downs she 'said "no" … so we didn't do it'. In another former dual-earner household, C1, the woman said that she did 'anything on the computer' and managed the spending on everyday items; her partner paid the bills. In C7, the man managed the household finances, but the couple had a spreadsheet for their budget, which they reviewed together; and the woman seemed to be able to veto decisions on drawing down assets with which she was uncomfortable.

In former male-breadwinner households, in contrast, the man's control of household finances tended to be the norm. If there were superannuation assets they often belonged to him, and he tended to have the most say in managing these and other financial assets. Negotiation of financial matters thus tended to be relatively limited and the woman's capacity to influence household spending often seemed to depend on whether she had some assets of her own (e.g. through inheritance).

A common technique for managing and monitoring household financial assets in former male-breadwinner households was the use of separate accounts for different types of spending, set up and monitored by the man. In one relatively wealthy such household (W2), the man allocated a budget from his superannuation for household expenses and the woman did the shopping, handing him receipts to account for her personal spending on clothes, etc. In another former male-breadwinner household, C2, the man allocated his partner a housekeeping allowance from his superannuation and some 'play money', which she used to buy things for her own personal needs but also spent on others, such as their grandchildren. He had his 'golf money'.

The importance of entitlements

This difference in the general pattern of decision-making across the former dual-earner and former male-breadwinner households reflects different mutually accepted entitlements to determine how financial assets are used. Because superannuation assets are primarily accumulated via employment relationships, they are typically owned individually – and, importantly, they are also seen to be so (Joseph and Rowlingson, 2012, report similar findings on perceptions of who owns pension assets in UK working-age couple households). As a result, the pattern of financial decision-making on such assets within the households generally tended to reflect the partners' paid work roles prior to retirement.

In the former dual-earner households, the partners typically perceived that they were both entitled to a say in how superannuation assets were used, even though such assets were inevitably individually owned, and this fostered a more cooperative approach to the management of household financial assets. In one such household, W3, the partners had shared the paid and unpaid work associated with supporting and raising their children. As a result, their superannuation assets were relatively evenly distributed at retirement. Guided by a norm of fairness, this couple also took steps to keep the balances on their individual superannuation accounts equal post-retirement. Having a relatively equal distribution of superannuation wealth, together with the experience of jointly acquiring and managing property assets, appeared to contribute to a perception, shared by the partners, that they were entitled to an equal say in how financial assets were used.

In another former dual-earner household, C7, the woman was strongly of the view that the contributions to the household's financial assets and thus the entitlements to household superannuation assets were equal. She explained how 'somebody said, when we retired, "well, it's his money, he can invest some of it". And ... I thought, "no, it's not his money, it's our money" ... I don't have a right over it ... and I don't think he does, but we have rights over it together'.

In the former male-breadwinner households, in contrast, the mutually accepted entitlement to superannuation assets tended to lie with the man and it was often easiest for his partner if she fell in with his plans for how they would be used in retirement. Importantly, the pattern of entitlement to superannuation assets did not appear to be affected by the transfer of legal ownership of such assets between partners after retirement. As noted earlier, such transfers are possible in Australia and can be financially advantageous to the couple. However, in C5, a couple in which such a transfer took place, the woman only joked about such assets being hers; and her partner described the fund as being the money *he* received upon retirement. He said that she would propose spending from this fund and he would resist. In M2, the woman smiled broadly when she described how they acted on the advice of a financial planner to transfer her partner's 'super' to her; but then said: 'it's all his, as far as I'm concerned anyway, even though it's in my name'. In C2 the woman did not know the balance on the superannuation account in her name and she had little to no influence on how this money was used. She put spending 'on the agenda', but her partner ultimately decided what was bought. She struggled with the tight budget that he imposed to preserve the household's substantial superannuation assets but seemed unable to effect change.

Other factors affecting the negotiation of financial resources in older couple households

Older couples' approaches to managing financial assets might well also reflect the habits of decision-making set up prior to retirement (see Bisdee et al., 2013, on the similarity between pre- and post-retirement approaches to managing income). It is difficult to disentangle the effects of entitlements to assets previously accumulated and previous habits of decision-making within the couples. Both are likely to be important, especially for women's participation in decision-making in older couple households and their wellbeing in later life; both are linked to the earlier paid and unpaid work roles of the partners, and they generate differences between former dual-earner and former male-breadwinner households.

Variations in how financial resources are negotiated *within* these groups of former dual-earner and former male-breadwinner households point to the likely influence of additional factors. In low-resource households within each group, women played a relatively large role in deciding how financial resources are used (also see Bennett et al., 2010, on women's roles in low-income households). In M1, for example, the woman managed the superannuation and bank accounts, kept track of income and spending and paid the bills. She said that the couple talked about investments and large expenditures, such as on household appliances, but also went on to say that sometimes she buys larger items without consulting her partner. In this household, the man said that he was happy to leave the management of financial assets to his spouse. Both partners perceived that she was more skilled in financial matters: he said, 'she's the smart one'; and she said, '[He] has no idea about anything'.

Dealing with, and negotiation about, financial assets were also affected by poor communication and conflicting preferences. In former dual-earner household C1, for example, the partners had different ideas about the level of household spending that was appropriate for their needs, and this appeared to make negotiation difficult. He was reluctant to spend if this involved drawing down more than the minimum amount from their superannuation accounts; she identified projects around the home that she thought needed doing that he was reluctant to finance. He said: 'it's not the case that we haven't got the money, it's just that I'm not that interested, I don't want to do it'. The disagreement between these partners over spending was not resolved through talk, highlighting the negative impact of poor communication. He said that his approach to negotiating conflict was to 'manage to squash it for the moment'. She responded by sometimes withdrawing money from her own superannuation account in order to achieve what she believed should have been joint spending.

Implications for policy and future research

Our research has shown how financialised retirement systems, by creating assets that individuals need to manage when they retire, require people to deal with risk, but that this is difficult, especially for people brought up to be workers rather than investors. Needing to make decisions about financial assets is clearly also a potential source of intra-household conflict, especially if household members have different ideas about the use of such assets and different levels of economic resources. Financialised retirement systems result in individual ownership of assets and gender and intra-household inequality in this ownership, reflecting the unequal distribution of wages. The capacity of older women to influence financial decision-making within their households is limited as a result.

Our findings suggest some avenues for future research, mainly to investigate policies that might help to rectify some problems of the present system, including its obvious gender inequalities.

To a large extent the causes of such gender inequalities lie outside the retirement funding system itself, in unequal lifetime earnings consequent upon unequal gender roles. These will not be rectified by changes within the current superannuation system. Measures that promote equality between working-age partners in their paid and unpaid roles would work towards equalising the gender distribution of superannuation assets, which would be positive for older women's wellbeing in particular.

Less reliance on superannuation for retirement funding and a greater role for a non-means-tested old age pension would assist women, help to equalise partners' retirement incomes within couple households and reduce the need for older couples to navigate decisions about the use of financial assets. Preliminary work in Australia has identified how, if set at a reasonable level, such a pension could be funded by progressive taxes on retirement income (Account Plan, 2020); but additional modelling is needed to assess its likely effects. More broadly, there is a need for investigations into the effect of contributory and non-contributory (including means-tested) state old age pensions on intra-household inequality.

The gendered pattern of work roles is likely to change only slowly and the entrenched power of the financial organisations involved means that the trend towards the financialisation of retirement incomes is likely to be difficult to reverse. It is therefore important to also consider whether modifying such systems can address the problems they create. In particular, research is needed into measures to address the circumstances of the *current* generation of older women and protect future generations of women with an unequal share of their household's superannuation assets, given that this inequality will inevitably persist for many years, even if to a diminishing extent.

Reforms such as care credits towards retirement provision for periods spent caring for children or adult family members – paid for by the state – could boost women's financial resources in retirement and thus enhance their role in household decision-making processes (see International Social Security Association, 2017: 18, for policy measures for improved gender equity in retirement in other contexts). However, how to implement such credits so that they close asset gaps but do not further entrench unequal employment and caring roles is not obvious and requires further research, including detailed policy simulations.

Superannuation transfers between spouses can also be positive in reducing gender asset inequality. However, if they were framed differently, not as opportunities to maximise benefits (as they are currently in Australia) but as a measure to promote sharing and equality, these effects could be larger. There is scope for research on whether framing equalising superannuation within couple households as the normal arrangement (or set as the default) would improve older women's financial position by changing their sense of entitlement to transferred assets and an income of their own.

There is also need for research into the role and impact of policy measures that might improve individuals' access to information on their partners' superannuation and other financial assets. Our results suggest that it is not uncommon for older women to have little to no knowledge of their partner's superannuation assets, and this is an obvious barrier to their ability to have a say in how such financial resources are used. A broader body of research (see, for example, Castilla and Walker, 2013) has identified how partners can conceal financial resources from each other and in so doing skew the allocation of household resources in their own favour. However, other research (Eroğlu, 2009) has highlighted the importance of privacy for women's outcomes, with some achieving financial agency through the use of a 'secret kitty' – savings that are squirrelled away unbeknownst to one's spouse.

Recent legislative change in Australia has improved individuals' access to information on their partner's superannuation assets in situations of relationship breakdown, in response to research showing that the process for obtaining a share of superannuation assets was complex to navigate for women

(Commonwealth of Australia, 2021; Women's Legal Services Victoria, n.d.). However, currently those within continuing relationships have no such rights and there is a lack of research on how changing such rights might affect processes and outcomes within households.

Policy measures that address barriers to communication about financial resources within older couple households also warrant consideration. Our data show that, even in relatively long-lasting partnerships, couples can struggle to discuss money and/or resolve disagreements over finances. Consequently, potential gains from cooperation (such as the sharing of knowledge or skills to help manage risk) go unrealised in some older couple households – delivering poorer financial and other outcomes to both partners. In some older couple households, the most that could be said about cooperation between the partners is that the one who was not happy with arrangements did not think it worth complaining.

A key limitation of each of these possible directions for research and policy is that they tend to reinforce the notions of individual responsibility inherent in a financialised approach to retirement income – that couples might be able to, if better equipped, sort out the issues involved in managing financial assets in retirement.[6] Of course, given the complex issues associated with managing financial assets, many couples will still struggle with such tasks, and interventions that focus on, for example, couples' relationships, will achieve little if not accompanied by measures that address the structural inequality in resources. There is, therefore, an ongoing need for research into 'alternative' approaches to retirement income, including contributory and non-contributory state old age pensions, as discussed above.

More broadly, there is a need for additional studies of older couple households, and of negotiation about assets in households in different life stages. International comparisons of financial negotiations among older couples would be especially valuable, as these would help to illuminate the impacts of specific national approaches, including Australia's combination of a defined contribution superannuation system with a means-tested state pension. Such studies could also help to identify possible differences in the management of assets, as compared to income, in older couple households.

Finally, more research is needed on cooperation within older couple (and other) households. Much economic research on households takes cooperation for granted, fails to distinguish between different types of cooperation that may take place within households and tends to assume that all forms of cooperation are desired and desirable. None of the key theoretical models of the household (namely unitary and cooperative and non-cooperative bargaining models) provides guidance on factors that might increase or decrease cooperation within couple households, including policies. Yet our results and an emerging body of research (Iversen et al., 2011; Udry, 1996) show that cooperation within households is far from guaranteed and this suggests a need for new theoretical approaches as well as additional empirical investigations to achieve richer understandings. As part of this effort, it would be useful to conduct studies exploring the likely relevance of trust, communication, interdependence, previous gender roles and the distribution of assets, as well as studies exploring how different circumstances (for example, the existence of children from previous relationships versus shared biological children) affect cooperation in the management of resources in older couple households.

Acknowledgements

The authors acknowledge Ray Broomhill, who helped to design and implement the research underpinning this chapter and whose friendship and support were so important to their work.

Notes

1. Across the Organisation for Economic Co-operation and Development, the share of pension fund money in defined benefit schemes fell to its lowest level on record in 14 out of 19 reporting countries in 2020 (OECD, 2021a: 39).
2. For employees earning more than AUD450 per month, until July 2022, when the threshold was abolished.
3. Beneficiaries with high superannuation assets (over AUD1.7 million) are liable to a tax.
4. In 2015–2016, less than 0.1 per cent of fund members made a direct contribution to their partner's superannuation account (Australian Taxation Office, 2016: Table 23).
5. In many other jurisdictions lump sum withdrawals are constrained (see OECD, 2021b: 25).
6. We thank the editors for highlighting this important point.

References

Account Plan. (2020). 'Mercer slams means test, strongly urges universal age pension' at https://accountplan.com.au/mercer-slams-means-test-strongly-urges-universal-age-pension/ (accessed 8 September 2022).

Austen, S., Broomhill, R., Costa, M. and Sharp, R. (2022). 'Living with risk: Retired couples' experiences of a financialised retirement income system'. *Economic and Labour Relations Review*, 33(4): 737–775.

Australian Taxation Office. (2016). *Taxation Statistics 2015–16*, at https://data.gov.au/data/dataset/taxation-statistics-2015-16 (accessed 31 October 2021).

Bennett, F., De Henau, J. and Sung, S. (2010). 'Within-household inequalities across classes? Management and control of money'. In J. Scott, R. Crompton and C. Lyonette (eds), *Gender Inequalities in the 21st Century: New Barriers and Continuing Constraints*. Cheltenham, UK and Northampton, MA, USA: Edward Elgar Publishing, 215–241.

Bisdee, D., Daly, T. and Price, D. (2013). 'Behind closed doors: Older couples and the gendered management of money'. *Social Policy and Society*, 12(1): 163–174.

Broomhill, R., Costa, M., Austen, S. and Sharp, R. (2021). 'What went wrong with super? Financialisation and Australia's retirement income'. *Journal of Australian Political Economy*, 87: 71–94.

Castilla, C. and Walker, T. (2013). 'Is ignorance bliss? The effect of asymmetric information between spouses on intra-household allocations'. *American Economic Review: Papers and Proceedings*, 103(3): 263–268.

Clare, R. (2022). *Developments in Account Balances*. Sydney: The Association of Superannuation Funds of Australia (ASFA).

Commonwealth of Australia. (2021). *Improving the Visibility of Superannuation Assets in Family Law Proceedings* at https://treasury.gov.au/consultation/c2021-177055 (accessed 8 September 2022)

De Deken, J. (2017). 'The challenges posed by the unintended universal financialization of retirement provision', in D. Natali (Ed.), *The New Pension Mix in Europe: Recent Reforms, The Distributional Effects and Political Dynamics*. Bern: PIE Peter Lang, 145–176.

Eroğlu, Ş. (2009). 'Patterns of income allocation among poor Gecekondu households in Turkey: Overt mechanisms and women's secret kitties'. *The Sociological Review*, 57(1): 58–80.

Fleming, R. (1997). *The Common Purse: Income Sharing in New Zealand Families*. Auckland: Auckland University Press.

Gibson, J., Trinh, L. and Scobie, S. (2006). 'Household bargaining over wealth and the adequacy of women's retirement incomes in New Zealand'. *Feminist Economics*, 12(1–2): 226–246.

James, H. and Agunsoye, A. (2022). 'The gendered construction of risk in asset accumulation for retirement'. *New Political Economy*, 28(4): 574–591.

International Social Security Association. (2017). *Mega Trends and Social Security: Family and Gender*, at www.issa.int/sites/default/files/documents/publications/2-Megatrends%20Gender%20Family-Final-217637.pdf (accessed 10 September 2022)

Iversen, V., Jackson, C., Kebede, B., Munro, A. and Verschoor, A. (2011). 'Do spouses realise cooperative gains? Experimental evidence from rural Uganda'. *World Development*, 39(4): 569–578.

Joseph, R. and Rowlingson, K. (2012). 'Her house, his pension? The division of assets among (ex-)couples and the role of policy'. *Social Policy and Society*, 11(1): 69–80.

Lim, H., Shin, S. and Wilmarth, M. (2022). 'Who decides? Financial decision-making among older couples'. *Journal of Family and Economic Issues*, 43(2): 310–337.

Lundberg, S. and Stillman, S. (2003). 'The retirement-consumption puzzle: A marital bargaining approach'. *Journal of Public Economics* 87(5–6): 1199–1218.

Myer, R. (2022). 'Australians have become super savers with billions stashed away'. *New Daily*, 1 September, at https://thenewdaily.com.au/finance/superannuation/2022/09/01/australians-are-saving-super/ (accessed 12 September 2022).

OECD (Organisation for Economic Co-operation and Development). (2021a). *Financial Incentives for Funded Private Pension Plans: OECD Country Profiles 2021*, at www.oecd.org/daf/fin/private-pensions/Financial-Incentives-for-Funded-Pension-Plans-in-OECD-Countries-2021.pdf (accessed 5 August 2022).

OECD (Organisation for Economic Co-operation and Development). (2021b). *Pension Markets in Focus 2021*, at www.oecd.org/daf/fin/private-pensions/Pension-Markets-in-Focus-2021.pdf (accessed 31 August 2022).

Tennyson, S., Yang, H. and Woolley, F. (2022). 'My wife is my insurance policy: Household bargaining and couples' purchase of long-term care insurance'. *Research on Aging*, 44(9–10): 692–708.

Thinking Ahead Institute. (2021). *Global Pension Assets Study*, at www.thinkingaheadinstitute.org/research-papers/global-pension-assets-study-2021/ (accessed 31 August 2022).

Udry, C. (1996). 'Gender, agricultural production, and the theory of the household'. *Journal of Political Economy*, 104(5): 1010–1046.

Women's Legal Services Victoria. (n.d.). *Improving the Disclosure of Superannuation Fund Information in the Family Law System*, at www.womenslegal.org.au/~womensle/wp-content/uploads/2021/04/Small-Claims-Large-Battles-Briefing-Paper.pdf (accessed 30 September 2022).

14. The gendered effects of joint assessment for couples claiming means-tested benefits

Rita Griffiths

Introduction

Assessment of a couple's entitlement to means-tested[1] state financial help using some form of test of joint income and assets is not unusual in the benefit systems of most western countries.[2] For couples sharing the same household, this means that their 'resources',[3] as well as their needs (together with those of any dependent children), are aggregated. Such aggregation runs counter to the trend across many Organisation for Economic Co-operation and Development (OECD) countries towards greater individualisation in fiscal regimes, in which the resources of each partner in a couple are assessed separately for income tax[4] (Dingledey, 2001). Joint assessment also creates asymmetry in the context of individual-level work conditionality for benefit receipt, which now applies in many western nations' welfare regimes (Ingold and Etherington, 2013), and sits uneasily alongside the movement towards greater independence and privacy in money matters in the context of social citizenship and human rights (Alston, 2019).

Yet, while views of the appropriateness of specific spousal and familial responsibilities have changed considerably over recent decades, joint assessment and means testing have shown remarkable resilience (Sleep et al., 2006). Indeed, on the assumption that income is pooled and resources shared within couple households, across most OECD countries, for means-tested benefits, the nuclear family of a 'husband and wife' – typically comprising a couple, married or cohabiting, with or without dependent children – is the norm for the purposes of assessing eligibility and entitlement[5] (Frericks et al., 2016). This matters because the 'unitary household' model underlying joint means testing effectively ignores the importance of receiving a personal income and the potentially unequal sharing of resources inside couple households, affecting women in particular (Howard and Bennett, 2021).

This chapter explores joint means testing in literature and research and draws on United Kingdom (UK) empirical research to highlight the issues that it can raise for the distribution of household resources, including evidence of both direct effects on women's incomes and indirect effects on family formation and on employment decisions of partners in couples. Joint assessment is examined empirically chiefly through the lens of UK means-tested benefits, because such benefits have come to occupy a much more central position there in maintaining incomes for people without, and increasingly also with, earnings (Millar, 2003). Although historically non-means-tested (including, for certain periods, earnings-related) benefits have played an important role, the availability and generosity of contributory benefits have been declining in many countries, with much stricter eligibility conditions and time limits (Gaffney, 2015).[6] In the UK, this has significantly increased the number and proportion of working-age people affected by means testing (SSAC, 2022). With increasing pressures on the financing of contributions-based and other non-means-tested benefits (OECD, 2019), and growing international interest in the more targeted approaches underpinning means-tested benefits, exploration of the UK context is particularly salient.

Joint and individual units of assessment

In most OECD countries, some benefits are based on individual assessment and others on joint assessment of the couple.[7] Individual assessment, which applies mainly to contributory (often earnings-related), categorical (for example, due to a disability) and universal benefits, is based on criteria such as an individual's employment record, health, the presence of children, citizenship status and/or other qualifying conditions (Adema et al., 2014).

Couple (or family) units of assessment – meaning couples sharing a household, with any dependent children – are more typically associated with means-tested benefits, based on the aggregated income and assets of the partners (and, in certain cases, other non-dependent adults in the household). Recipient numbers and proportions of social security expenditure for means-tested benefits are comparatively much higher in the UK and other Anglophone countries such as Australia, New Zealand and Canada than in most European countries. Scandinavian countries operate on a more individual basis, with far fewer financial support or resource-sharing obligations on couples unless they are legally married (Frericks et al., 2020). In the United States, benefits are means-tested jointly for married, but not cohabiting, couples (Gennetian and Knox, 2003).

In Australia, where there are no non-means-tested benefits, concerns about the disincentives to paid work created by benefit entitlement conditions for low-income couples led the government to reform its method of means testing couples in the 1990s (Saunders, 1995). The introduction of a new Partner and Parent Allowance in 1995 granted the partners in a low-income couple partially individualised entitlement to means-tested benefits, subject to certain conditionality requirements and earnings limits.[8] With these changes to the joint income test, Australia has a partially individualised system of means-tested benefits in one area of its operation.

Why do these differences matter? The use of different units of assessment is not merely a technical distinction but crucially affects who is eligible to claim, whose income and assets are used for determining eligibility and amount of entitlement, whose needs are taken into account when calculating this entitlement and who receives the payment (Roll, 1991). What may often be viewed as administrative decisions are therefore in practice important policy matters, reflecting wider assumptions about the balance of financial responsibilities in a household between state, family, couple and individual (Eardley, 1996). In couple households, joint assessment may therefore influence the ways in which money may be acquired and distributed between the partners and accessed by them. Research also shows that aggregation and joint means testing can have direct effects on partnered women's incomes (Griffiths, 2017), as well as indirect effects on family formation and dissolution (Griffiths, 2017, 2019) and on the labour supply decisions of (so-called) 'second earners'[9] in couples, a majority of whom are women (Thomas and O'Reilly, 2016).

Literature and research

Who is eligible to claim, and who receives payment of, a benefit are issues that have attracted considerable policy interest and scholarly attention; but there has been much less focus recently on whose needs, income and assets are used to assess eligibility and entitlement (Frericks et al., 2016). Extant literature on joint assessment and means testing is therefore mainly dated. The two-volume survey by Eardley et al. (1996a, 1996b) categorises and compares institutional features of social assistance schemes in OECD countries and their application in different welfare state contexts in the mid-1990s. The survey by McLaughlin et al. (2001) of European social security systems focuses on units of assessment and includes in-depth case studies of the degree of aggregation and individualisation in social security systems in Ireland, the Netherlands and the UK (as well as Australia). Although these studies are comprehensive and detailed, significant changes to the benefit systems of many countries in recent decades mean that they are now out of date.

From the 1970s, an important strand of feminist literature sought to challenge the assumption that men's financial support obligations towards women and women's economic dependence on men are natural and/or unproblematic (Lister, 1990; Lundberg and Pollak, 1996). Using the nuclear family as the unit of assessment also raises the knotty administrative problem of how to determine when two people living in the same household constitute a couple for this purpose (McLaughlin et al., 2001). The scrutiny, moral censure and surveillance of lone mothers suspected of cohabiting were denounced as sex snooping – akin to forcing women into 'prostitutional dependence' on the men they slept with (McIntosh, 1978). Researchers have explored the experiences of women prosecuted for benefit fraud for failing to disclose a partner in the UK, Canadian and Australian social security systems, which all have similar rules (Little and Morrison, 1999; Kelly, 2006; Tranter et al., 2008).

Lister's research resulted in her recommendation that means-tested benefits should place much greater emphasis on financial support between partners in practice, rather than just in principle (Lister, 1973). Unlike child maintenance, for example, which requires evidence of financial contributions from the non-resident parent, there is no legal obligation on claimants assessed jointly in a couple to transfer any benefit monies received to their partner. Moreover, unlike the usual situation for spouses, cohabitees are under no legal obligation to financially support each other. Joint assessment was also criticised for eroding social and citizenship rights, particularly for women (Lister, 1990).

A separate, influential body of sociological research from the same period threw doubt on the extent of income pooling in couples, thereby undermining a large part of the justification for aggregating couples' resources. Pahl and Vogler provided evidence that equal sharing of household income is much less common than often assumed, and that pooled income does not necessarily benefit all family members similarly (Pahl, 1989; Vogler, 1989; Pahl and Vogler, 2008). Other studies exploring gendered patterns of intra-household money management in different national contexts have similarly discredited the notion of egalitarian income pooling (Bourguignon et al., 1993; Burgoyne, 2008).

Some feminists campaigned in favour of 'disaggregation' in both social security and income tax regimes, arguing that structural reform was needed to tackle the inequity and underlying assumption of economic dependence inherent in the model of the couple as a means-testable unit (McIntosh, 2006). Independent taxation was introduced from the 1990s in the UK and a number of other European countries, meaning that, whether married, cohabiting or in a civil partnership, the partners are taxed as individuals on the basis of their own earnings and income and regardless of any income pooling which may occur.[10]

Esam and Berthoud (1991) examined options for treating 'husbands and wives' as separate units, suggesting different ways in which the UK benefit system might be reformed. Millar's later explorations of means testing in the UK and Australia concluded that the Australian system of partial individualisation could have positive effects on women's incomes and employment participation (Millar, 1998, 2003). However, in the UK, calls for greater individualisation found little political traction and were rejected in successive reviews on the grounds of cost and the inequality that would arise from paying means-tested benefits to women and men with high-earning partners. In addition, many within the women's movement argued that individualising means-tested benefits (or 'disaggregation of supplementary benefit', as it was inelegantly known in the UK at the time) would not create independent rights to benefits and that other solutions were preferable.

The more recent cross-country overview of ten European welfare states by Frericks and colleagues found considerable variation in the degree to which the income and assets of different family members are taken into account in social security systems, both between countries and between policy areas (Frericks et al., 2016, 2020). Their analysis showed that there is no country which has a fully individualised means-tested benefit system, nor is there any general trend observable towards greater individualisation (Frericks et al., 2020). The authors also confirm the observation above that recent empirical studies about these issues are rare.

Research on the effects of joint assessment on access to and distribution of resources within the household

To help fill the evidence gap, we now turn to two empirical studies which explore the effects of joint assessment and means testing on access to and distribution of resources within households. The first is a doctoral study completed in 2016 examining the influence of UK means-tested benefits and tax credits on partnering and family structure for low-income mothers (Griffiths, 2016). The second is a qualitative longitudinal research study, conducted between 2018 and 2021, exploring experiences of couples jointly claiming Universal Credit, the UK's main working-age benefit (Griffiths et al., 2020, 2022).

Effects of joint means testing on family formation and dissolution decisions

Doctoral research based on face-to-face qualitative interviews in 2012/2013 with a sample of 52 low-income mothers living in England explored the extent to which claiming means-tested benefits, as a lone parent or joint claimant or both, may have influenced the decision to cohabit, live apart from or separate from a partner (Griffiths, 2016). The research found that the joint means test, which could remove or reduce a woman's personal income if she started to cohabit, was a significant deterrent to family formation. Ceding responsibility for safeguarding the family's financial security to an unreliable 'breadwinner', or a new or unproven partner (whether earning or unemployed) who was not the biological father of her child/ren, was often seen to pose a significant risk to both her own and her children's wellbeing. Some lone mothers ruled out any form of partner relationship while reliant on benefits.

The mother's inability to access the family's benefit income when claiming jointly had also destabilised some married and cohabiting couples' relationships, sometimes contributing to separation and/or divorce (Griffiths, 2019). Regardless of whether earnings and/or benefit entitlements were paid separately into an individual bank account or pooled in a joint account, many partnered women experienced difficulties in accessing an equitable or fair share of household income. Joint accounts provided no guarantee that both members of the couple had access to, or an equal allocation of, household money. A male partner's tendency to withhold earnings or retain benefit income for personal use, before rent and important household bills were paid, was cited as a common reason for relationship tensions, leading in some cases to partnership breakdown. After claiming benefits as a lone parent, many women found themselves to be financially better off, mainly due to personal access to and greater control over household income – a finding reflected in other research (Bradshaw and Millar, 1991).

In this research, the propensity to repartner was also strongly influenced by the rules governing claims by couples. Referred to by Webb as 'creative claiming strategies' (Webb, 1991: 41), some women with children whose partners were unemployed or working in low-paid or insecure jobs opted to live apart from these men, which allowed them to continue to claim benefits legitimately as lone mothers. While residing at a different address from their partner enabled these women to retain an independent income, doing so had, in some cases, placed an additional burden on the state, through supporting two sets of personal benefits and compensation for housing-related costs – for the mother and for her partner. For other couples, maintaining separate households had reduced the non-resident parent's ability to contribute financially, practically and emotionally to their children's upbringing. Perversely, living apart had prevented some couples from becoming committed and managing resources jointly, the very behaviours necessary for pooling resources and assuming shared responsibility for household finances and children (Griffiths, 2017).

The research showed that, whilst those aspects of the benefit system facilitating a mother's access to an independent income served mainly to strengthen couple relationships and encourage family formation, those aspects reinforcing financial dependence on a partner – in particular joint assessment – were apt to destabilise relationships and discourage lone parents from repartnering. To the extent that benefit systems influence how and by whom money in the household is acquired, accessed and controlled, how much financial independence women can exercise in different partnership states and household configurations could be seen as having indirect effects on family structure.

Effects of aggregation and joint means testing in Universal Credit

Universal Credit is the UK's main means-tested working-age benefit. Replacing six means-tested benefits and tax credits[11] with one benefit per individual or couple, assessed monthly, its gradual introduction from 2013 further extended aggregation (Bennett, 2012), with potentially far-reaching consequences for resource distribution inside couple households (Bennett, 2021). Paid in arrears, usually monthly, to mimic receipt of a salary, and integrating elements for housing, children, childcare costs and disability/incapacity in one household payment, Universal Credit is paid to eligible individuals and couples with and without dependent children, both in and out of work.

Universal Credit and couples

Couples living together must claim jointly and are assessed jointly for Universal Credit. However, in a significant departure from the previous ('legacy') system, it is paid monthly by default in a single household payment into one bank account. Couples can choose whether payment is made into an individual or joint account but, other than by discretionary, temporary arrangement in exceptional circumstances,[12] couples can no longer decide to whom different part(s) of the benefit are paid. Automated deductions for sanctions and to repay loans and debts, taken at source from the monthly payment, are another distinguishing feature of Universal Credit. In couples, these too are aggregated, including benefit overpayments and debts which may be 'inherited' from a partner (Griffiths and Cain, 2022).

Critics have argued that a single monthly household payment can exacerbate the challenges faced by partnered women in achieving a personal income (Howard and Bennett, 2021). Absorption of benefits intended for housing, children and childcare costs into one household payment contrasts with the legacy system, which allowed separate benefits to be paid to the members of a couple, enabling each partner to have an income (Bennett and Sung, 2013). It also runs counter to the principle that child-related benefits should be paid to the main carer.[13] Compared with the legacy system, Universal Credit also weakens work incentives for many 'second earners' in couples – a majority of whom are women (Finch and Gardiner, 2018).

Qualitative longitudinal research conducted between 2019 and 2021 exploring experiences of 90 participants with a joint claim for Universal Credit found that money concentrated in the hands of one payee was problematic for women in unequal or abusive relationships[14] (Griffiths et al., 2020). Some women, now separated, said that their former partner had mismanaged or misappropriated the couple's benefit payment. Some were left with significant liability for debts and rent arrears. The greater autonomy and financial independence they gained by claiming as a lone parent or single person made them wary of claiming jointly in future. Joint liability for repaying a partner's debts was seen as particularly egregious, especially when these 'inherited' debts related to a period before the couple had even met (Griffiths and Cain, 2022). Both demeaning and potentially destabilising for relationships was having to ask, or rely on, a partner for money – especially for couples for whom Universal Credit was their main, or only, source of income.

For the majority of couples in this research who reported their relationship as stable and trusting, a single monthly payment proved less problematic. If one partner had no income whilst the other had earnings, the non-earning partner was typically nominated as benefit payee. By sharing passwords and bank cards, online and mobile banking apps enabled couples to transfer money between accounts to pay rent and bills and other household essentials regardless of which partner received Universal Credit or was earning. In this context, the payee and type of bank account made little practical difference to the ways money was accessed by and distributed between partners. However, women in particular valued an individual bank account (also found by Bennett and Sung, 2013) and were generally wary of joint accounts, which very few couples had, unless the female partner had a separate one in addition. Having their own bank account was said by these women to allow them to create their own financial 'footprint' for residence, loans and benefits in their own right, which was felt to be important not only for equality and financial independence but also as useful insurance in case of possible separation.

The same research explored work and care decisions in couples and the extent to which Universal Credit encouraged or discouraged paid work or increased hours and earnings (a fundamental policy objective). This showed that the aggregation of earnings and joint means testing could reduce women's incomes and discourage 'second earners' from entering paid work or increasing their hours (Griffiths et al., 2022). Because women were more likely to be the Universal Credit payee, they were disproportionately affected by any reduction in benefit entitlement resulting from an increase in their own, or their partner's, earnings. Contrary to Universal Credit's main policy objective, this led some women to reduce working hours or withdraw from the labour market, eroding their individual access to income. 'First earners' – a majority of whom were men – could also be discouraged from earning more in cases where the Universal Credit payment was received by their partners, as this meant it would be reduced or might cease altogether.

Regardless of their own circumstances, many couples in this research felt that Universal Credit failed to reflect contemporary relationships in which both partners want and expect a personal income, through their own earnings and/ or benefits. There was also a strong desire to resist being or becoming economically dependent on a partner. This finding is reflected in other research. For example, when new Universal Credit claims surged in 2020 in the COVID-19 pandemic, large numbers found that they were ineligible for means-tested help due to a partner's earnings, income or savings being too high (around 45 per cent of refusals) (Baumberg Geiger et al., 2020); and among unsuccessful applicants, the indignity and perceived risk of enforced financial dependence on a partner were some of the key issues raised (House of Commons Work and Pensions Committee, 2020: 17). This suggests that, though generally ignored by policymakers, aggregation and joint means testing for couples remains a live, unresolved policy issue.

Policy implications

The findings here reinvigorate arguments in favour of reforming means-tested benefits in ways which increase the financial independence of both partners in a couple. So what are the options and how can reform be argued for in the current fiscally constrained policy environment? A fully disaggregated and individualised benefit system which removes joint/family-based means testing wholesale is likely to be prohibitive on the grounds of cost. However, no account has previously been taken of the hidden social and economic costs of joint means testing and of the potential savings that could be made through reductions in entitlement to housing-related benefits, benefit fraud investigations and prosecution costs, and this needs further investigation. And, as noted above, some means-tested benefits in Australia are partially individualised.

Although much contested, the idea of a Universal Basic Income (UBI) could potentially be a means of ensuring that both partners in a couple have access to an independent income. Being universal and unconditional, the advantage of a UBI over the individualisation of means-tested benefits is the elimination of means testing. A UBI would also remove the disincentive effects of means testing in terms of partnership formation, as well as in relation to paid work by either partner in a couple. Although studies suggest that UBI may show promise in this regard, the issues it raises from a gender perspective are far from straightforward. The greater potential incentive for women to stay out of the labour market, for example, could reinforce the gendered division of labour (Lombardozzi, 2020). Non-means-tested contributory benefits (potentially also related to earnings), in addition to non-means-tested non-contributory benefits, could be another important part of the solution to increasing women's (partnered individuals') access to an independent income (Bennett, 2017).

Opportunities for future research

Given the generally dated nature of much literature and research in this field, a useful starting point to inform and underpin policy reform would be to update the surveys and studies which categorise and compare the ways in which different units of assessment operate in different welfare state contexts. Empirical research is also needed to explore the extent to which benefit rules governing couples' eligibility and entitlement in different countries may affect access to and distribution of income between the partners, as well as how unintended effects of joint assessment may influence, for example, the partnering decisions and living arrangements of couples. It would also be useful to model the costs of individualising means-tested benefit systems in different welfare state contexts, taking into account the potential savings to the public purse if couples wanting to live together were not discouraged from doing so by benefit rules (see Avram and Popova, this volume, on the potential of microsimulation).

With benefit eligibility and entitlement increasingly contingent upon recipients' work-related behaviour, another important area of research would be to investigate the effects of joint means testing on the labour market decisions of partners. A key opportunity would be to learn more about the Australian system of partial individualisation of means-tested parenting benefits. Since reforms to the joint means tests were introduced in 1995, there has been a large increase in two-earner households, raising the question as to whether the change encouraged more partnered claimants into work. To date, no evaluation has been carried out, nor any systematic exploration of the feasibility of transferring elements of the Australian model for parenting payments to other countries. In the French benefits system, too, a bonus is paid when a second earner in a couple enters work (Perivier, 2012). Empirical research to explore the effects of partial individualisation and second-earner disregards on the incomes, earnings and employment behaviour of partners in couples could usefully fill the gap in evidence.

The COVID-19 pandemic highlighted the importance of social insurance schemes, different versions of which operate in most European welfare states (Beland et al., 2021). Drawing on international literature and research, further investigation is needed into how social insurance schemes operate in different national contexts, and for men and women in couples, including those elements which aim to cater for those whose earnings potential may be limited by caring responsibilities.

Notes

1. Also known as 'income-based' or sometimes 'income-related' (not to be confused with earnings-related) benefits.
2. See Benassi (2010) on the historical origins of joint assessment in benefit systems.
3. By 'resources' we generally mean a couple's earnings and other income, but in some countries it also includes their assets.

4. In most European countries, married couples are no longer assessed jointly for income tax purposes, but in some countries they are; in others, there are transferable tax allowances between husbands and wives. See Christl et al. (2021).
5. Eligibility refers to whether an individual or couple meets the criteria for a benefit. Entitlement refers here to the amount of benefit an eligible individual or couple is calculated as being entitled to.
6. See Hills (2004) for a discussion of the contributory principle in the UK benefit system.
7. There is insufficient space to explore differences in the social security systems of OECD countries. Interested readers should refer to Eardley et al. (1996a, 1996b). Although dated, these sources provide very useful reference material. The OECD (Benefits and Wages) and International Social Security Association databases also contain detailed, country-level information on benefit levels and expenditure.
8. A joint income test operates for higher-income couples. For a detailed explanation of partial individualisation in Australian social security, see Saunders (1995).
9. The term 'second earner' refers to the person in a two-earner couple whose earnings and/or hours of work are generally lower than that of her or his partner. In male/female partnerships, particularly those with children, 'second earners' tend to be women.
10. See Christl et al. (2021) for a cross-country comparison of the fiscal treatment of married and cohabiting couples. In the UK, changes since the 1990s mean the couple is treated as a unit in relation to some income tax measures.
11. The six 'legacy' benefits Universal Credit is replacing are: Income-Related Employment and Support Allowance, Income-Based Jobseeker's Allowance, Working Tax Credit, Child Tax Credit, Income Support and Housing Benefit for those of working age.
12. Exceptional circumstances include when there is proven financial mismanagement and/or domestic or financial abuse, when claimants have been sanctioned, when there is fraud and, for households with children, when there is a risk of claimants losing their home. Northern Ireland gives a wider choice of payment than in Great Britain.
13. An online prompt at the start of the claim now 'nudges' couples with children to nominate the designated 'lead carer' as payee for the whole Universal Credit amount. Typically, this is the female partner.
14. That the single monthly payment may reinforce or facilitate financial abuse by a controlling partner is a topic covered separately in this volume (see Howard and Sharp-Jeffs).

References

Adema, W., Fron, P. and Ladaique, M. (2014) 'How much do OECD countries spend on social protection and how redistributive are their tax/benefit systems?', *International Social Security Review*, 67(1), 1–25.

Alston, P. (2019), *Report of the Special Rapporteur on extreme poverty and human rights*, United Nations A/74/493, General Assembly, 11 October.

Baumberg Geiger, B., Scullion, L., Summers, K., Martin, P., Lawler, C., Edmiston, D., Gibbons, A., Ingold, J., Karagiannaki, E., Robertshaw, D. and de Vries, R. (2020), *At *the edge of the safety net: Unsuccessful benefits claims at the start of the COVID-19 pandemic*, London: The Health Foundation.

Beland, D., Cantillon, B., Hick, R. and Moreira, A. (2021) 'Social policy in the face of a global pandemic: Policy responses to the COVID-19 crisis', *Social Policy and Administration*, 55(2), 249–260.

Benassi, D. (2010) '"Father of the welfare state"? Beveridge and the emergence of the welfare state', *Sociologica Fascicolo, Italian Journal of Sociology*, 3.

Bennett, F. (2012) 'Universal Credit: Overview and gender implications', in M. Kilkey, G. Ramia and K. Farnsworth (eds) *Social policy review 24: Analysis and debate in social policy*, Bristol: Policy Press, 15–34.

Bennett, F. (2017) 'The developed world', in *Megatrends and Social Security: Family and Gender*, Geneva: International Social Security Association, 10–26.

Bennett, F. (2021) 'How government sees couples on Universal Credit: A critical gender perspective', *Journal of Poverty and Social Justice*, 29(1), 3–20.

Bennett, F. and Sung, S. (2013) 'Gender implications of UK welfare reform and government equality duties: Evidence from qualitative studies', *Oñati Socio-Legal Series*, 3(7), 1202–1221.

Bourguignon, F., Browning, M., Chiappori, P.-A. and Lechene, V. (1993) 'Intra household allocation of consumption: A model and some evidence from French data', *Annals d'Economie et de Statistique*, 29, 137–156.

Bradshaw, J. and Millar, J. (1991), *Lone parent families in the UK*, Research Report no. 6, London: Department of Social Security.

Burgoyne, C. (2008) 'Modern couples sharing money, sharing life', *European Societies*, 10(3), 509–511.

Christl, M., De Poli, S. and Ivaškaitė-Tamošiūnė, V. (2021), *Does it pay to say 'I do'? Marriage bonuses and penalties across the EU*, JRC Working Papers on Taxation and Structural Reforms No. 07/2021, Seville: European Commission.

DHSS (Department of Health and Social Security) (1978), *Social assistance: A review of the Supplementary Benefit scheme in Great Britain*, London: DHSS.

Dingledey, I. (2001) 'European tax systems and their impact on family employment patterns', *Journal of Social Policy*, 30(4), 653–672.

Eardley, T. (1996) 'Means testing for social assistance: UK policy in an international perspective', in N. Lunt and D. Coyle (eds) *Welfare and policy: Research agendas and issues*, London: Taylor & Francis, 58–77.

Eardley, T., Bradshaw, J., Ditch, J., Gough, I. and Whiteford, P. (1996a), *Social assistance in OECD countries, Volume I: Synthesis report*, Department of Social Security Research Report 46. London: HMSO.

Eardley, T., Bradshaw, J., Ditch, J., Gough, I. and Whiteford, P. (1996b), *Social assistance in OECD countries, Volume II: Country reports*, Department of Social Security Research Report 47. London: HMSO.

Esam, P. and Berthoud, R. (1991), *Independent benefits for men and women: An enquiry into options for treating husbands and wives as separate units in the assessment of social security*, London: Policy Studies Institute.

Finch, D. and Gardiner, L. (2018), *Back in credit? Universal Credit after Budget 2018*, London: Resolution Foundation.

Frericks, P., Hoppner, J. and Och, R. (2016) 'Institutional individualisation? The family in European social security systems', *Journal of Social Policy*, 45(4), 747–764.

Frericks, P., Och, R. and Hoppner, J. (2020) 'The family in minimum income benefits in Europe: An institutional analysis', *Social Politics*, 27(3), 615–642.

Gaffney, D. (2015), *Welfare states: How generous are British benefits compared with other rich nations?*, London: Trades Union Congress.

Gennetian, L. A. and Knox, V. (2003), Staying single: The effects of welfare reform policies on marriage and cohabitation. The Next Generation: Working Paper Series No. 13, *MDRC*, University of Texas.

Griffiths, R. (2016), *No love on the dole: The influence of the UK means-tested welfare system on partnering and family structure*, doctoral thesis, University of Bath.

Griffiths, R. (2017) 'No love on the dole: The influence of the UK means-tested welfare system on partnering and family structure', *Journal of Social Policy*, 46(3), 543–556.

Griffiths, R. (2019) 'For better or for worse: Does the UK means-tested benefit system encourage partnership dissolution?', *Journal of Poverty and Social Justice*, 28(1), 79–98.

Griffiths, R. and Cain, R. (2022) 'Universal Credit, deductions and partner inherited debt', *Journal of Social Welfare and Family Law*, 44(4), 431–454.

Griffiths, R., Wood, M., Bennett, F. and Millar, J. (2020), *Uncharted territory: Universal Credit, couples and money*, Bath: Institute for Policy Research, University of Bath.

Griffiths, R., Wood, M., Bennett, F. and Millar, J. (2022), *Couples navigating work, care and Universal Credit*, Bath: Institute for Policy Research, University of Bath.

Hills, J. (2004) 'Heading for retirement? National Insurance, state pensions, and the future of the contributory principle in the UK', *Journal of Social Policy*, 33(3), 347–371.

House of Commons Work and Pensions Committee (2020), *What we learned from our survey into people's experiences of the benefits system during the coronavirus outbreak.* https://publications.parliament.uk/pa/cm5801/cmselect/cmworpen/correspondence/coronavirus-survey-responses.pdf (accessed 9 May 2023).

Howard, M. and Bennett, F. (2021), *Distribution of money within the household and current social security issues for couples in the UK*, London: Women's Budget Group. https://wbg.org.uk/wp-content/uploads/2021/01/Money-in-the-household-FINAL-with-cover-2.pdf (accessed 9 May 2023).

Ingold, J. and Etherington, D. (2013) 'Work, welfare and gender inequalities: An analysis of activation strategies for partnered women in the UK, Australia and Denmark', *Work, Employment and Society*, 27(4), 621–638.

Kelly, S. (2006), *Ruling on cohabitation: A critical study of the cohabitation rule in UK social security law*, doctoral thesis, University of Edinburgh.

Lister, R. (1973), *As man and wife? A study of the cohabitation rule*, London: Child Poverty Action Group.

Lister, R. (1990) 'Women, economic dependency and citizenship', *Journal of Social Policy*, 19(4), 445–467.

Little, M. and Morrison, I. (1999) 'The pecker detectors are back: Changes to the spousal definition in Ontario welfare policy', *Journal of Canadian Studies*, 34(2), 110–136.

Lombardozzi, L. (2020) 'Gender inequality, social reproduction and the Universal Basic Income', *The Political Quarterly*, 91(2), 317–323.

Lundberg, S. and Pollak, R.A. (1996) 'Bargaining and distribution in marriage', *Journal of Economic Perspectives*, 10(4), 139–158.

McIntosh, M. (1978), *The state and the oppression of women*, London: Routledge and Kegan Paul.

McIntosh, M. (2006), *Feminism and social policy*, Cambridge: Polity Press.

McLaughlin, E., Yeates, N. and Kelly, G. (2001), *Social security units of assessment: An international survey of the UK, Netherlands, Republic of Ireland and Australia and its implications for UK policy reform*, London: Trades Union Congress.

Millar, J. (1998) 'Reforming welfare: The Australian experience', *Benefits*, 23, 32–34.

Millar, J. (2003) 'Squaring the circle? Means testing and individualisation in the UK and Australia', *Social Policy and Society*, 3(1), 67–74.

OECD (2019), *OECD employment outlook 2019: The future of work*, Paris: Organisation for Economic Co-operation and Development.

Pahl, J. (1989), *Money and marriage*, Basingstoke: Macmillan.

Pahl, J. and Vogler, C. (2008) 'Money, power and inequality in marriage', *The Sociological Review*, 42(2), 263–288.

Perivier, H. (2012) 'Work or get married! Gendered regulation of poverty in France and the United States', *Travail, genre et societies*, 28(2), 45–62.

Roll, J. (1991), *What is a family? Benefit models and social realities*, London: Family Policy Studies Centre.

Saunders, P. (1995) 'Improving work incentives in a means-tested welfare system: The 1994 Australian social security reform', *Fiscal Studies*, 16(2), 45–70.

Sleep, L., Tranter, K.M. and Stannard, J. (2006) 'Cohabitation rule in social security law: The more things change the more they stay the same', *Australian Journal of Administrative Law*, 13(1), 135–146.

SSAC (2022), *The future of working age contributory benefits for those not in paid work: A study by the Social Security Advisory Committee*, Social Security Advisory Committee Occasional Paper 26, London: Department for Work and Pensions.

Thomas, A. and O'Reilly, P. (2016), *The impact of tax and benefit systems on the workforce participation incentives of women*, OECD Taxation Working Papers No. 29, Paris: OECD.

Tranter, K., Sleep, L. and Stannard, J. (2008) 'The cohabitation rule: Indeterminacy and oppression in Australian social security law', *Melbourne University Law Review*, 32(2), 698–738.

Vogler, C. (1989) 'Labour market change and patterns of financial allocation within households', ESRC Social Change and Economic Life Initiative Working Paper 12, Oxford: Nuffield College, University of Oxford.

Webb, S. (1991) 'Social security policy and the division of income within the family', in M. Pearson, S. Smith, S. Stark and S. Webb (eds), *Economic policy and the division of income within the family*, Report series 37, London: Institute for Fiscal Studies.

15. Temporality and the meaning of social security money within households

Kate Summers and David Young

Introduction

Much analysis of social security[1] money within the household has a clear, but often underacknowledged, temporal dimension. This chapter aims to analyse temporality and social security money within the household and consider the implications for future research and policy agendas. Our focus is both substantive and methodological. We ask: how does temporality relate to intra-household dynamics; and what does it mean, analytically, to take temporality seriously when studying how social security money is dealt with within the household? We also ask about the methodological tools best suited to prioritising this temporal focus.

We pursue these questions by first reviewing the literature on temporality and social security money, with a focus on the United States (US) and the United Kingdom (UK), countries with relevant policy examples and in which recent sociological or psychological studies have analysed aspects of temporality. Key aspects highlighted here include the waiting periods often associated with applying for and managing social security claims and the timing of payments. Next, we consider an example of research making use of qualitative methods to investigate aspects of time when studying social security money within the household. Such qualitative longitudinal methods, including income and expenditure diaries, can give insights into intra-household dynamics and money management. We end by considering ways forward for this research agenda and for policy.

Focusing on temporality within the household means attending to the dimensions relating to claiming, receiving, organising and spending social security money. These include, for example, the time taken to apply for an entitlement, assessment periods and time limits, when and how often payment is received, the periods over which social security money is organised and tracked within the household and the time over which it is spent. This is important in relation to not only the given number of relevant units of time but also the *nature* of these – how does it feel (and what does it mean within the context of people's wider financial and social lives) to receive, organise and spend money within particular temporal structures? Within an intra-household context, how do temporal dynamics relate to relationships and roles, who do household members think money belongs to and is *for* and are income and spending viewed as joint or individual?

Overview of existing research

A concern with temporality is evident in recent research on social security policy. Patterns of benefit payment are said to exert an 'iron grip' on recipient families (Daly and Kelly, 2015), whose financial lives are dictated by the rhythms of money coming in. Payment patterns feed through into strategies for managing and spending money within households, which have strong temporal dimensions. These strategies have been shown to involve 'juggling' (Kempson, 1996; Patrick, 2017) – trying to synchronise income and outgoings over time; using 'adaptive strategies', including going without or bulk buying to deal with financial 'pinch points' (e.g. when payment patterns mismatch key outgoings such as rent or utilities, bills or when money runs out before the next instalment) (Pemberton et al., 2017: 1164); or establishing 'strict routines' (Shildrick and MacDonald, 2013: 288), by timing spending to exert control over finances. Central to these strategies are short-term horizons (Hecht and Summers, 2021). Living 'day to day' is a necessary way of managing scarce resources when planning ahead is not possible (Pemberton et al., 2017: 1164–1167). This shorter-term budgeting can be in tension with the relatively longer timelines of social security payments (Hartfree, 2014). While previous research has often emphasised such strategies as responses to low income, the focus here is on timing or patterns of payment, not just amounts.

Research on the effect of waiting is limited. Waiting can refer to the time after beginning to consider applying for benefits but before doing so (Baumberg Geiger et al., 2021); the time between applying for and receiving payments, at the beginning of the application process or during a continuing claim; and the time between enacting some administrative process and attaining a resolution (e.g. reporting a change in circumstances, or requesting information). However, most research on waiting has not considered its differential impacts within households. Studies by Wacquant (2009) and Reid (2013) conceptualise it as a form of 'temporal domination' (Reid, 2013: 742): the person who waits is subjugated to the person enforcing the wait. The experience of waiting can vary: for claimants in Australia, for example, Peterie et al. (2019) show such experiences ranging from being frustrating and an inconvenience to being demeaning and more seriously injurious.

Waiting is baked into multiple stages of the administrative design of social security payments. This might be waiting on the telephone or in person, for example, for help with maintaining one's claim, or when going through an appeals process. For example, the 'in arrears' payment design of the UK's Universal Credit, with a month's assessment calculation period, results in at least five weeks' wait before the first payment (although a repayable advance can be requested). Claimants also find themselves queuing to access charitable support or independent advice, in places where the third sector fills the gaps in formal welfare provision (Edmiston et al., 2022).

Bennett et al. (2009) examined time as a 'compliance cost' of claiming benefits and tax credits and cited the Netherlands where the government has attempted to measure 'administrative burdens on citizens' (59), including 'hours spent' on administrative tasks and waiting for responses (63). A study of the 'administrative burden' of waiting in Israel detailed short- and long-term waits to access and interact with National Insurance and Employment Services and the psychological costs that came with 'waiting for the state', especially under conditions of uncertainty (Holler and Tarshish, 2022). Administrative burdens have also been associated with benefit take-up rates, with low burden benefits such as the Earned Income Tax Credit (EITC) in the US leading to higher take-up (Herd and Moynihan, 2019: 194). Administrative burdens such as waiting were found to have a bigger impact on the 'least advantaged' (6). But there is a lack of research examining intra-household dynamics. An important layer to add to such analyses is therefore *who* within the household takes on navigating a wait, taking a place in a queue or finding alternative sources of income, as well as psychologically shouldering the burden of delays and associated uncertainties.

There is a likelihood that such experiences are unequally patterned within as well as across households, as suggested by a number of investigations of social security payments. Female members of couples have been found in some UK studies to be more likely to manage the burdens and stresses of claiming social security (Bennett and Sung, 2014; Griffiths et al., 2022). Griffiths and colleagues (2020) found the women in their study disproportionately likely to shoulder the burden of intra-household money management and benefit changes such as moving on to Universal Credit and the online tasks and waiting periods coming with that (102). The unequal nature of these burdens was found to cause intra-household conflict and in some cases lead to relationship breakdown and separation (152) (Howard and Sharp-Jeffs, this volume). Previous literature also finds that this gendered burden relates to credit and debt decisions (Goode 2010), spending decisions (Vogler et al., 2008) and the source and recipient of income (Goode et al., 1998, 1999).

Different households, and different members of households, have differing roles and capacities to deal with enforced waiting. For example, claimants have an unequal ability to smooth income through borrowing, relational support and/or use of savings (Young, 2022), which influences intra-household dynamics (for example, *who* has to call on relational support, or coordinate formal or informal borrowing); while those with caring responsibilities or chronic illness may find their time constraints impeding their ability to navigate and resolve a period of waiting. Unpaid care responsibilities in particular are unequal between men and women (Ophir and Polos, 2022) and are therefore likely to influence an individual's capacity to enact income-smoothing strategies within their household. However, studies that directly target the intra-household effects of waiting periods are scant.

Research on a second key aspect of temporality – the timing of social security payments – has also, thus far, neglected intra-household effects. Internationally, there is substantial variation in the payment frequency of different social security payments, with these being part of a wider mix of means-tested, contribution-based and categorical or universal benefits in each country. Within the UK, low-income, working-age households have increasingly relied on means-tested benefits over recent decades (Gardiner, 2019: 29). A headline feature of the UK's Universal Credit scheme was that it would be paid monthly, replacing previously separate benefits paid through a mixture of weekly, fortnightly and four-weekly payments (with often some choice of payment frequency). The monthly design was justified as a simplification, and as reflecting the supposedly typical temporal pattern of in-work income from wages and salaries; this matches the wage patterns of the majority of claimants in work (Bell et al., 2020). It would also fit with the 'real-time information' from employers about earnings used to calculate entitlement (Millar and Bennett, 2017; Griffiths et al., 2023).

Research on Universal Credit has emphasised both positive and negative effects of the new temporal pattern of payments. Critics pointed to the proportion of low-paid work paid daily, weekly, fortnightly or four-weekly rather than monthly, as well as the challenges of claimants having to budget over a longer period (Hartfree, 2014). For some claimants, the monthly lump sum makes it clearer how much money is available and fits well with receipt of other income and previous experience of monthly money management (Howard and Bennett, 2020; Summers and Young, 2020). However, those on the lowest incomes often match their expenditure patterns with the arrival of different income sources (Harris et al., 2009) – and the type of income and who earned it can also influence how it is spent (Goode et al., 1998). A key conclusion of this research is the need for the design of Universal Credit to pay more attention to the ways temporal aspects of benefits are experienced by claimants and their households (Millar and Bennett, 2017; Summers and Young, 2020).

There is evidence that payment frequency can influence how resources are allocated within the household. Social security income consisting of different payments has been shown to fit with 'juggling' approaches to budgeting (Patrick, 2017) and the timing of income can shape these practices (Hickman et al., 2014: 39). Research shows that household budgeting for those receiving means-tested social security payments in the UK tends to revolve around days and weeks rather than longer stretches (Hills et al., 2006; Hickman et al., 2014). While the level of social security is a central issue in budgeting decisions, the timing of payments (not just the amount, but *when* money arrives) matters far more than is often acknowledged. Further, this links with patterns of receipt of wages. The different income sources and their pay frequencies can mean a claimant receiving monthly income from work and benefits having a patchwork of payments within any month. Adding the intra-household layer, this patchwork might be doubled in complexity; and each payment, both 'officially' and unofficially, will be owned by or allocated to a specific household member or members within the household. Who has access to, and control over, a given tranche of money will vary; and the implications will differ depending on when that money is arriving and therefore, taken together, how that money can and will be used.

Payment patterns intersect with household budgeting strategies. A key work on the temporality of social security monies and its impact within the household is Daly and Kelly's examination of the financial lives of low-income families in Northern Ireland. They summarise how, 'In effect, money defined the practices and rituals of family life in fundamental ways. One could speak of "money rhythms". These are daily and weekly but fan out also to encompass the entire year' (Daly and Kelly, 2015: 48). Within these rhythms of receipt and spending money was 'earmarked' for certain purposes (e.g. 'food money', 'children's school money', etc.). This earmarking communicates functional but also relational distinctions, whereby a given pot is laden with personal, familial and social values, dictating how and by whom it should be managed, spent and (de) prioritised within the household (Daly, 2017). Earmarking is influenced by the rhythms of income receipt in that anticipated needs at specific times (e.g. 'children's school money') are matched with expected income (e.g. Child Benefit payments). Budgeting cycles also begin with the receipt of different payments, rather than specific days (Daly, 2017); and Daly and Kelly (2015) describe a cycle comprising receipt of different income sources, a period when these are spent and a period of being 'broke' (49). This mirrors previous research that found income receipt guiding expenditure, including debt repayments (Kempson et al., 1994; Harris et al., 2009). This research shows how temporal aspects may be at the heart of intra-household money management, informing and to some extent defining practices.

The perspective in this chapter attends to the 'social meaning' of money which is 'profoundly shaped by cultural and social-structural factors' (Zelizer, 2011: 379). Work on the Earned Income Tax Credit (EITC) in the US emphasised the importance of this approach. The EITC is paid to low- and middle-income individuals and couples on the basis of their income and number of children in the form of a refundable tax credit applied for annually by recipients through their tax return. Halpern-Meekin et al. (2015) combine insights from behavioural economics and sociology to understand the 'social meaning' of the EITC. The authors find that the meanings attached to the EITC relate to it being understood as money that recipients earned themselves, and that this is linked to their status as workers and contributors to society and their households. Highlighting the importance of temporal factors, the authors show how the EITC, by being paid as a large lump sum 'windfall' once a year that is combined with ordinary tax refunds, contributes to it being seen as a reward for work and a chance to spend or save towards an improved future. Taken together, these findings suggest that temporal (as well as other) aspects of the payment matter for how that money is perceived and used. Some money is earmarked for special purposes (e.g. buying treats for children), while a large chunk is dedicated to 'getting ahead', for example by buying durable goods, a second-hand car or dealing with debts (Halpern-Meekin et al., 2015). The perceived nature of the EITC as a 'reward for work' may also reinforce the dominant role of a male 'breadwinner' within households and influence what and whom money is spent on. This may in turn be reinforced by the timing and nature of receipt: a large lump sum, paid to one person within a household. Indeed, it has been found that additional income received as a lump sum generally yields more utility than an equivalent stream of regular payments (Kahneman and Thaler, 1991). An intra-household perspective involves considering *who* within the household directly benefits from such payments. The way sources of income are paid, including their temporal dimensions, thus relates to the meanings assigned to them and therefore also to intra-household allocation and management, all of which express aspects of familial and social roles and identities.

The temporal features of social security policy shape how money is *perceived* and used within the household. The 'policy' and 'within household' worlds can complement and support each other, or conversely, these two worlds can be in tension, and the work involved in then negotiating and reconciling mismatches may fall on specific members of a given household and reinforce existing power relations. Returning to the example of Universal Credit in the UK, Griffiths and colleagues (2020) found that the women in their study of couples balancing work, money and care were usually responsible for money management, including the extra burden of the single monthly payments and related administrative tasks. Against this backdrop, identifying and under-standing (in)congruities between the temporal patterns of policy design and the ways in which households handle money over time is an important task for policy analysis, and one which we argue is under-addressed in recent intra-household literature.

Temporality clearly plays a role in decisions about the handling and use of money in the research described above. However, as noted, this tends not to be the focus of social security policy research, perhaps because 'time is such an obvious factor in social science that it is almost invisible' (Adam, 1990: 3). We next reflect on a recent study that did have this focus. The study used qualitative longitudinal methods to explore aspects of the social meaning(s) of social security money in the UK. We use it to consider how the substantive concerns described above interlink with choices about research methodology, and suggest directions for future research.

Lessons from a longitudinal diary study

The study was centrally concerned with temporality and used financial diary methods to investigate how claimants of means-tested benefits (including Universal Credit) experienced income and expenditure changes over rela-tively short periods. Fifteen working-age claimants of means-tested benefits with a good knowledge of their household finances were recruited via advice, support and housing organisations and asked to attend up to four monthly interviews and to complete income and expenditure diaries. All participants completed at least one face-to-face semi-structured interview, nine were inter-viewed more than once and five were interviewed three or four times and fully completed income and expenditure diaries for periods of up to five months.

The sample consisted of four couples with children and 11 single people (six with children). The multi-person households within this sample (n = 10) allowed for in-depth analysis of their finances and intra-household dynamics over relatively short time periods. The combination of diary-based methods and regular interviews facilitated examination of multiple dimensions of temporality.

The financial records and experiences of the households reveal a complex picture of interacting pay periods and habits that shape financial management within households. Short-term practices were guided by different sources of income and their receipt dates, alongside the relative needs of household members, usually involving the prioritising of children. All multi-person and couple households had a female money manager, and in the four couple households they self-identified as the better money manager and as wanting to oversee all income and expenditure. Within these households, men had a limited administrative role in money management practices (such as transferring money); but the amount and timing of their wages played an important temporal role (for example, what was paid and when).

Relational dynamics and the relative value of different income sources shaped household money management; but so did the timings of income and outgoings and how these changed. For one household (the Bevans),[2] the mother (Sue) did more child care and less waged labour, with a smaller wage coming in, providing a gendered context for their money management strategies. They earmarked money from 'sub-pots', including Sue's and her partner's wages as well as two benefit payments. Sue explained how they matched pots of income with major outgoings: 'I actually pay the rent when he gets paid, because he gets paid more than I do, so I can pay the whole amount' (Young, 2021: 162). This practice thus appeared to be an ongoing 'matching' exercise based on the level of his income. However, it also relied on his income being matched to the timing of payments. Moreover, as this study reveals from focusing on a period of up to 15 weeks, this changed as his job changed from four-weekly to weekly paid. Through negotiating with their landlord, the Bevans started to pay weekly rent just after his wage became weekly. This adaptation shows how pay periods can provide a structure for money management practices within a gendered household context. Waiting also played a part in the Bevans' experience, with a ten-week wait for their first Universal Credit payment, as two of Sue's wages were counted in one monthly assessment period. During this period, the family relied on financial support from Sue's mother to cover the expenses usually covered by Sue's wages.

Wages also changed within the Lennon household and interacted with social security payments, within the context of gendered relational dynamics (and conflict). Crucially, diaries showed here how income changed over time and what this meant for internal dynamics and money management within the household. While wages and Universal Credit were paid into Paul's bank account, Samantha retained his bank card and was responsible for paying all the bills. Because of Paul's fluctuating wages and their interaction with Universal Credit, the Lennons were finding money management challenging. During the research period (14 weeks), they experienced a very high-income period followed by a very low-income period. This increasing and decreasing income was accentuated by the assessment and monthly-in-arrears payments of Universal Credit. A high-income month was followed by a low-income month – as well as a low Universal Credit payment, calculated on the basis of the previous month's income. Universal Credit was accentuating the volatility of wages and therefore damaging their income security. Gaps between payments were also experienced as waiting periods by the Lennons, who would sometimes receive nothing because of the previous month's wage and then have to wait until the following month for their Universal Credit payment. These waits were significant in the couple's arguments about the money they each brought in, with heavy reliance on Paul's wages when Universal Credit payments were low.

These examples show how the timing and level of social security payments and waiting periods place temporal restrictions on individuals within households and can require them to negotiate how such resources will be used. There was also relational tension within both households, with gendered and temporal elements. In both the vast majority of caring and financial management responsibilities fell on the female partner, while the male partner was either the sole wage earner (Lennons) or carried out the most paid work (Bevans); relational tensions around these issues coincided with periods of low income. For the Lennons, their insecurity caused conflict between the partners, with income changes often a precursor to conflict, involving Samantha expressing feelings of being devalued as a woman and reporting Paul feeling devalued by his experience of work. A related dynamic was Paul's long working hours and lack of perceived financial benefit and his view that Samantha should contribute more to household finances, underlining the importance of the source and 'earner' of household income to relationships and dynamics within the household (Goode et al., 1999).

This study adds to the existing literature by detailing how emotional and relational ups and downs are influenced by periods of waiting and the timing of social security payments and other income. These relational stresses shape intra-household dynamics and money management decisions. Being aware of these aspects is important in better understanding the impact of social security payments. In particular, the income fluctuations documented are a particular challenge for households like the Lennons and the Bevans. One assumption behind Universal Credit's monthly assessments and payments is that claimants will smooth their consumption by saving when income is higher and spending when it is lower. However, when income is consistently low in an absolute sense and also uncertain, managing fluctuations becomes particularly challenging, especially when Universal Credit exacerbates those fluctuations. The section below will consider how policy might address these issues.

Policy implications and directions for future research and methods

A central point is that temporal aspects of social security policy and how these affect household dynamics have more impact on intra-household management and distribution of resources than is widely acknowledged, and future research should focus on this. The management and use of money *within* the household reflect the work – often negotiation – of household members to establish and operate within various rhythms and rules, while social security policy also sets money rhythms and rules. These money rhythms and rules influence each other: they may be in tension, or they may be mutually reinforcing; and in turn they relate to the roles of different household members in managing and spending money. Temporality is not, as sometimes assumed, a bland, neutral or unimportant aspect of policy. This has implications for policy design and is also an important avenue for future research for which we must continue to hone our methodological tools.

We have highlighted two specific temporal issues: waiting as a feature of social security design; and payment receipt and expenditure patterns. Integrating different benefits into one, as with Universal Credit, has increased payment intervals for some households and posed further challenges. While some households receive non-means-tested benefits and wages at different frequencies alongside their Universal Credit, others rely on it as their only substantial income. The monthly assessment of Universal Credit also posed challenges to income stability, with fluctuations dependent on both which month a wage payment falls into and its amount (see Bennett and Millar, 2022, for a discussion of policy challenges posed by Universal Credit design). Research and policy should also focus on how different household members experience common social security waiting periods (e.g. while a claim is processed, or advice or support is sought) and how administrative and temporal burdens are shared within households.

The longitudinal diary-based study shows how research methods can be used to focus on temporality, policy and intra-household dynamics. This highlights temporality in the everyday, showing that payment frequency, and its intersection with the complex work of managing, strategising and spending money, really matter. This example highlights two main methodological points. First, it is important to study the longitudinal nature of intra-household dynamics to understand the meaning of changes over time. Second, household income is also dynamic, and change over short periods of time can be tracked with diaries alongside qualitative interviews.

To continue this agenda, these tools should be expanded and refined further, by considering how to embed temporality in research designs through methodological innovation (Treanor et al., 2021). There is currently a lack of longitudinal tools to capture within-year income changes alongside claimant experience. Moving beyond default static 'point in time' data collection techniques towards trying to capture policy and financial lives 'in motion', whilst recognising the complexity of the intra-household context, is key.

Whilst the study discussed here produces insights into intra-household dynamics, further studies could use different methodological approaches. This could involve, for example, innovative diary-based or online approaches or adapted interviews, to better access dimensions of temporality such as changes in income and circumstances. These approaches must consider who within the household would fill in diaries, or participate in other data collection, at what time intervals and the implications for research findings. Another methodological addition would be to consider the unit of analysis, for example by pursuing couple or family interviews, and/or interviewing each household member separately (see Griffiths, this volume), alongside longitudinal and diary-based approaches. There should also be full use of administrative and secondary data (e.g. from banking or consumer sources) that might offer different insights into income and spending behaviours, with triangulation with in-depth qualitative work. The future research directions suggested here are based on appreciating the links between temporality, social security policy and handling money in the household, and on pursuing a methodologically sensitive research agenda exploring these dimensions and their interrelationships, with the goal of better informing policy debates.

The key policy implication of this chapter is that, when designing social security policy, more attention should be paid to how low-income households actually organise their finances and lives – especially the temporal obstacles posed when managing low and uncertain income and how these have intra-household significance. A longer averaging period for assessing entitlement may provide a better understanding of how income works over longer periods and avoid low benefit payments coinciding with low wage payments. Access to financial services and products providing a better fit with financial realities for low-income families could also help. Indeed, there is much to learn from the informal borrowing available to some low-income households (from close family) based on short-term need and relational understanding. The social security system should (re)consider the role of non-repayable grants, alongside loans, targeting particularly difficult periods and helping avoid cycles of debt.

A key lesson from the discussion above is that timing should be considered as more than a functional concern in relation to social security systems, being bound up instead with familial and social contexts, and the roles people play within their household. Research and policy should focus on: the ways temporality in policy shapes the temporality of household finances and thus intra-household dynamics and money management; methods that can examine different aspects of temporality and incorporate policy, income and personal circumstances; and moving beyond the primary focus here on the UK and US to policy and research contexts elsewhere.

Notes

1. Social security here means cash transfers paid from the state to individuals or households. We chose this term to avoid direct association with stigmatised representations of welfare, though 'benefits' is sometimes used. The focus is predominantly social security for working-age people and children.
2. All participants were assigned a pseudonym.

References

Adam, B. (1990) *Time and Social Theory*. Cambridge: Polity Press.
Baumberg Geiger, B., Scullion, L., Summers, K., Martin,, Lawler, C., Edmiston, D., Gibbons, A., Ingold, J., Robertshaw, D. and de Vries, R. (2021) *Non-Take-Up of Benefits at the Start of the COVID-19 Pandemic*, Salford: Welfare at a (Social) Distance and Health Foundation: https:// www .distantwelfare .co .uk/ take -up (accessed 22 February 2023).

Bell, T., Cominetti, N. and Slaughter, H. (2020) *A New Settlement for the Low Paid: Beyond the Minimum Wage to Dignity and Respect*. London: Resolution Foundation.

Bennett, F. and Millar, J. (2022) *Inflexibility in an Integrated System? Policy Challenges Posed by the Design of Universal Credit*. Barnett House Working Paper 22-0. Oxford: Department of Social Policy and Intervention, University of Oxford.

Bennett, F. and Sung, S. (2014) 'Money Matters: Using Qualitative Research for Policy Influencing on Gender and Welfare Reform'. *Innovation: The European Journal of Social Sciences* 27(1): 5–19.

Bennett, F., Shaw, J. and Brewer, M. (2009) *Understanding the Compliance Costs of Benefits and Tax Credits*. London: Institute for Fiscal Studies.

Daly, M. (2017) 'Money-Related Meanings and Practices in Low-Income and Poor Families'. *Sociology* 51(2): 450–465.

Daly, M. and Kelly, F. (2015) *Families and Poverty: Everyday Life on a Low Income*. Bristol: Policy Press.

Edmiston, D., Robertshaw, D., Young, D., Ingold, J., Gibbons, A., Summers, K., Scullion, L., Baumberg Geiger, B. and de Vries, R. (2022) 'Mediating the Claim? How "Local Ecosystems of Support" Shape the Operation and Experience of UK Social Security'. *Social Policy and Administration* 56(5): 775–790.

Gardiner, L. (2019) *The Shifting Shape of Social Security: Charting the Changing Size and Shape of the British Welfare System*. London: Resolution Foundation.

Goode, J. (2010) 'The Role of Gender Dynamics in Decisions on Credit and Debt in Low Income Families'. *Critical Social Policy* 30(1): 99–119.

Goode, J., Callender, C. and Lister, R. (1998) *Purse or Wallet? Gender Inequalities in Income Distribution within Families on Benefits*. London: Policy Studies Institute.

Goode, J., Callender, C. and Lister, R. (1999) 'What's in a Name? Gendered Perceptions of Benefit Income amongst Couples Receiving IS/JSA and Family Credit'. *Benefits* January/February: 11–15.

Griffiths, R., Pearce, N. and Wood, M. (2023) *Monthly Assessment in Universal Credit for Working Claimants*. Bath: Institute for Policy Research, University of Bath.

Griffiths, R., Wood, M., Bennett, F. and Millar, J. (2020) *Uncharted Territory: Universal Credit, Couples and Money*. Bath: Institute for Policy Research, University of Bath.

Griffiths, R., Wood, M., Bennett, F. and Millar, J. (2022) *Couples Navigating Work, Care and Universal Credit*. Bath: Institute for Policy Research, University of Bath.

Halpern-Meekin, S., Edin, K., Tach, L. and Sykes, J. (2015) *It's Not Like I'm Poor: How Working Families Make Ends Meet in a Post-Welfare World*. Oakland, CA: University of California Press.

Harris, J., Treanor, M. and Sharma, N. (2009) 'Below the Breadline: A Year in the Life of Families in Poverty'. Ilford: Barnardo's: 1–70.

Hartfree, Y. (2014) 'Universal Credit: The Impact of Monthly Payments on Low Income Households'. *Journal of Poverty and Social Justice* 22(1): 15–26.

Hecht, K. and Summers, K. (2021) 'The Long and Short of It: The Temporal Significance of Wealth and Income'. *Social Policy and Administration* 55(4): 732–746.

Herd, and Moynihan, D. (2019) *Administrative Burden*. New York: Russell Sage Foundation.

Hickman,, Batty, E., Dayson, C. and Muir, J. (2014) '*Getting-By*', *Coping and Resilience in Difficult Times: Initial Findings*. Sheffield: Centre for Regional Economic and Social Research, Sheffield Hallam University.

Hills, J., Smithies, R. and McKnight, A. (2006) *Tracking Income: How Working Families' Incomes Vary through the Year*. Case Report 32. London: Centre for Analysis of Social Exclusion, London School of Economics.

Holler, R. and Tarshish, N. (2022) 'Administrative Burden in Citizen–State Encounters: The Role of Waiting, Communication Breakdowns and Administrative Errors'. *Social Policy and Society*, 1–18. Doi: http://doi.org/10.1017/S1474746422000355

Howard, M. and Bennett, F. (2020) 'Payment of Universal Credit for Couples in the UK: Challenges for Reform from a Gender Perspective'. *International Social Security Review* 73(4): 75–96.

Kahneman, D. and Thaler, R. (1991) 'Economic Analysis and the Psychology of Utility: Applications to Compensation Policy'. *American Economic Review* 81(2): 341–346.

Kempson, E. (1996) *Life on a Low Income*. York: York Publishing Services for Joseph Rowntree Foundation.

Kempson, E., Bryson, A. and Rowlingson, K. (1994) *Hard Times: How Poor Families Make Ends Meet*. London: Policy Studies Institute.

Millar, J. and Bennett, F. (2017) 'Universal Credit: Assumptions, Contradictions and Virtual Reality'. *Social Policy and Society* 16(2): 169–182.

Ophir, A. and Polos, J. (2022) 'Care Life Expectancy: Gender and Unpaid Work in the Context of Population Aging'. *Population Research and Policy Review* 41(1): 197–227.

Patrick, R. (2017) *For Whose Benefit? The Everyday Realities of Welfare Reform*. Bristol: Policy Press.

Pemberton, S., Fahmy, E., Sutton, E. and Bell, K. (2017) 'Endless Pressure: Life on a Low Income in Austere Times'. *Social Policy and Administration* 51(7): 1156–1173.

Peterie, M., Ramia, G., Marston, G. and Patulny, R. (2019) 'Emotional Compliance and Emotion as Resistance: Shame and Anger among the Long-Term Unemployed'. *Work, Employment and Society* 33(5): 794–811.

Reid, M. (2013) 'Social Policy, "Deservingness", and Sociotemporal Marginalization: Katrina Survivors and FEMA'. *Sociological Forum* 28(4): 742–763.

Shildrick, T. and MacDonald, R. (2013) 'Poverty Talk: How People Experiencing Poverty Deny Their Poverty and Why They Blame "the Poor"'. *The Sociological Review* 61(2): 285–303.

Summers, K. and Young, D. (2020) 'Universal Simplicity? The Alleged Simplicity of Universal Credit from Administrative and Claimant Perspectives'. *Journal of Poverty and Social Justice* 28(2): 169–186.

Treanor, M.C., Patrick, R. and Wenham, A. (2021) 'Qualitative Longitudinal Research: From Monochrome to Technicolour'. *Social Policy and Society* 20(4): 635–651.

Vogler, C., Lyonette, C. and Wiggins, R.D. (2008) 'Money, Power and Spending Decisions in Intimate Relationships'. *Sociological Review* 56(1): 117–143.

Wacquant, L. (2009) *Punishing the Poor: The Neoliberal Government of Social Insecurity*. London: Duke University Press.

Young, D. (2021) 'Managing Insecurity and Change: Low-Income Households and Social Security'. Doctoral research, University of Bath: https:// www .bath .ac .uk/ projects/managing-insecurity-and-change-low-income-households-and-social-security (accessed 6 April 2023).

Young, D. (2022) 'Income Insecurity and the Relational Coping Strategies of Low-Income Households in the UK'. *Journal of Social Policy*, 1–19. doi:10.1017/ S004727942200006X

Zelizer, V. (2011) *Economic Lives: How Culture Shapes the Economy*. Princeton, NJ: Princeton University Press.

Index